MANY REASONS WHY

Many Reasons Why

The American Involvement in Vietnam

Michael Charlton & Anthony Moncrieff

HILL AND WANG · NEW YORK
A division of Farrar, Straus and Giroux

© Michael Charlton and Anthony Moncrieff 1978
All rights reserved
First American edition, 1978
Published simultaneously in Canada by
McGraw-Hill Ryerson Ltd., Toronto

The two extracts from President Nixon's interviews
with David Frost are printed in Chapter 9 with the kind permission of
David Paradine Productions Inc.

Printed in the United States of America

Contents

Introduction *page vi*

Maps *pages x and xi*

Biographical notes on principal contributors *page xii*

1
1945: the untold story *page 1*

2
The return and defeat of France *page 21*

3
Creating a State—South Vietnam *page 39*

4
The New Frontiersmen hold the line *page 59*

5
Trying to win with LBJ *page 101*

6
Gulliver in Lilliput *page 133*

7
Protest at home *page 150*

8
The Pentagon Papers *page 168*

9
Trying not to lose *page 187*

10
South Vietnam—shadow or substance? *page 211*

11
The fall of Saigon *page 227*

Indexes *page 247*

Plates *between pages 14/15 and 46/47*

Introduction: Anthony Moncrieff

The eleven chapters in this book are based on the radio programs which were written by Michael Charlton and broadcast during September, October and November 1977 by BBC Radio Three. The programs were subsequently made available abroad through the BBC Transcription Service. A shortened version of the series was scheduled by BBC Radio Four during July, August and September 1978, and repeated a few weeks later by BBC World Service; shortened versions of the scripts of the programs of the original Radio Three series were printed in *The Listener*.

The form of MANY REASONS WHY is largely chronological, thirty years 1945 to 1975, from the OSS involvement in Indo China at the end of World War II to the fall of Saigon. The first-hand testimony comes from the men who either made or largely shaped the crucial decisions during this period—the men of the White House, the State Department, and the Pentagon, who are still alive today, including Dean Rusk (about whom more below), George Ball, General Maxwell Taylor, William Bundy, Henry Cabot Lodge, Fritz Nolting, Paul Warnke, Warren Nutter, Graham Martin, Roger Hilsman, General Ed Lansdale, J. K. Galbraith and William Colby. But there are also separate sections, between the chapters on the White House years of Lyndon Johnson and Richard Nixon, given over to a long interview with General William Westmoreland about fighting the war, to the role of television and to protest 'at home'—and there is on my files much about the anti-war movement within the United States it would be tedious now to publish—and to the story of *The Pentagon Papers*. There is also a long interview with Nguyen Cao Ky, former Premier and Vice President of South Vietnam, the most senior surviving Vietnamese political leader currently willing to talk.

Michael Charlton conducted all the interviews of contributors in the United States during December 1976 and May 1977. Other interviews took place in London, Somerset and Paris during 1977, except for the French politicians who were recorded in 1975. Professor Walt Rostow, although supporting this project since its beginnings, in the

INTRODUCTION

event declined to be interviewed but authorized our use of extracts from his television lectures to students at Austin, Texas, in March 1974. Other contributions are from the Radio and Television Archives of the BBC.

As the producer of the series I want to state briefly how the project began. The Honorable Dean Rusk, Secretary of State 1961 to 1969, throughout the Presidencies of Kennedy and Johnson, kept no diary and has written no memoirs. He told me he left office without any official papers except appointments books. We first met in London on 3 July 1974, and I secured his agreement to give BBC Radio Two substantial interviews—about his eight years as Secretary of State and about the American involvement in Vietnam, speaking (as he remarked) as the senior surviving decision maker. I am especially grateful to Dean Rusk because I am sure that during a visit to the United States in October 1974 many other former American decision makers were good enough to meet me and agree to contribute to the project because of the participation of the former Secretary of State, whether or not they always agreed with him. Subsequently when I met Dean Rusk again in Athens, Georgia in June 1975, not long after Saigon had been captured by the Communists, he felt it was unfair to give the BBC two interviews when, with rare and often brief exceptions, he had declined to do so to the American media since leaving office. We settled for one BBC interview. This eventually took place with Michael Charlton in Washington in December 1976, and lasted 75 minutes. The more general material was broadcast in 1977 by Radio Three on 20 March and 2 April, and by Radio Four on 31 August. The questions and answers about the American involvement in Vietnam are included in this book.

Many of Michael Charlton's other interviews lasted an hour or more. While we were putting these together for the radio series in June and July 1977 we found we had often prepared programs too long to claim attention by ear alone. For this publication I have restored a great deal of this evidential material which had to be cut from the Radio Three programs. My other editorial changes from ear to eye relate to inserting names and dates, to greater use of substantive nouns than we all use in conversation, and to some minor adjustments of language to try to make the texts more readable. Otherwise the contributions retain the advantages and disadvantages of their origin as tape recorded interviews.

The interviews, however, are what Michael Charlton and I regard as the strength of this offering in understanding: we have tried to explain a series of complex and difficult decisions changing and deepening the American involvement in Vietnam through the minds and voices of the surviving decision makers themselves—all of whom were given the opportunity to vet the broadcast scripts for publication. Whatever our personal views on the Vietnam wars, none of us ought lightly to judge the men who bore those responsibilities. Time for judgment will be when more documentation, and perhaps personal testimony, becomes available from North Vietnam. Our job has been to elucidate evidence, first-hand where possible.

But meanwhile several of our contributors did attempt to put the American involvement in Vietnam into perspective in the final chapter of this book. Was the action of Congress cutting off aid to South Vietnam more of a slap at Nixon than a deliberate attempt to abandon an ally, which General Taylor thinks it was? And he expects the United States to be watched to see whether Americans can be counted on the same way as in the past. Both Air Marshal Ky and Senator Fulbright draw the parallel between Vietnam and Angola. Dr Henry Kissinger is credited with describing what happened in Vietnam as 'a cruel side-show' in the new world-wide policies of the United States. Sir Robert Thompson, who headed the British Advisory Mission in Vietnam, judges the conflict as probably being the most decisive war of this century and doubts that if the Americans had come out of Vietnam successfully in 1972 there would have been a 1973 Middle East war. Senator Mike Mansfield argues that the American people want to forget Vietnam, but he himself regards it as one of the most tragic, if not *the* most tragic episode in American history and adds: 'It was just a misadventure in a part of the world which we should have kept our noses out of.' As might be expected, Dean Rusk does not share this view—although because we have not yet seen the end of the story in all sorts of directions 'it may be twenty years before we can make a judgment'. But he does think the withdrawal from Saigon marked the end of a chapter which the United States 'would be called upon to undertake major responsibilities relatively alone'. As the editor of a previous BBC series, *Suez—Ten Years After*, I find this judgment about Vietnam an uncanny echo of the British lessons of 1956.

Finally, since this is not a BBC publication, I want to record my personal thanks to my immediate boss at the BBC, George Fischer, for sustaining this project through so many vicissitudes; and to the Controller of Radio Three, Stephen Hearst, who patiently accepted so many delays. And both Michael Charlton and I are indebted to our production secretary Valerie Simmonds, who also had to cope with the extra problems of my absence ill while the first half of the series of programs was completed and broadcast.

Broadcasting House, London: January 1978

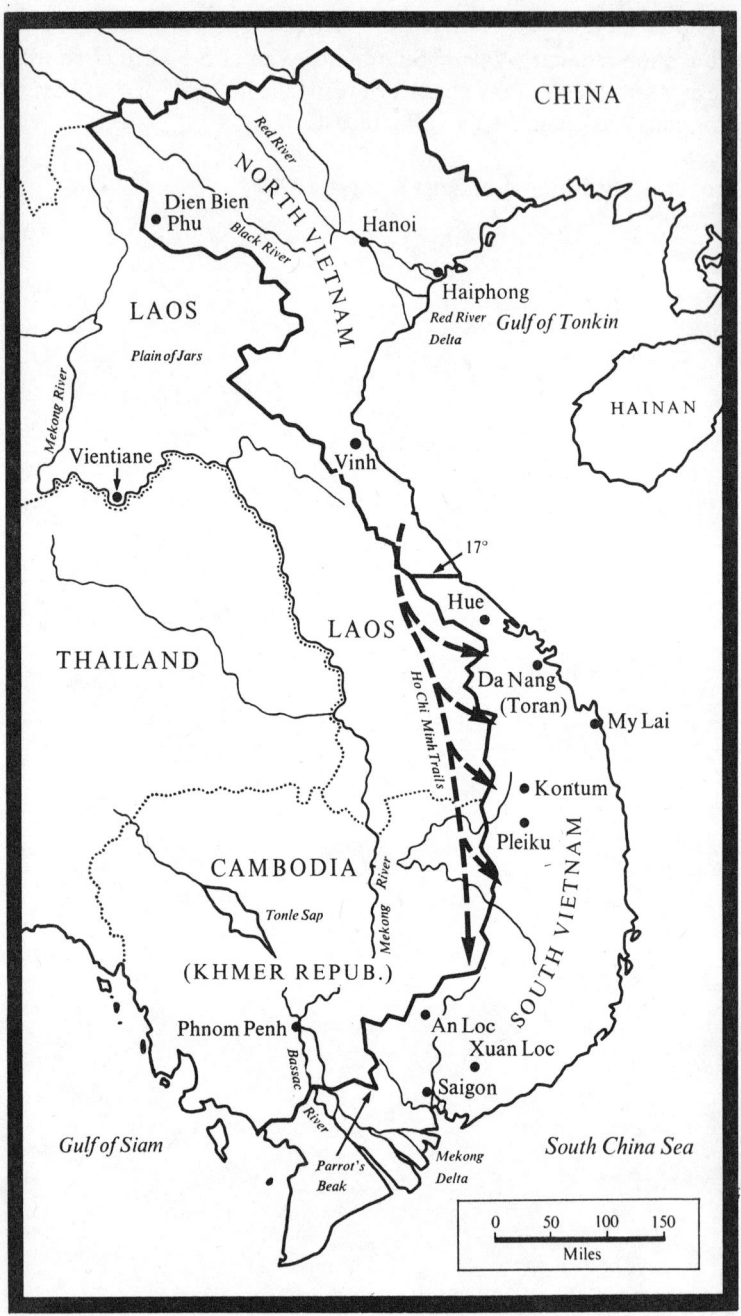

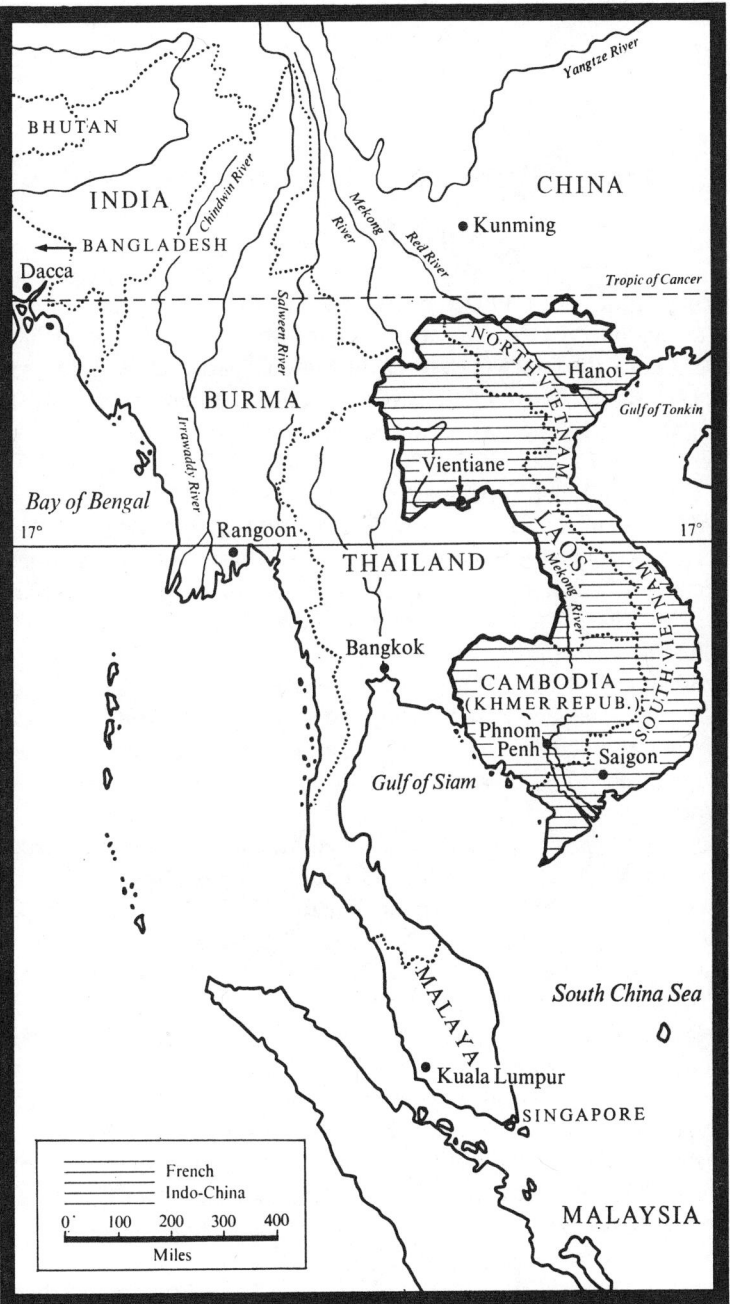

Biographical notes on principal contributors

George Ball. Born 1909; general counsel French Supply Council, Washington 1945–46; Undersecretary of State for Economic Affairs 1961; Undersecretary of State at the State Department 1961–66.

Robert Bowie. Born 1909; Director policy planning staff at State Department 1953–55; Assistant Secretary of State 1955–57; Director Center for International Affairs at Harvard University 1957–72. Director National Foreign Assessment Center at CIA 1977–

William Bundy. Born 1917; with CIA 1951–61; Deputy Assistant Secretary and Assistant Secretary of Defense for International Security Affairs at the Pentagon 1961–64; Assistant Secretary of State for East Asian and Pacific Affairs at the State Department 1964–69; editor *Foreign Affairs* 1972–

William Colby. Born 1920; 1st Secretary American Embassy Saigon 1959–62; chief Far East Division, CIA, Washington 1962–67; Ambassador Director Civil Operations and Rural Development Support, Saigon 1973–77; Director CIA 1973–76; now practising law in Washington.

Tran van Don. Born France 1917; educated in Paris; joined French Army 1939; in early 1950s transferred to Army of Republic of Vietnam. Retired 1963 as Lieutenant General; Minister of Defense 1963–1964; Deputy Prime Minister 1974–75; left Vietnam 1975 and now runs restaurant in Washington DC. Author *Our endless war inside Vietnam*, Presidio Press 1978.

Dennis Duncanson. Born 1917; Malayan Civil Service (Chinese Section) 1946–57; Government of Hong Kong 1957–61; Diplomatic Service 1961–67 (British Advisory Mission to Vietnam 1961–65); Reader in South East Asian Studies, University of Kent 1969–

Daniel Ellsberg. Born 1931; with Rand Corporation, California 1959–1964, 1968–69; special assistant to Assistant Secretary of Defense for International Security Affairs at the Pentagon 1964–65; with State Department in Vietnam 1965–67.

William Fulbright. Born 1905; US Senator from Arkansas 1945–74;

BIOGRAPHICAL NOTES ON CONTRIBUTORS xiii

Chairman Committee on Foreign Relations 1959–74; now practising law in Washington.
John Kenneth Galbraith. Born 1908; American Ambassador to India 1961–63; Chairman Americans for Democratic Action 1967–68.
Roger Hilsman. Born 1919; Director Bureau Intelligence and Research at State Department 1961–63; Assistant Secretary of State for Far Eastern Affairs 1963–64.
Nguyen Cao Ky. Born 1930; educated Hanoi; conscripted into army and commissioned; flight training Marrakech, Morocco, and in France 1951–54; advanced through ranks to command air force of Republic of Vietnam, with rank of Air Vice-Marshal; Prime Minister 1965–67; Vice President 1967–71; left Vietnam 1975 and now lives in California.
Edward Lansdale. Born 1908; served in Philippines during Hukbalahap rebellion; assigned South Vietnam 1954–56; special assistant to American Ambassadors in Saigon 1965–68.
Jean Letourneau. Born 1907; served in French governments 1946–53; (High Commissioner for Indo-China 1952).
Henry Cabot Lodge. Born 1902; US representative at the United Nations 1953–60; American Ambassador to South Vietnam 1963–64, 1965–67; member US delegation to Vietnam Peace Talks, Paris 1969.
Eugene McCarthy. Born 1916; US Senator from Minnesota 1958–70; ran for President 1976.
Michael Mansfield. Born 1903; entered Congress 1943; House Foreign Affairs Committee 1943–52; US Senator from Montana 1952–76; majority leader in Senate 1961–76; member of Senate Foreign Relations Committee 1952–76; now American Ambassador to Japan.
Graham Martin. Born 1912; with US foreign service 1947–77; American Ambassador to Thailand 1963–67; to Italy 1969–73; and to Vietnam 1973–75.
Ho Thong Minh. Born 1920; Minister of Defense 1954; left Vietnam 1955; has subsequently lived in France.
Frederick Nolting. Born 1911; with US foreign service 1946–64; American Ambassador to Vietnam 1961–63; now Professor of Business Administration at University of Virginia.
Warren Nutter. Born 1923; CIA 1952–53; Assistant Secretary of Defense for International Security Affairs at the Pentagon 1969–73; Professor of Economics at University of Virginia 1958–
Archimides Patti. Born New York City 1913; educated US and Italy; US Army 1936–57; worked with British Intelligence Services 1942–44; directed OSS special operation in French Indo-China October 1944

to October 1945; Planner, Department of Army 1958–59; Executive Office of President 1959–71.

René Pleven. Born 1901; twice Prime Minister of France; also served as Minister of Defense 1952–53 and 1954; Foreign Minister 1958.

Walt Rostow. Born 1916; deputy special assistant to President for National Security Affairs 1961; counseler to Chairman Policy Planning Council at State Department 1961–66; special assistant to President 1966–69; now Professor of Economic History at University of Texas.

Dean Rusk. Born 1909; served with AUS 1940–46; joined State Department 1946; Assistant Secretary of State for Far Eastern Affairs 1950–51; President Rockefeller Foundation 1952–60; Secretary of State 1961–69; now Professor of International Law at University of Georgia.

Jean Sainteny. Born 1907; banking career in Indo-China 1929–31; and Paris 1932–39; served in French Resistance; French Commissioner to China 1945; to Tonkin and Anam (Vietnam) 1945–47; arranged secret meetings between Dr Henry Kissinger and North Vietnamese representatives in Paris from 1969; died February 1978.

Maurice Schumann. Born 1911; BBC French Service 1940–44; Deputy Minister for Foreign Affairs 1951–54; Minister 1969–73.

Maxwell Taylor. Born 1901; Chief of Staff US Army 1955–59; military representative of President 1961–62; Chairman Joint Chiefs of Staff 1962–64; American Ambassador to Vietnam 1964–65.

Sir Robert Thompson. Born 1916; served government of Malaya after Second World War until 1961; head of British Advisory Mission to Vietnam 1961–65; consultant to Presidents Kennedy and Nixon.

Paul Warnke. Born 1920; general counsel Department of Defense 1966–67; Assistant Secretary of Defense for International Security Affairs at the Pentagon 1967–69; now Director Arms Control and Disarmament Agency.

William Westmoreland. Born 1914; Commander US Military Assistance Command, Vietnam 1964–68; Chief of Staff US Army 1968–72.

Adam Yarmolinsky. Born 1922; special Assistant to Secretary and Deputy Secretary of Defense 1961–64; principal deputy Assistant Secretary of Defense for International Security Affairs at the Pentagon 1965–66; currently Counsellor US Arms Control Agency.

Publisher's note

In order to distinguish between Michael Charlton's roles of interviewer and commentator, a bold mark has been placed in the margin at the beginning of each passage of narrative and summary. Materials taken from the BBC Archives have been set in italics.

1
1945: the untold story

DECLARATION OF INDEPENDENCE OF THE DEMOCRATIC REPUBLIC OF VIETNAM

All men are created equal. They are endowed by their Creator with certain unalienable rights, among these are Life, Liberty and the Pursuit of Happiness.... These are undeniable truths.

Nevertheless, for more than eighty years, the French imperialists, abusing the standard of Liberty, Equality and Fraternity, have violated our Fatherland and oppressed our fellow citizens. Their acts are the opposite of the ideals of humanity and justice.

In the field of politics, they deprived us of all liberties. They have enforced inhuman laws... they have built more prisons than schools. They have mercilessly slain our patriots; they have drowned our uprisings in rivers of blood.

We are convinced that the Allies who recognized the principle of equality of all the peoples at the Conferences of Teheran and San Francisco cannot but recognize the independence of Vietnam...

Vietnam has the right to be a free and independent country; and in fact is so already.

Hanoi, 2 September 1945

▌With those words, echoing the famous phrases and political ideals of the American Declaration of Independence, a little known political force, the Vietminh, seized power in Hanoi and proclaimed the independent Republic of Vietnam on 2 September 1945. A memorable photograph the day those words were spoken shows the Vietnamese Communists giving their clenched fist salute as the new red flag with the yellow star unfurled above the citadel of the once French colony of Indo-China [see fig. 1]. By the side of these new Communist leaders that day also saluting the new flag were American officers in uniform.

This episode was a first landmark in the American involvement in Vietnam. At first hand it has hitherto been a largely untold story. It concerns essentially three men, two of whom tell it here in their own words. The Communist leader with that proclamation of Vietnam's

Independence was Ho Chi Minh—who died in 1969. Our two contributors are the American intelligence officer who helped Ho to write it, Major Archimedes Patti; and the Frenchman Jean Sainteny, Commissioner for Indo-China, who watched that day while what he calls 'the infantile anti-colonialism of the Americans' helped to power a movement dominated by Communists with incalculable consequences, a movement which the United States would spend most of the next thirty years trying either to dislodge or contain.

The context which culminated in these fateful proceedings took shape in 1944. By then the defeat of Germany was assured. The Allies started to concentrate on the defeat of Japan. Japan occupied French Indo-China, and much of the other colonial empires in South-East Asia too. President Roosevelt's antipathy to the return of the French to their former possession Indo-China is a matter of record. In January 1944 he minuted his Secretary of State, Cordell Hull:

France has had the country—thirty million inhabitants—for nearly one hundred years, and the people are worse off than they were at the beginning... France has milked it for one hundred years. The people of Indo-China are entitled to something better than that.

Later at Yalta on the afternoon of 8 February 1945, Roosevelt, who was in his terminal illness, had an exchange with Stalin about Indo-China. He told Stalin that the Americans were unable to find any ships to transport French troops back to Indo-China.

Churchill, who did not wish to see any precedents established in Indo-China which would affect Britain's position and authority in Asia, spoke with familiar voice:

I have not become the King's first Minister in order to preside over the liquidation of the British Empire.

So Britain supported France and became engaged in what can only be called a running battle with the Americans over the post-war order in Asia. President Roosevelt's opposition to the re-establishment of the pre-war status of the colonial empires was comprehensive. It went for the British and the Dutch too. Roosevelt saw a post-war order based upon the self-determination of peoples. In the resultant Balkanizing of the old imperial systems the peace would be kept by the authority of a new world body, the Security Council of the United Nations, a concept which was soon to be doomed by the onset of the cold war and by the Russian veto. But in 1944 and 1945 with victory approaching the Americans considered it their international right and their national interest where possible to thwart the return of the colonial powers, by getting back into South-East Asia first.

With Japan undefeated and still in control of Indo-China it was the intelligence services of the Allied powers who were crucial in determining what happened next. British, Americans and French secret service men were flying, parachuting or infiltrating into southern China and Indo-China. They had a common enemy, Japan, against whom they wished to enlist and promote resistance. But they had rival perceptions of what was to follow victory. They were all poised in 1944 and 1945 in their missions on the frontier with Indo-China. They were preparing for the seaborne invasions by Allied forces which would wrest control from the Japanese. That would come first and then the political future could be settled in its successful aftermath at more leisure.

But in 1945 events suddenly greatly accelerated. Roosevelt died in April. President Truman in August took the decision to drop the atomic bombs on Hiroshima and Nagasaki. No invasions were necessary. Japan instantly surrendered. That sudden vacuum of power in Indo-China caught the Allied policy makers off balance, and no one moved with greater swiftness and sureness into that vacuum than a little wisp of a man who at this time had lived outside his native country for nearly thirty years, his identity lost in a labyrinthine confusion of political aliases. He was almost totally unknown to his Vietnamese countrymen yet he soon established himself as a national figure—Ho Chi Minh.

Dennis Duncanson is one of Ho's biographers.

Duncanson: I think one can say without much risk of challenge that Ho Chi Minh followed the course of action of Lenin more faithfully than any other Communist leader has ever done. Now that was not entirely to his credit. He wanted to do it but also he had the good fortune to be in a position to do it; and that's precisely what he did —to seat the Communist Party in power in his country. National liberation meant that seating—not simply getting rid of the colonial power, that's only half of it, in fact the lesser half of it. The real important point was that the end result should be that there was a Communist Party in power.

Charlton: How did Ho Chi Minh convert this apparent disadvantage that he was outside the country, and presumably almost unknown for thirty or forty years, and yet suddenly in this very short space of time presented himself and apparently was accepted significantly, if not widely, as a liberating patriot?

Duncanson: It arose from the fact that the country had been occupied by the Japanese, that the Japanese were then defeated and that Ho Chi Minh was able to represent himself coming into the country from outside. If he'd been there all along he wouldn't have been able to pose in this convincing guise. He could come in from the outside as one of the victorious Allies along with particularly the Americans, and incidentally the British and the Russians and the Free French and the Chinese.

Six months before they surrendered the Japanese had set out to extinguish French power in Indo-China. They interned the Vichy French administration who had been their collaborators. The Japanese confirmed the Vietnamese emperor Bao Dai and his ministers in a measure of self-government under Japanese suzerainty over the North, but not the South of Indo-China.

In this humiliation of the French lay the origins of a national excitement and exuberance among the Vietnamese. But the Imperial government proved unable to substitute its authority for that of the French. In the northern provinces on the Chinese frontier the Communist-led guerilla bands had begun agitation and armed propaganda campaigns with assassination of government officials. In the months before the Japanese surrender Indo-China was drifting into a state of anarchy. This was the wind Ho Chi Minh rode to political power. In 1944 and 1945 the allied intelligence missions based at Kunming in Southern China had no reliable intelligence of what was happening in Indo-China. They all turned to the underground network of the Communists as a source. It was that which first brought them into contact with Ho Chi Minh.

As events following the surrender of Japan quickly unfolded the French-American rivalry to determine the outcome in Hanoi intensified. The Americans who controlled the air transport at Kunming in China prevented the quick return to Hanoi of the representative of France and the Head of their Intelligence, Mission Five, by then designated Commissioner for Indo-China, Jean Sainteny.

Sainteny [translation]: Our role in Kunming, where we were based, the capital of Yunnan, was to observe the Japanese troops who were occupying Indo-China and, naturally, to maintain information networks to help the Allies and to prepare France's eventual return, either if there was fighting—which we thought was inevitable—or if there was a rapid peace settlement, which turned out to be the case. You know that at Kunming there were practically four headquarters: the Chinese headquarters, British headquarters, and American headquarters; and a commanding French headquarters—which was in reality Mission Five.

❚ What instructions had Sainteny received about his return to Hanoi, the French colonial capital of Vietnam?

Sainteny: Well, look, in this case I'm forced to be severe towards my country and the government of the time. I had practically no instructions. The only telegram I received at the time of the Japanese capitulation, after the bombing of Hiroshima and Nagasaki, 6 and 9 August, was—well, we've been overtaken by events. We are counting on you to ... the actual wording was 'to deal with the most urgent matters first'—*parer*—you know what that means—to make ready in order to cope with events; in short, manage on your own.

❚ What seemed to Jean Sainteny the part played by Major Patti of the American OSS? There are photographs showing this American Major Patti, head of an American intelligence mission which had returned to Hanoi from Southern China, with him standing by the side of and shaking hands with the Communists under Ho Chi Minh at the moment they announced their seizure of power.

Sainteny: There's an even more startling photograph, showing Patti with his two aides by the side of the famous General Giap, saluting, but you can't see what they're saluting; I can tell you what they're saluting, it's the unfurling of the Communist colors over the Hanoi citadel. And so the American Mission endorsed this Communist takeover by being at the side of Giap, who wasn't Minister of War at the time but Minister of the Interior. So, what was Patti's role at Kunming, in the American headquarters there? He was, I believe, very much on his own. He came under the OSS and because being of Italian origin, I think, it was thought he would get on better with the French! I don't know—but, anyway, he was the one who dealt with liaison with my headquarters, with my associates. I had very little to do with him and, clearly, the United States' hostility towards France's eventual return to Indo-China went through Patti. Did Patti do it spontaneously? I don't think so because this hostility was such that it could only have been the result of general directives issued much higher up.

▌ How Archimedes Patti of the OSS, the Office of Strategic Services of the United States, America's first central intelligence agency, came to be in the area and the instructions he took with him now form the most important part of this story, how Patti took with him his own ideals of emancipation—his grandfather had fought with Garibaldi's Red Shirts during the Italian revolution—and how he interpreted in practice Roosevelt's espousal of righteous causes. Major Patti as he was then—now Colonel Patti in retirement in Florida, surrounded by a personal collection of documentation, from which he is writing his own account of events—was recalled in 1944 from service in Europe and given new orders by the Head of OSS, General Donovan:

Patti: I arrived about mid-June, in Washington DC, and there I had lunch with General Donovan where he said, 'Well look, the mission is a very simple one, but it's a very difficult one. I need special people that can handle this, and I think that you're it. And what is it? It'll be the job of setting up an intelligence organization in Indo-China.' To be quite honest about it, I wasn't very sure where Indo-China was at that particular moment. I had an idea it was out in Asia somewhere. But we finally got that out of the way and he explained that the President had called him about the question of the French in Indo-China; what should we do, what should our policy be, and how should it be handled. Without referring specifically to the documents which I do have here now, which are part of my files, it appears that President Roosevelt was very anxious that we, the Americans, did not become involved in French 'Anamese' problems, that we stick strictly to the issue of fighting the Japanese, our enemy at the time.
Charlton: How did you interpret that, not to become involved in French 'Anamese', that is to say Vietnamese, problems?
Patti: I interpreted that literally. I mean it was an instruction from General Donovan, and I accepted it. I wasn't aware of the implications until several days after, in fact several weeks after, going over the files, what it really was all about. I had an office in the Q Building, Constitution Avenue, in Washington, in the OSS, and there files were made available to me on Asia. These included many notes, letters, cables, from the various commanders in the Far East, to the White House, to the Joint Chiefs of Staff.
Charlton: When you went back to Washington for this special

mission which it was disclosed to you was the setting-up of an intelligence network in Indo-China, you were at once aware that this had the personal authority and backing of President Roosevelt. Can you just expand a bit on what you subsequently discovered the policy to be in detail? Roosevelt had said that it was an anti-Japanese mission, not to become involved in French/Vietnamese problems, but what was the policy as you understood it, given six months or so to study the background to it, that you took with you to Vietnam?

Patti: I'm sorry to say there was no policy spelled out in terms that could be really followed. It was a very nebulous policy. It was a series of statements made by Cordell Hull, by President Roosevelt, and by various members of the Joint Chiefs of Staff, and that's the way we pieced it together. We had no clear-cut policy.

Charlton: You must have taken instructions with you after this six months of briefing that you had had with access to all the Joint Chiefs of Staff documents in Washington. So what were the instructions you took, particularly in dealing with the French?

Patti: Well, specifically we formulated a policy concept—since again I repeat we had no specific written policy at the time—we formulated a concept that our mission to Indo-China was to set up an intelligence net against the Japanese. But at the same time, on General Donovan's direct and explicit instructions, we were not to become involved in Indo-Chinese/French politics, nor in Chinese Communist/Nationalist politics or any other for that matter. We were to steer clear of any group that had any political inclinations other than to assist the military in fighting in the war.

Charlton: Yes, but you weren't meant to be neutral about the French. You were specifically ordered not to align yourselves with them, is that correct?

Patti: Yes, that is correct. We were specifically ordered—I was specifically ordered, by General Donovan—that on the President's instructions, we were not to assist any French objective to re-enter Indo-China with American or lend-lease equipment.

Charlton: You were to see to it that the French were not armed?

Patti: The policy was—and as given to me by General Donovan—that in my mission in the Far East I was not to support the French objective of retaking their former colony, nor necessarily to assist the Vietnamese in achieving their independence.

Charlton: When and how did you come to meet Ho Chi Minh?

Patti: I first heard of Ho in the fall of 1944, while reviewing some of the files in the OSS office, Washington. In reviewing these files I came across the name of Ho Chi Minh, in some State Department cables; and it was spelled various ways, but it all came out Ho Chi Minh. I was looking for contacts in Indo-China, and Ho was one of them.

Charlton: So you are saying that you were aware before you went to Kunming in 1944, that you believed as a result of your study of these files, that Ho Chi Minh was sympathetic to the Americans?

Patti: That is correct, yes.

Charlton: He was in conformity with the policy you were taking with you? [Yes.] You knew him to be anti-French?

Patti: We knew that, but that did not play an important role at that time. And as a matter of fact it never did. Our interest was to find some contacts in Indo-China who could help us in setting up intelligence operations in the area.

Charlton: Did you have any specific orders and instructions in dealing with him, with Ho Chi Minh?

Patti: No, no, that was left entirely up to my discretion.

Charlton: Were you aware of his background as a Communist?

Patti: Yes, I was aware of his background as a Communist, that is in having been to Moscow and to having worked for the Comintern for a number of years; and that was based again on some of the rather sketchy files that we had.

Charlton: So, when and how did you come to meet him personally?

Patti: I first met Ho the last days of April 1945 or perhaps maybe the first or second day of May. I don't recall just exactly the day, but it was in that five-day span. I was doing a field survey of southern China, with respect to our field operations, and there I met one of our agents on the way to Indo-China who was accompanying a gentleman, Ho Chi Minh, who had been working for the office of war information in Kunming. They were returning to Indo-China to set up—or at least for our men to set up—an escape and evasion network in the area. Ho would assist him in getting the necessary.

Charlton: An escape network for pilots who were shot down?

Patti: For pilots that were shot down, that is members of the 14th Air Force and members of the Navy that were flying in the area.

Charlton: In the first meetings you had with Ho Chi Minh, what impression did he make on you?

Patti: Really he didn't impress me very much, to be honest about it. To me, he was just another old Vietnamese. Except for one thing, that in parting he had said: 'Now if you need any help, contact the following people.' and he gave me a list of names, which at the time meant nothing to me, in Kunming. Well sure enough, those people started to come into Kunming headquarters at our compound and brought us some interesting order of battle information on the Japanese in Indo-China. So we were beginning to get information which was free—no charge connected with it, which was unusual. It was reasonably accurate. At first we paid no credence to it at all. But it contradicted the French intelligence. And we were more or less compelled after a while to really read the information that was coming from the Vietnamese, and it was good.

Charlton: Did you speak to him directly or through an interpreter?

Patti: I spoke to him directly in English, and then we interspersed it with French, but he was very uncomfortable in French. He was more comfortable in English, perhaps because he was speaking to an American, or because really he preferred to speak English rather than French.

Charlton: So what was the flavor and the substance of your reporting about Ho Chi Minh at this time? How would you characterize that? What were you telling your Government about him and his followers?

Patti: I was telling my Headquarters in Chungking, with respect to Ho Chi Minh he was definitely a Communist, no question in my mind about it. But he was not a Moscow Communist. He was more of a nationalist who was using the Communist techniques and methods to achieve his ends.

Charlton: Did he specifically disavow his interest in and connections with the Soviet Union? Did you talk to him about Russia?

Patti: Yes, there was a period of August and September while I was talking to Ho, he told me on several occasions that he had nothing to expect from, could expect nothing from Russia and the Soviet Union, since the Soviet Union was in a bad way, in a bad state after the war, so he could expect no help from them. With respect to his being a Communist he said: 'Yes, I put in fifteen years of service to the party and I believe I paid my debt. From now on I am independent, and I can do as I find best for my country.'

Charlton: He had convinced you of an allegiance which conformed to the interests of the United States?

Patti: Allegiance is a hard word really, but he asked me on a number of occasions during the period of August and September 1945 that if the United States would provide the expertise of American technology he was more than happy to receive the Americans. And I asked about the French; and he said the French could come too. 'I have no objection to the French coming as advisers and to help us set up our country, but I don't want them here as colonial rulers.'

Charlton: But he had made it clear to you, presumably, that he regarded you Americans at this time with your Mission in Kunming as the advanced guard of a power and an army which would help him to power in Indo-China. Is that correct?

Patti: No, that is not correct. No. I am sorry, but he didn't regard us as a power to help him take over or to achieve independence, because he knew we were not going to provide him with unlimited arms and equipment to fight the French since the French were our allies. Actually he expected moral support. As a matter of fact he said to me on more than one occasion: 'Why can't you look at us as you do the filipinos, you promised them independence, you have given them independence and here they are.' He said: 'Why don't you live up to the provisions of the Atlantic Charter. Have you forgotten the Fourteen Points of Wilson? Why don't you just support us? All we want is moral support. We don't want money, arms or equipment from you, all we want is moral support.'

Charlton: Were you personally attracted by those arguments?

Patti: Yes, I was personally attracted. I thought they were reasonable and I presented them as such to Chungking and to Washington and London to the point that I received a cable from my own offices: 'For God's sake stop sending any more wires to London and Washington on this subject.'

Charlton: Was it obvious to you that the Americans were vital to Ho Chi Minh in helping him to establish his authority as a leader? After all, the man was completely unknown inside Indo-China, do you agree with that?

Patti: Yes, that is true. He did use us, and I know it. I knew he was using us, and I didn't mind frankly because the use he made of us was more one of image rather than substance. Really what he was trying to do was to say: 'Well look, even the Americans believe in my cause'—when speaking to the Vietnamese. But at the same time he did use us, yes.

Charlton: Now, you were deeply into this Mission. You had set up your intelligence network, the original charge that you were sent to Indo-China to implement. I would like to know whether you feel that from round about this time the Vietminh and their relationship with OSS—with you—had a wider objective than just the defeat of Japan, that you were beginning to think now of the succession to colonial rule in Indo-China?

Patti: In retrospect, yes of course, I can see it now very clearly. Then of course they not only were willing to provide us with what we wanted, but at the same time taking advantage of the opportunity to train their own people and to be prepared to take over from the French, or from the Japanese, or whoever was in power at the time.
Charlton: But were you aware of that at the time?
Patti: No, I wasn't really too much concerned with it, let's put it that way. I was not really concerned with that.
Charlton: Now at this time the French and their Intelligence Mission under Jean Sainteny, Mission five at Kunming, were desperately trying to get back into Indo-China, immediately following the news of the Japanese surrender, and re-establish French contact with the Vietnamese. So here was a crucial test for American policy, which from the beginning had been to refuse to align itself with the return of the French. Was that still the policy, now that Roosevelt was dead?
Patti: Yes, it definitely was the policy. I had daily, almost hourly, contact with Chungking on the subject of what to do with this French Mission in Kunming. They wanted to return to Hanoi, they wanted to return to Indo-China and they were seeking my help. I was told to keep my hands off, and that as far as the French were concerned, they'd have to find their own way. And the only way that there was at the time was to approach General Chiang Kai-shek, the Commander in Chief of the area.
Charlton: Now the corollary of that of course was going to be that the Vietminh led by Ho Chi Minh were going to get to Hanoi first. Do you agree?
Patti: I agree with that, yes, definitely.
Charlton: And were you instructed to assist that?
Patti: No, we were not instructed to assist Ho Chi Minh or any other group to go into Indo-China at any time. They went in on their own.
Charlton: On the other hand, one of your subordinate officers, Major Thomas, accompanied Giap and his Vietminh guerillas south to Hanoi, didn't he?
Patti: Correction. They assisted Giap in his forays against the Japanese on the way south.
Charlton: Some of the history disputes that, and says that the Vietminh themselves were burning villages as a means of establishing their authority.
Patti: Well, there might have been some of that.

Patti had flown into Hanoi taking the representative of France, Sainteny, with him on the plane. The Americans had deliberately delayed this French return and Sainteny has said he was in effect under American guard on the plane.

Patti: We got there on 22 August on the same plane together, holding hands if you want to put it that way. Sainteny approached me sometime around 10 August right after the word got out that the Japanese were ready to surrender. He said, 'I must get back into Indo-China and contact the Vietnamese. I have been delegated by Paris to try to smooth the way for the French return to Indo-China.' I said 'Oh, hold it, I can't help you here, this is not my area of responsibility.' But Sainteny tried very hard, and he even suggested at one point that I let him use American uniforms. He could dress as an American officer and so could his men and they could go in there as Americans. And I said: 'Never, never, never, it will never happen, we can't do it. I can tell you that basically you will not do it that way.'

Charlton: Now, we're coming to the fascinating episode of the use by Ho Chi Minh, as he seized power in Hanoi, of the famous wording of the American Declaration of Independence.

Patti: He actually called me in one afternoon and we discussed among many things the preparation of the text of the Declaration of Independence and he asked me to help him, and I told him point blank that there was very little that I could do to help him because I didn't remember it verbatim.

Charlton: Were his motives clear to you for using it at all?

Patti: At this point I'd like to agree with Major Sainteny, that I perhaps was somewhat naive at that point in time with respect to intent and purpose in using the words.

Charlton: What is your answer to Sainteny's charge, which he has made in his own record of these days, that you were guilty of an adolescent anti-colonialism which provided this very small band of Communists with an advantage that they should never have possessed?

Patti: Well, that's a matter of opinion. Major Sainteny has the right to his own opinion on that subject, but I felt very strongly that the Vietnamese had a legitimate gripe or claim, if you like to put it that way, to really govern themselves. After all what was this war all about? Self-determination of people to govern themselves, etc., etc. We've been through two wars fighting for the very same principle, so if you call that naive, well I guess that's alright, but I believed in it.

Charlton: What can you tell us about the day when Ho Chi Minh actually seized power in Hanoi?

Patti: I'd like to make a point clear: I've heard this so many times, that Ho Chi Minh seized power. Ho Chi Minh did not seize power. The power came about by the existence of a vacuum between the time of the Japanese acceptance of surrender terms and the time that the Japanese actually surrendered in fact, which was several weeks later. The vacuum was created by the Japanese withdrawing their administrative control of the major cities and by the fact that there was no one to take over. The Bao Dai Government itself just fell apart. The Vietminh were the only ones to present a concrete solid program. It was accepted.

Charlton: Accepted by whom?

Patti: Well accepted by the people in Indo-China itself, in Hué, in Vinh, in Touran, in Hanoi, everywhere, Haiphong. I mean there was really no such thing as either a formal coup or a takeover.

Charlton: But it was done under duress wasn't it? Bao Dai did it because he was told that they would make a Romanov of him if he didn't?

Patti: Bao really had not much to say about it. He had done nothing to start with, except in playing puppet to the Japanese. Therefore there was nothing he could do about it.

Charlton: But all the time this man, Ho Chi Minh, and his followers were transforming themselves into national leaders, largely because of the authority that—as many would suggest—you gave them as allies, that they could do this because you were always at their side.

Patti: Well that's a slight exaggeration—I wasn't always at their side. I was there in Hanoi for the specific purpose of making the arrangements for the surrender of the Japanese to Chiang Kai-shek. I was there for the specific purpose of assisting the allied POWs to be repatriated. So really I wasn't there at the side of Ho Chi Minh or of the Vietminh.

Charlton: But you appeared with them on the day that they proclaimed a Democratic Republic?

Patti: Oh yes. I appeared as a matter of courtesy at many occasions when called to do so.

Charlton: Incidentally, what can you tell us about the passage overhead of a flight of American aircraft which were taken, weren't they, by this rather confused crowd as more evidence that the Americans were supporting what was happening?

Patti: That was a quirk of fate, that was just one of those things that happens once in a million years, I suppose. During the speech that Ho was delivering from the rostrum, way up high, a flight of P.38s—I believe they were—came overhead. Sure enough, they were curious, I suppose about the huge crowds below and I can imagine what a pilot might do. 'Say, what's going on down there?' And they must have dipped down to look and many people interpreted that to be a dip of a salute.

Charlton: But that was just an accident?

Patti: Oh that was simply an accident. I never did find out where they came from or where they were going.

Charlton: How did you come to leave Hanoi, having seen the installation of this new government and having seen it take power?

Patti: I had received word that the OSS would be disbanded on the last day of September and were to be out of the area by 1 October. So on 30 September I took my leave from Ho and made arrangements to leave on the day that it was predetermined. And of course my last meeting with Ho was a rather sentimental one, if you want to call it that, because he really opened up and told me quite a bit of his background and his family and his own political problems and his own doubts at times of the way he was going and what was in the future for him. At the time he made it quite clear that it looked almost impossible for a peaceful transition for his country, that he would have to fight for it. As a matter of fact some of the last words he said were: 'I'm sorry to say that we're going to have to go it alone because we cannot depend on Russia. Of course, we cannot depend on the British or the United States to support us militarily, but the French have agreed to come back in force—we know that.'

In all that confusion of these first days of liberation following Japanese surrender in 1945 there is supporting evidence of the consummate skill with which Ho Chi Minh tipped the balance to his cause by conveying to the wondering and exuberant crowds that the unfamiliar faces of the Vietminh enjoyed the support of the victorious Allies. The apparent American benediction on Ho Chi Minh's men deeply impressed the Vietnamese. One of them, later to be a senior general and political figure in South Vietnam, was Tran Van Don. When did he hear the name Ho Chi Minh?

Don: His name was only known in 1945. People like myself discovered that there was a leader, who came and took over control of Hanoi, with the name of Ho Chi Minh, leading an organization. We didn't

Figure 1. Vietnamese Communists salute the new flag of the independent Republic of Vietnam, 2 September 1945 (Archimedes Patti)

Figure 2. Buddhist monk immolates himself as a protest against the Diem regime, 11 June 1963 (Keystone)

1945: THE UNTOLD STORY

know how big, but especially we knew at that time that this organization was backed by the Americans.

Charlton: And that was the crucial fact?

Don: Yes. That was the crucial fact, because in that time we were surprised to know that some Vietnamese organization, led by the name Ho Chi Minh, was backed by an American organization. We didn't call them CIA, we didn't call them OSS. We called it Secret American Organization.

Charlton: So you think the principal reason for Ho Chi Minh's sudden acceptance as a National Leader for North Vietnam was due more or less entirely to the fact that he was visibly being supported by the victorious Americans rather than any popular sentiment or uprising among the people?

Don: I am convinced about this, because at that time even Bao Dai as an Emperor, when he knew that this group led by Ho Chi Minh was backed by the Americans, said that is the best way to get independence. And he resigned very fast. He said there is nothing to say against these people because they are fighting for independence and the Americans are supporting these people.

Much the same appraisal of the effect on the crowds of seeing the Americans and Vietnamese Communist leaders like Ho—and the famous General Giap who was to be the victor of Dien Bien Phu—standing together as the independent Republic of Vietnam was proclaimed has come from General Ed Lansdale who was to become a legendary figure in the American involvement in Vietnam nine years later. Graham Greene based some of the characters in *The Quiet American* on Lansdale, who learnt from eye-witnesses about Patti's activities.

Lansdale: The people up in the North whom I talked to—those who were part of the early government and later quit, those who were parts of political organizations up there, non-Communist ones, nationalist ones and people in all walks of life up there—were positive that the Ho Chi Minh group were alright because of US support and as such could be trusted entirely; and said that if that hadn't happened they wouldn't have had a government that was viable at all with the people.

We were trusted as idealists who would help people, and not just with the material things but with a representative government, and so on, that we would favor. And they said that the sense came when they brought some of the US aircraft out of China and did a fly over Hanoi just as people were deciding whether or not to go ahead and form a new government with Ho Chi Minh and party, and that this sort of tipped the balance. The Americans were on the balcony, were riding their jeep around Hanoi and so on; it very definitely gave an impression of American support.

❙ After the Japanese surrendered in 1945, the apparent enthusiasm with which the first Americans to go into Indo-China, and Major Patti in particular, appeared to endorse the Vietminh, and his zeal in doing so, shocked the French community. Did Jean Sainteny have the impression that Patti was improvising policy on the spot or carrying out instructions?

Sainteny: I don't think he improvised. I think he had instructions, but he went beyond his orders. That is to say he overdid the instructions he had, maybe out of personal resentment towards France, I don't know. But the fact remains that he behaved towards us as a deliberate enemy, because when I was incarcerated by the Japanese and by the Vietminh, together with my associates in the Governor-General's palace, as I was French representative, it was therefore rather a special incarceration. I was permanently guarded by Japanese sentries, with fixed bayonets, and Patti used to come regularly to make sure we were really properly guarded by the Japanese—our common enemy—who had capitulated two weeks earlier. When you come to think of it, it really was abnormal. Were there instructions? I think there were; but I repeat, I think these instructions were exceeded by Patti who was overdoing things.

❙ Major Patti recalled clearly the conversations he had with General Donovan, that the instructions they were carrying out in Indo-China to frustrate the return to power of the French came directly from Roosevelt himself. Roosevelt had died by the time Ho Chi Minh seized power. Did Patti exceed those instructions? There seems little doubt that he and other American intelligence officers succumbed when they were with him not just to Ho Chi Minh's impressive determination and abilities but to his charm and flattery of them too. Ho perceived that it was the Americans, not the Russians, who would determine events in the immediate future in Indo-China, Ho saw that a short cut to power lay through them. Patti frankly concedes that he may have been naive. At a classical revolutionary moment

perhaps a certain lack of discipline in representational behavior, together with those national characteristics giving expression to individuality and enthusiasm which marked the Americans, may have overstepped the bounds of political caution.
  The fact is that it was the Americans who literally took revolution by the hand and accompanied it into Hanoi. The visible support of the Americans and their apparent benediction upon the proceedings gave Ho Chi Minh the political initiative, an apparent legitimacy and a hold on power he never let go. Dean Rusk, who later became President Kennedy's Secretary of State, was at this time Deputy Chief of Staff in the China-Burma-India theater in charge of American military intelligence for South-East Asia.

Rusk: We on the American side believed that the great colonial areas of Asia would have of necessity become independent. Franklin Roosevelt bumped his head against your Mr Churchill quite hard on that at times. Mr Churchill didn't yield on it. As a matter of fact while we were in India we had considerable friction with some of your people because we tried to explain to the Indians that we were there solely for the purpose of fighting the Japanese and that we were not involved in their relations with the British at the end of the war. Franklin Roosevelt had the idea that India, Burma, Ceylon, Malaya, Indonesia, Indo-China should emerge from World War II as independent nations. Somewhere along the way, perhaps around January of 1945, he seemed to give up on this idea. He lost interest in it. Whether that was because he was getting old and tired or had other preoccupations I just don't know. Then after his tragic death, Mr Truman was so heavily involved in becoming President and looking after problems arising from the occupation of Germany and the continuation of the war against Japan that he did not pick up the same policy attitude and press it forward.
Charlton: But it was an absolutely vital period this, wasn't it?
Rusk: Yes, it was. You see out in that part of the world the combined Chiefs of Staff had delegated command responsibility to the British Chiefs of Staff, so that when an American President lost interest in pressing matters of this sort then the command responsibility really rested with Mr Churchill.
Charlton: But can you help as to why Roosevelt as you say gave up on this idea because, as you point out, his view is well attested that the United States did not wish the colonial powers to return particularly in South-East Asia. Cordell Hull in his memoirs quotes Roosevelt as

saying that the French milked Indo-China for a hundred years and the Indo-Chinese were entitled to something better than that. And at the same time, at this time of course the United States was giving support to Communist guerillas in Vietnam through the OSS, the forerunner of the CIA's early mission. What do you think forced the abandonment of that position?

Rusk: I think it was possibly because Mr Roosevelt was losing his powers at that time but also I think there was some thought on the American side that with the coming of Mr Attlee to the Prime Ministership that as far as the British areas were concerned this problem was probably going to be solved within the British system itself and they needed no outside help. We did have further problems with regard to Indonesia, and with the French in Indo-China. I remember very clearly Secretary of State George Marshall, who after all had something of an understanding of military matters, telling our friends the Dutch that they could bleed themselves white and still not succeed in restoring their control of Indonesia. Therefore they had to get out because no one else would help them, you see. Well, the French as it turned out were somewhat in the same position, but governments in France during much of this period were too weak to make the tough decisions with respect to Indo-China. So there was a possible turning point in history that somehow didn't quite come out the way at least Franklin Roosevelt had in mind.

▎But when did Dean Rusk think it was apparent to the Americans that Ho Chi Minh was less interested in independence from colonial rule in Indo-China than with the creation of a Communist-organized state?

Rusk: Oh I think that became apparent as early as 1946 and 1947. Actually I was among those who authorized the dropping of arms to Ho Chi Minh during World War II, because we were ready to help anybody who would shoot at the Japanese at that period. If there was ever any chance of helping Ho Chi Minh to move off in a different direction, it would have been I think late 1945 and early 1946 and that opportunity was lost if there ever was one.

▎As down the long tunnel of the years the nature of Ho Chi Minh's swift and sure seizure of the moment and the hour in Hanoi becomes clearer, it has claimed close attention and many judgments.

Dennis Duncanson: The program that Ho Chi Minh had been working to during the Second World War was that he would be seated in power in Hanoi along with other Communists, by Chiang Kai-shek. That the KMT, the Nationalist Party of China and its army, was going to invade Indo-China. The Nationalist government were going to invade Indo-China, and they were going to set up in Indo-China a regime which would supersede the French. They would be out for good. At this time, when the plan was hatched, the French were still in power; they hadn't been unseated by the Japanese. They would be driven out on the grounds that they were Vichy supporters—in that respect I suppose Vichy comes to be of some significance: they were anti-Ally and pro-Axis—they would be driven out and a Chinese protectorate would be restored of even greater significance perhaps than the Chinese protectorate of the nineteenth century. Under this protectorate Ho Chi Minh would set up an autonomous government which would hope eventually to see the Chinese depart.

Now during the course of the war of course the Chinese element became less and less significant and the Americans moved in, and they became the allies. But there's no question that the Communist Party, or Ho Chi Minh personally, or anybody else, actually won power in Indo-China simply by sentimental appeal to the mass of the people. Politics isn't of that kind, and no Communist has ever supposed that it was. Politics grows out of the barrel of a gun, and the strength that Ho Chi Minh and his followers could look for, his central committee round him, would derive from whatever outside power would support them.

Charlton: And that was the Americans, as the victors over the Japanese?

Duncanson: Particularly since Chiang Kai-shek was also negotiating with a rival Vietnamese faction and trying to seat that in power: and Ho Chi Minh had no intention of sharing power. Nationalism is all very well, but it's no good if somebody else ends up by exercising it.

Charlton: What comment do you have in retrospect on the audacity and success of Ho Chi Minh's tactics at this time? He had eluded successfully accommodation with the Chinese occupying army in North Vietnam, he had eluded successfully a coalition with nationalists like the Kuomintang. He had made a successful and confusing appeal to the Americans, particularly to their intelligence services. What in retrospect appears to you to be the dimensions of his success with a very small following apparently, on his own admission?

Duncanson: Five thousand at most, five thousand at most. Well, if

I may express it in Machiavellian terms and not with a view to my own prejudices in the matter, I would say that it was sublime. I think that it partakes of a sublimity even greater than that of Lenin. I would put Ho Chi Minh's capacity in the actual exercise of power in his narrow field as more remarkable than Lenin's. Of course Lenin was on a much broader canvas, and Lenin was a great literary figure and so on, which Ho Chi Minh was not: Ho Chi Minh wrote very little as you know and was not a great intellect. But in his narrow field where he could operate he was, I would say, as a political manipulator, sublime.

2

The return and defeat of France

▌ So Indo-China in 1945 saw the Americans saluting a new red flag flying above the citadel in Hanoi. This chapter deals with the complete reversal in America's attitude, the return of the French and their ultimate departure after the battle of Dien Bien Phu. In taking his swift and sure step to power Ho Chi Minh had followed the course of action laid down by Lenin more faithfully than any other Communist leader. The personality of Ho and his political skills dominated the immediate future and the next twenty-five years in Vietnam. What he stood for, his beliefs and methods of realizing them, therefore deserve closer attention. They were what first the French, and then the Americans, came up against. The background has been sketched-in by Dennis Duncanson.

Duncanson: 1923—he went off to Moscow; and there he was put into the machine and used as a figurehead for the founding of the Peasant International. That's when Ho Chi Minh began to be famous. I don't think there is much doubt that he was singled out as a bright young man. There was no question whatever he was. He was one of the great figures of the twentieth century in my opinion, I have a great admiration for him. I mean I don't approve of his unscrupulousness but it was in its way very admirable and very successful. He moved to and fro between Paris and Moscow, until they decided how to fit him into the oriental operation. One has to remember what Lenin's objectives were. Lenin was quite explicit about this! He looked forward to a world state in which all nations could be abolished. Just as classes would be wiped out, so he said nations will be wiped out, and there will be one universal state with its capital somewhere in Europe. I think his first choice actually was London and his second choice was Berlin. Reluctantly for the time being he had to accept that Moscow was the capital, but sooner or later the whole world was to be drawn in.

The first place in the caditalist world to be drawn in was Germany. Unfortunately that failed in 1923; the revolution in Germany was a fiasco. So Lenin and his comrades moved to the second target which was China. China's situation was one of pretty frightening chaos. Ho

Chi Minh was to be an employee of that mission in Canton, and incidentally to do what he could to subvert and make Communist recruits of some of the young students who were known to be present in South China in those days from all over South-East Asia, and also from Korea, Indonesia, Malaysia, Indo-China, Thailand and so on.

Charlton: Was he throughout this period, in your view, anything other than an instrument of Soviet diplomacy, Soviet power?

Duncanson: In my opinion, no. They were his employers and that was the job that was in hand. I notice that in 1922—to put a precise date on it, the issue of 25 May 1922—he wrote an article in *L'Humanité* in which he discussed the question of nationalism in colonies and said that this was a great danger to the revolution and ought to be nipped in the bud. Rather an interesting point, which is I think one of the few pieces that really pinpoint this question of nationalism. I know in after years he said it was 'nationalism that led me to Lenin'; it would be far truer to say it was Lenin who led him to nationalism and the use of nationalism in temporary revolutionary fronts and maneuvers.

Charlton: How did they proceed to go about winning power in Vietnam?

Duncanson: By any means that came to hand. Lenin's method of getting power in Russia had been to turn the imperialist war into a civil war.

Charlton: In 1945, at this very early period when the boundaries of the post-war world were being drawn up between the victors and the vanquished or between the victors in particular, the success of Ho Chi Minh rested upon the boldness of his claims to have a relationship with the victors. But how significant do you think it was going to prove from this moment on in all the subsequent treaties—be they the Geneva Accords of 1954 and everything that preceded them—that somehow Ho Chi Minh had won a legitimacy as the authorized government of North Vietnam?

Duncanson: I think he'd won legitimacy in the outside world rather than in his own country. I think that people give him great credit for having been an exponent of guerilla warfare like Mao Tse-tung, but I think that even more he deserved credit for his guerilla diplomacy. He had very much in his mind that the way to get power was to consolidate it bit by bit. At no time did he ever lose sight of world revolution and every pronouncement always mentions world revolution at the end as a primary objective. We should never forget that, never focusing solely on the national territory. What happened to him was that he was able to establish a position each time from which the international community, and especially those of liberal tendency in the international community like myself, would regard it as illegitimate to try to evict him, and then he would use such a base to make another forward movement. The Vietnamese have a very nice pithy phrase for this; it is 'Hoa de tien', which means each peace agreement is a springboard for a further advance. So he got out of the Americans a consolidated position of establishing in the world eye— and got recognition from people like Pandit Nehru and so on—that he had a government in Tonkin. That fact that Truman then withdrew the Americans and said: 'You've overstepped your brief, now you've got to push off, we're going to withdraw you before you do any further damage', doesn't matter all that much. They'd served their purpose, and now he cosied up the next stage to first the Chinese and then the French.

Now, the Chinese were there as an occupying force disarming the Japanese, and repatriating their troops. So what he had to do now was make use of the Chinese in order not to get rid of the French but to get concessions out of the French. He didn't want to get rid of anybody for the prime reason that there was no money in the treasury and he'd got to have foreign money to keep his government going. If he couldn't keep his government going the people, the mass of the people, wouldn't obey him. So he had to get money, and he used in the next few months a most skilful double negotiation with the French and the Chinese to play off each of them so that he got the maximum advantage out of them. But he never failed throughout to play the card that because of his success in setting up a government with American backing in September 1945, he was a legitimate government in the eyes of the outside world and a lot of people so recognized him.

Charlton: Do you believe in view of his repeated appeals to the Americans for support, these now famous letters of appeal that he addressed to them, that there was an opportunity for the Americans to agree at this very early stage to the establishment of something like a Titoist brand of Communism which was divorced from Soviet strategic imperatives, which would have been broadly consistent with American aims had the Americans been alert to the actual situation inside the country?

Duncanson: No I don't. He was never a Titoist of course and always condemned Tito as roundly as Mao Tse-tung condemned Tito. This is a nice pious hope. Ho Chi Minh wanted a monopoly of power, and the establishment of Communist Party rule in his territory. Now what happens (and this is the true explanation of what is called multipolarity in the Communist world, the underlying reason for the Sino-Soviet dispute, for Tito's dispute, for the attempts at independence of Rumania and so on) is of course if you have a Communist party and a forthright leader, a leader of character, in charge of it in any country naturally he's going to have his own ambition. To the extent that he had his own ambition he's going to appear to be independent. But on the other hand his independence is going to be circumscribed by his dependence on outside aid, and Ho Chi Minh would have, of course, taken outside aid from anywhere he could get it; but he would never have sacrificed to it his own monopoly of power, the monopoly of power of his party and a monopoly of power of himself within his party. That was the ultimate irreducible objective, and if we suppose that somehow or other he would have turned into a bourgeois democrat or something like that because really he was a patriot—this I'm afraid is all for the birds.

Charlton: No, but he might have served the objectives of the containment as the Americans broadly saw it, had he been a client of the Americans. Do you believe that that was remotely feasible, that he could have served the objectives of the containment of the larger power and authority of the Soviet Union and China?

Duncanson: No, I don't think so at all. I think he would have taken whatever help he could that the Americans were willing to give him. Then when Mao Tse-tung came to power in the end of 1949 he would have made common cause with Mao Tse-tung—even if he had not at that time simply been a guerilla fighting in the hills, even if he had been in power. He would still have made common cause with Mao Tse-tung at that time—I think that is absolutely certain, and in solid alliance with the Soviet Union. China and the Soviet Union at that time were absolutely one, and I think that Communist Indo-China would have been alongside them.

▌Ho's policy, as we have seen, was to do nothing to assist, and some things to frustrate, the return of France to Indo-China and to allow things in Indo-China to take their course. Roosevelt thought that Indo-China should be taken away from France, and given full independence after a period under international trusteeship. American views on independence for the 'colonies' were strongly resisted by the British who did not wish to see any precedent established in Indo-China which would challenge their own role in South-East Asia. They saw the question of independence as self-government within the framework of empire: and so did the French.

It is important to recall how sharp those arguments about colonialism between the Allies were. Something of their flavor was contained in a jibe the Americans often made about the joint United States/British South-East Asia command set up under Mountbatten, or SEAC. It was known to the Americans as 'Saving England's Asiatic Colonies'. The strong views Roosevelt entertained about Indo-China in particular had not been shared by his own State Department, who thought that France should be allowed to return to Indo-China in return for a pledge about eventual self-government —when qualified for it—along the lines of the Philippines.

Cordell Hull, the Secretary of State in 1944, had pointed out to Roosevelt that while America was seeking the closest possible cooperation with the parent colonial powers they could not alienate them in the Orient and still expect to work closely with them in Europe. Successive French Leaders, Petain, Giraud and de Gaulle, had been told, as official American policy, that America supported the return of France to her Empire overseas. These documents show clearly that the Americans were conscious that they were trying to balance two conflicting policies. When Roosevelt died something of the priority that he was giving to the anti-colonial issue was removed too. At Potsdam, the military conference between the big powers in 1945, it was agreed that Britain would disarm the Japanese army following surrender south of the sixteenth parallel in Indo-China, and the Chinese Nationalists would do the same north of the sixteenth parallel. And so it was that with the arrival of a British general to take the Japanese surrender in Saigon came the return of the French to Indo-China. The historical anti-colonialism of the Roosevelt period shifted in emphasis decisively with the onset of the cold war. In the same month, September 1945, that Ho had seized power in Hanoi, there was a conference in London of the foreign ministers of the big powers—a political conference to succeed the military one at Potsdam. By this time much of what Roosevelt had hoped would be possible in agreement with Stalin had begun to evaporate.

In the summer of 1945 Truman, now President, had failed to get the Russians to comply with the agreements made at Yalta which provided for free and unfettered elections as the basis for self determination of peoples. Stalin was setting up new governments uniterally in Eastern Europe demanding the return of refugees to the Soviet Union. The whole atmosphere between the big powers changed in the first and now substantial chill of the cold war. Byrnes, the American Secretary of State at the London conference which followed Potsdam, told Truman that, as he put it, 'the Russians are welching on all their agreements'. It was this above all which threw American policy over Indo-China into disarray.

George Marshall and Dean Acheson were the principal influences on American foreign policy during this period, and Dean Rusk has noted the differences between them.

Rusk: This turned a bit on personalities. Secretary Marshall had a pretty comprehensive view of the world. Secretary Acheson was very much a North Atlantic kind of man and he was so anxious to have close French cooperation with you and with us in the formation of NATO and the Marshall Plan and great enterprises of that sort.

Charlton: There was the prospect then, wasn't there, of a Communist government in France?

Rusk: That is correct, yes. That was one of the real possibilities. So Mr Acheson's interest in Indo-China was a kind of by-product of his interest in France you see. Even so we did press the French rather strongly at times to go ahead and make a political solution with the three states of Indo-China, even while we were helping France through the Marshall Plan and military assistance and other things, with the kind of aid that they transferred to some degree to Indo-China.

Charlton: Why did the United States approve return of the French to Indo-China do you think, given that it must have been pretty obvious that meant war in Vietnam?

Rusk: Well, we did not take the view that it was really our choice. We couldn't order the British to stay out of India and Burma, Ceylon, Malaya. We couldn't issue orders to the Dutch to stay out of Indonesia and the French to stay out of Indo-China.

Charlton: But France could not have returned without the material aid and support that Marshall was prepared to give them.

Rusk: Perhaps, perhaps. Certainly the situation in France would have been very serious indeed without that help. But I think if there is a criticism of US policy on that point during that period it was that we tried to straddle something that couldn't be straddled. We tried to keep one foot in both points of view and that is rather tough to do.

Charlton: But is it right to suggest that what made it impossible for the United States to support Ho Chi Minh was that here was the convinced Marxist-Leninist, who saw the key to change as a class struggle and revolution as the path to independence, and the United States, while willing to encourage independence, could not grant it by those means, in fact was opposed to them?

Rusk: I think, yes. We were not embarked upon a crusade against Communism as an ideology, but there were times when public opinion became involved in just that issue. For example, when we first consulted with Senator Arthur Vandenberg about the Marshall Plan, he said: 'Well gentlemen, if you want that kind of money out of the Congress, you have got to scare the hell out of them'—and to some extent NATO was a by-product of the Marshall Plan, because it helped to put that entire effort on security grounds you see . . .

Charlton: You had to demonstrate a threat.

Rusk: That's right. And a threat, as it turned out, was there.

Thus it was in the bleak context of the cold war that the Americans reconsidered their anti-colonialism or at least the priority that it had had in their foreign policy. Western Europe, not Asia, had first claim now on their attention. Rusk's words remind us of the special influence personalities had in contributing to the change. General George Marshall who had personal contacts with Mao Tse-tung in China, had given way to Dean Acheson, President Truman's Secretary of State. Acheson was an Atlanticist and he gave an urgent emphasis to the recovery of Western Europe to be achieved economically by the Marshall Plan and militarily by NATO as the foundation of the western alliance.

In the building of the military alliance France assumed a particular importance for American policy as the only continental nation, in the days well before German rearmament, which was capable of making a sizeable contribution of troops.

The situation in France itself was cause for concern. The large French Communist Party was expanding; it had played a major role in the Resistance. There were Communist ministers in the first postwar government. There was the prospect that in the coming elections in France the Communists would do well enough to win. The French Communists were naturally opposed to conflict with Ho Chi Minh in Indo-China. The Americans had withdrawn from active intervention on the spot in Indo-China. Under the British aegis, French authority was by now re-established in the south of Indo-China. In the north, Ho Chi Minh was not yet as powerful as he became in the 1950s with military victory. Ho had to concede that the best way to negotiate successfully the withdrawal of the Chinese Nationalist occupying army which took the surrender of the Japanese in the north was to acquiesce in the return of the French.

But the weakness of the French position and the strength of Ho Chi Minh's appeal to nationalist Vietnamese opinion was that France was offering a qualified form of something they already claimed to have seized—independence. Jean Sainteny was the representative of France who negotiated with Ho Chi Minh the conditions of the French return, culminating in agreements in March 1946. To what extent was French policy at this time influenced by the domestic political scene in France? Sainteny answers first in terms of Indo-China.

Sainteny [translation]: It's obvious that we didn't think it unnatural that a Vietnamese government, with authority north of the 16th and 17th parallels, should have Communist ministers in it. We had some in our government in France at the time. In any case, what we were seeking was to avoid conflict. It was certain that if we could avoid this trial of strength at the price of accepting a Vietnamese government which included four or five Communists—even if the head of this government was himself a Communist, in the person of Ho Chi Minh—that didn't seem to me too high a price to pay. We'd fought side by side with the Communists. They were our comrades in battle.

❚ In France too, where Thorez was leader of the large and expanding Communist Party, there seemed the possibility at the time of a Communist majority in government. Psychologically, had Jean Sainteny and his contemporaries been prepared to accept Communists?

Sainteny: Absolutely. Don't forget that Maurice Thorez was at the time Vice President of the Council of Ministers. He himself had become much more of a nationalist than a Communist. And, undeniably, the French Communists who were part of the French government were urging an understanding with the Vietnamese Communists, who were part of the Vietnamese government. It was perfectly natural. But apart from a few militants who were blinded by partisan passion, the Communist members of the French government did not encourage the Communist members of the Vietnamese government to adopt an attitude pressing for war; rather they encouraged them to try and find grounds for understanding.

❚ In northern Indo-China, Sainteny, as the representative of the French government, had worked out in 1946 the outlines of a political settlement—'freedom within the French union'—with Ho Chi Minh, which lasted only a few months. What had been the meaning of the agreements he signed with Ho Chi Minh in March 1946?

Sainteny: Let me rectify that: I didn't sign an agreement with the Communists. I signed an agreement with the government I found there when I arrived in Hanoi. This government was Communist-led of course, but it was a government which was trying to be one of national union. Was it really that? No, of course not. When the Communists are in government, they are the ones who pull the strings. But, in fact, apparently there were as many nationalists as Communists in this government. Consequently, the government with which I signed the famous agreements of 6 March 1946, after months and months of extremely difficult negotiations—you can imagine—was a government of national union. I had, moreover, refused to sign anything with a government composed exclusively of Communists.

▎Had Ho been led to believe that France would accept *unification* under the Communists, in order to maintain the French position in Indo-China?

Sainteny: Let's go back in this respect to a proposal which had been secretly made to me by Ho Chi Minh, whereby it was understood that Indo-China would keep a status of federation, including the former parts of French Indo-China, and that this federation would have its place in the French union. Consequently, there was no question of handing over—it was said so afterwards on different occasions—of handing over Indo-China to the Communists. In this federation, there was to be a part of Indo-China which normally had to be north of the 17th or 16th parallels, which would have been ruled by a government in which there would have been Communists, in which, naturally, the Communists would have been in the majority; but there was no question of the rest of Indo-China coming under Communist authority; that was never in the minds of the French negotiators—in any case, not in mine.

▎At this time, 1946, had Jean Sainteny tried to remove the mass of the Vietnamese people from the Communist side, by dealing with the nationalists, for example?

Sainteny: No, and for good reason. The idea obviously occurred to us—or it did to me, at any rate, in particular. The nationalist parties were not sufficiently credible, on the one hand. Their leaders weren't up to much, and those who might have been were entirely in the hands of the Chinese. You see, they were people in the pay of the Chinese and whose real intentions weren't very clear, or rather, they *were* clear.

❙ The 'agreement' between the French government and Ho Chi Minh broke down after a few months in mutual distrust and bloodshed. While this fitful cooperation had lasted the French Army had helped Ho Chi Minh eliminate many of his adversaries, including pro-American nationalists. In the South, the French had set up an autonomous republic as a counterweight to Ho Chi Minh's independent republic in the North. By December 1946 the degree of French control was being contested. The Vietminh were shooting at the French in Hanoi and the French were bombarding the port of Haiphong to teach the Communists a lesson.

On 20 December Ho Chi Minh's government was swept aside and driven out of Hanoi by the incidents it had in part provoked. Ho went back to his guerrilla sanctuaries to begin protracted revolutionary war based on class struggle to decide the future of Vietnam.

While he was doing that—an event of transcendental importance changed the whole context in South-East Asia. The civil war in China which had begun in 1947 ended with victory for Mao Tse-tung in 1949—and we shall return to aspects of this in the next chapter. Ho Chi Minh's sanctuaries along the border with China were now guaranteed, and a constant and uninterrupted build-up of supplies was available to him for war against the French.

Despite the stance of cautious detachment from events in Indo-China, America was once again called upon to make a response. René Pleven, who was then Prime Minister of France, explained the circumstances of 1950.

Pleven: I think that the matter holds in a quite natural way, when discussing our military needs with the United States in the frame of the NATO arrangements. The United States were asking the Allies to increase their military power. Obviously we had to take into consideration the strain on our resources and our material which was caused by the Indo-Chinese war.

THE RETURN AND DEFEAT OF FRANCE 31

▌ In the early nineteen-fifties and with the cold war at its zenith, events in Indo-China were overshadowed by the significance and importance of the Korean War, and Communist China's intervention there with her armies across an Asian mainland frontier. This was the context which again triggered an American response in Indo-China. Jean Letourneau, the French Minister for the Associated States of Indo-China, explained when and how the first American aid came to Saigon.

Letourneau: The first American supplies arrived in Saigon on 29 June 1950. There was no discussion that time, it was entirely finished. Of course it was no more than the Americans were the givers, wanted to be perfectly sure of the exact destination of the aid they were supplying. But on the other hand it was normal too that France, who was alone bearing the weight of the war, and of whom alone the children were killed, asked to be the only consignée, for two reasons: she was using by herself arms and ammunitions, and she was responsible for the organization of the new national Vietnamese army—the decision of creating that army having been taken quite recently by agreement between His Majesty Bao Dai and the French government. Of course, the Pentagon maintained in Saigon a military mission for checking the arrivals of the supplies, but I have to say that relations between that mission and the French General Staff were always excellent.

▌ So President Truman authorized substantial aid to the French to allow them to carry on in Indo-China. By 1952 the Americans were contributing 400 million dollars a year. The Iron Curtain confronted the western alliance across eastern Europe. In Korea, the Chinese were negotiating—yet at the same time expanding both the scale and intensity of the fighting, during long months of intransigence at Panmonjom. American casualties were greater during the period of negotiations than they were before them—in conformity with the Communists' strategy of 'fighting to negotiate'. This and an expanding conflict in Indo-China were the circumstances in which the Americans begin to look at the vulnerability of all South-East Asia, and were conceiving the doctrine of containment and giving expression to it in the person of a new Secretary of State, John Foster Dulles, under a new American President, Dwight Eisenhower. The balance in Indo-China began to change against the French and the burden of fighting Ho Chi Minh's insurgent warfare was becoming too heavy to shoulder. In the French Empire in North Africa, unrest was taking root from Tunis to Casablanca. Professor Robert Bowie was at this period in charge of policy planning at the State Department; but he also speaks in this book for the late John Foster Dulles.

Bowie: I think the picture—and I think it was more like an image than a kind of specific analysis—was that these were weak governments through most of this area; that they were readily subject to internal or domestic subversion; and that if you had a beginning in which an area, a certain part of the area like Vietnam or Indo-China, became a center of Communist control, that it would probably be used as an effective base for further subversion outward, and that because of the weakness of these governments there was not any particular reason to suppose that they would be able to resist, and that they would therefore tend to come under domination one at a time. I think the fear was that this would be sort of a spreading kind of infection, and that the power of China wouldn't necessarily be exerted by any invasion or military action but rather simply by the existence of this vast powerful state to the north of many of them and that the combination of that plus the existence of an indigenous or local Communist power in Indo-China would probably act like pinchers politically, though not necessarily involving direct military aggression—probably more in the form of use of guerillas and local subversion and the like.

Charlton: So would it be true then to say that Dulles considered that China was the force driving the conflicts to come?

Bowie: I think that would be fair. I think the assumption was that the countries themselves were not very strong social orders and that it was not too hard to generate groups of dissent which could be converted into local guerilla actions—as was, indeed, happening of course in north-eastern Laos. But I think the assumption was that probably the energy, the driving force so to speak would be China, yes.

Charlton: And you don't think that Dulles considered China an expansionist power? Or did he have doubts about that?

Bowie: I think Dulles thought of it as expansionist probably in the sense of seeking to expand its influence. My recollection is that people didn't assume that China would mount military aggression and take over this area. There was a sort of assumption on the basis of history that China would like to have a predominant position in the area and that it would exercise the necessary influence or pressures to try to achieve that, but not that there would be direct military action, invasion by Chinese forces, unless it was provoked by external presence of much greater powers like the US or other forces.

▌ Now in the face of Ho Chi Minh's accelerating insurgency in the countryside of Northern Vietnam the French staked all by seeking a military trial of strength. In a large amphitheater of ground, surrounded by hills, shrouded in mist, and densely grown with jungle far away from the centres of population, near the border with Laos, the French deliberately issued an invitation to Ho Chi Minh's peasant army to come down and fight. They believed their apparent vulnerability would delude the Vietnamese Communists into accepting enticing odds, but that the firepower of a western garrison would prove decisive and make this place called Dien Bien Phu a killing ground. No greater misjudgment was made in war. Ho's army showed enormous endurance and capacities in manhandling many of their heavy guns across the mountains: the French garrison was cut off and beleaguered. Dien Bien Phu was not a killing ground but a trap. It fell and Ho Chi Minh's peasant army, commanded by General Giap, took ten thousand French prisoners. The French had made a desperate appeal to the Americans to help to save it by launching an air strike. One of the sustained myths about the Vietnam War is that France was made a positive offer of the atomic bomb to save the garrison at Dien Bien Phu. René Pleven had become Defense Minister at the time of Dien Bien Phu.

Pleven: My comment is that some people may have thought of it but that the French Government never requested the use of an atomic weapon against its adversaries in Indo-China.

▌ So, the French government didn't 'request' atomic weapons for use says the then Defense Minister. But, during the critical conversations about a possible air strike—carrier based—by the Americans, between Dulles and the French Foreign Minister's deputy, Maurice Schumann was present in the same room while the issue was being discussed. What did Dulles offer?

Schumann: He didn't really offer. He made a suggestion and asked a question, but he actually uttered the two fatal words 'atomic bomb'. I must say that the French Foreign Minister, Georges Bidault, whose deputy I was, immediately reacted as if he didn't take this offer seriously. It was never, never so far as we are concerned, it was never a practical proposal.

▌Robert Bowie, speaking for John Foster Dulles, was highly sceptical that an offer of nuclear weapons was ever actually made.

Bowie: I simply don't believe it, and if he did I don't believe he had any authority to do so. But I don't believe he did it, for two reasons: I'm perfectly clear that Eisenhower was not about to authorize any use of nuclear weapons; and second in my experience Dulles simply did not do things on his own authority which he knew the President was not prepared to support. He was meticulous in clearing with the President anything of any importance, that was my experience: and on a thing of this consequence which he knew perfectly well the President would not have authorized I don't believe for a minute that he would have done so.

Charlton: But if it wasn't ever meant to carry the force of executive action is it incredible that he may not have suggested this as part of the bluff, or to hint at the possible use of it, as a means of coercing China and the Soviet Union?

Bowie: I don't think that he would have used anything so precise. If Schumann's recollection is as you say, my guess is it would be more likely from conversations with somebody like Admiral Radford. It's quite conceivable to me that Radford—who couldn't possibly have said 'we will authorize it' because he couldn't have had that authority —might very well have talked about it with Ely, the French Chief of Staff; and I believe they had a rather continuous kind of contact during this period. Radford may well have said he would propose it or recommend it. I don't know. That's quite conceivable to me. But I don't see Dulles acting in that way: and while I think he was quite anxious to create this sense of concern on the part of the Chinese, I do not think he would have done so by anything so specific as that when he knew perfectly well that the President would not have been willing to approve it.

▌Maurice Schumann underlines the point made by Bowie that Eisenhower was determined against any unilateral action, that is to say without the support of allies, and that Eisenhower was the man in charge.

Schumann: I'm sure the President was opposed to any form of intervention. After all he'd been elected as you know to restore peace in

Asia, to end the Korean War. He was not the kind of man to start a new military commitment in the Far East. He was far more cautious than his successors were, and the fact that he was opposed was enough by itself to settle the problem. But I'm not quite sure that either Foster Dulles or Richard Nixon (who was Eisenhower's Vice President) were exactly in the same mood.

In February just before the battle for Dien Bien Phu fully developed, the big powers had met in Berlin. At the end of that conference they were deadlocked over the questions of German reunification and disarmament. The stalemate of the cold war would therefore continue on the European continent. But they did make a move to break that deadlock by convening a conference over Indo-China. They agreed to meet in Geneva in April 1954. By this time the battle for Dien Bien Phu was raging, the fall of its garrison approaching. The negotiating position of the Communist powers was being immeasurably strengthened, as the prospect advanced of the defeat in battle of the soldiers of the white colonial power on ground of its own choosing by an Asian peasant army supplied and armed from China and Russia. Dulles, Eisenhower's Secretary of State, was urgently trying to enlist some kind of joint effort among the Allies, including Britain.

Bowie: Dulles made a speech at the end of March about the necessity for dealing with the problem by 'united action', which was a very vague phrase. I do not think myself that he intended or expected that there would be military action. What I think was in his mind was that the French position was rapidly crumbling, that they were about to go to the Geneva meeting with virtually nothing to negotiate with, nothing in their hands. Their military position was extremely weak and he was fearful that the Chinese and the Soviets whom he saw basically in charge of the negotiating position on the other side would push their position to the limit, and perhaps bring about a takeover of the whole of Indo-China. So his tactic so to speak was to try to create a sense of concern or fear on the part of the Soviets and the Chinese that if they pushed too far they might provoke an actual military response by the West. I think myself that what he was trying to do was to create the uncertainty in the minds of the Soviets and the Chinese on this point.
Charlton: In other words it was a bluff at that time to warn the Chinese?
Bowie: In effect it was. Precisely.

▌Dulles' efforts to recruit Britain in particular for a joint initiative were rejected for reasons explained by Lord Avon in an interview in 1967. It is clear that he disagreed not just with the action proposed but also the fundamental tenet of the theory of containment in South-East Asia. Eden believed that if the Chinese did choose to expand it would not be southwards but to the west, in which case the Russians would have the most cause for concern.

Avon: Originally, when this problem arose in 1954, it seemed to us that the conflict was in its origins a colonial war. Maybe that the Communists were seeking to profit by it, was one aspect. And the other aspect which troubled us a good deal, it didn't seem to us that any of the actions then canvassed—such as an air strike at Dien Bien Phu—were likely to be effective. On the contrary, we thought it would get the worst of both worlds, because it wouldn't succeed. The only thing that could succeed, we felt strongly at the time, would be military action of all three arms on the scale of a Korean War, and we didn't think then that the world was prepared to do that. Nor did we think that was a policy we wanted ourselves to carry out.

Charlton: How do your views of what Chinese intentions are in South-East Asia differ from the American view?

Avon: I don't know that they do. I find it extremely difficult to make an assessment of Chinese intentions. I think everybody must. But what I do feel myself is that whatever Chinese ambitions may be they're likely to be linked with their population problem, therefore that they may be more interested in countries that lie westward of them than they are either in Indo-China or in India.

▌At the time of the fall of Dien Bien Phu the Americans had been supplying the French armies in the field for four years. That aid was on an ascending scale and at the end accounted for almost eighty per cent of French expenditure on the war. Dien Bien Phu was humiliation for France. It was also a reverberating defeat for American policy. How did it fit into the overall American assessment of what might be salvaged? For, from this time forward, the Americans had to take all their decision in the light of this Communist victory by force of arms. Sir Robert Thompson was later head of the British advisory mission in Vietnam, and also became a personal adviser to Presidents Kennedy and Nixon.

Thompson: The point about Dien Bien Phu was that it didn't win the war militarily. The French could have held on for a very long time, and might even have developed still quite a strong position in the South—because Dien Bien Phu was way up in North Vietnam. I don't necessarily think that it was as decisive as we make out in the military sense. Where it was decisive was it broke the French will to continue the war.

Charlton: Can a guerilla war ever be decisive in your view? Is it always a test of will rather than a trial of strength?

Thompson: That is true, because a guerilla war of this type is bound to be a protracted war lasting for five, ten, fifteen, twenty years, and it is a test of stamina.

Charlton: What was it about that war which was unappreciated, do you believe, by the Americans? Was it the protracted nature of the conflict?

Thompson: Oh yes. It's not only the protracted nature of the conflict but the political nature of the conflict. After all, what this war was about right from 1945 after World War II through the first Indo-China war and through the second Indo-China war was the succession to power in Indo-China after the French had left. The whole of this war right the way through was to decide in Indo-China as a whole, not just in Vietnam, who was going to succeed to French power. It was quite clear at the end of the war that though the French could fight a rear-guard action, and could play their part in deciding who succeeded to power, it was not going to be a French colony any longer. In other words, under direct French rule. You therefore had two forces in Indo-China: you had the well-organized guerilla forces of Ho Chi Minh which achieved an enormous coup in 1945 in their Declaration of Independence, but above all in the way they destroyed the leading members of the nationalist anti-Communist people amongst the South Vietnamese. What happened through the French war was that the French to a very large extent were able to build up Vietnamese forces, both military and political, which were not so much pro-French but were definitely anti-Communist and it was these forces which eventually centered into South Vietnam, because people came out of North Vietnam, and it was these forces that built up the South Vietnamese government after the Geneva Agreement in 1954.

▌In making this point that the war in Vietnam was the war to decide the succession to colonial power, Sir Robert Thompson illuminates what many hold to be the essential weakness of the American anti-colonial stance. The Americans believed that it was colonialism which was the reason for the Communist advance, and that once that was got rid of the Communists would be weakened and their appeal diminished. But in conformity with the principles of Lenin the war was for what was to *succeed* colonialism. The truce which followed the French collapse at Dien Bien Phu did not end the war in Vietnam. It removed one of the participants from the field, France. The collapse of the French in Indo-China, and the refusal of the British to become more closely involved (their hands sufficiently full countering the Communist insurgency in Malaya), left only the Americans, with the prospect of acting by themselves.

3
Creating a State—South Vietnam

▍After the Geneva Agreement of 1954, following the Communist armies' defeat of France at the battle of Dien Bien Phu, the United States moved towards the direct support of the separate non-Communist state of South Vietnam. For four years America had been heavily supporting France with aid; now they proceeded to give it directly to the nationalist, non-Communist Vietnamese.

The Geneva Agreement did not end the war in Vietnam. It led only to its abandonment by one of the principal contenders, the colonial power: France. With Britain and the Soviet Union as co-chairmen and Communist China a partner to the Accords the fifty-five day Geneva conference, like Solomon dividing the child, partitioned Vietnam into two zones at the 17th parallel. The partition line was not to be considered either a political or territorial boundary. The people were to be able to decide freely in which zone they wished to live. Both sides undertook to refrain from the threat or the use of force. And perhaps above all in importance a general election by secret ballot, and under international supervision, was to be held within two years—by July 1956.

John Foster Dulles, Eisenhower's Secretary of State, had believed that it was important for the elections to be held as late as possible after the cease-fire because, as he stated in cables to London and to his negotiators in Geneva, it was undoubtedly possible that the elections would result in unification of Vietnam under Ho Chi Minh and it was therefore of the utmost importance that France should secure a guarantee that they be held in conditions free from intimidation and under effective international supervision 'to give'—as Dulles put it in those cables—'the democratic elements the best chance'.

The United States—a non-belligerent—did not sign the Geneva Agreement; neither, incidentally, did the non-Communist Vietnamese. But in a special statement the Americans undertook to do nothing to disturb them, and they said further that any violation would 'be a matter of grave concern and seriously threaten international peace and security'. In those last sentences was a whiff of the brinkmanship with which Dulles had challenged the Communists at the time of the battle of Dien Bien Phu when the possibility of an American air-strike to save the beleaguered French garrison was being canvassed. It was this, seriously considered or not, which led the Russians and the Chinese to extract 'concessions' from the Vietnamese Communists on the timing of the elections in particular. So, Geneva gave a breathing space after battle. Was this therefore the time when Dulles realized that nationalist non-Communist Vietnam was a burden the United States would shoulder alone and that their involvement would become a unilateral commitment? As in the previous chapter, Robert Bowie speaks for Dulles.

Bowie: I think Dulles still didn't despair of somehow or other creating the feeling that it wasn't going to be merely unilateral response if things were pushed too far. I think he was conscious that all the initiative for even creation of an atmosphere was going to rest with him. Here I think there was basically a difference in conception and strategy between Dulles and Eden. Dulles seemed to me to believe that you weren't going to get a deal at Geneva that would be at all acceptable unless there was some sense of constraint on the part of the other side, and that the only way to create that was to create some sense of uncertainty or fear or concern by them as to what might be the result otherwise. That was, as I see it, the purpose of all the maneuvering.

Apparently Eden's conception was utterly different and I think the French to some extent. They saw any of this sort of thing as interfering with a possible deal. I don't quite understand what it was that Eden thought was going to cause the Chinese to make a reasonable deal and he took great pride later in his belief that he had been the one who had achieved the deal. I don't quite know what he thought he achieved it with. It seems to me that in fact he was trading at Geneva on the sense of uncertainty which Dulles had in fact created in the minds of the Chinese and the Soviets. So, as I see it, the atmosphere which was created was a contribution to the actual ultimate outcome.

Despite Dulles's hopes, which of course were not to be fulfilled, that there might be some way out, the United States began to supplant France as the principal influence in Vietnam at this moment. How did he view the prospect of the United States being seen to supplant France in Indo-China?

Bowie: I don't think there was any desire to do so at all. I think the feeling was that up until very near to the very end the French still conveyed to the local people the feeling that this was fundamentally a colonial war; and that this was a terrific handicap. I think the United States didn't adequately take in the fact that anyone who went there after the French would be seen inevitably in much the same light. I think the Americans had indeed seen themselves as anti-colonial, rather to the dismay of their allies in some cases, and that their own sense of self-righteousness on this count prevented them from seeing the fact that as a strong power who came in after the French they would be seen in much the same light. I think that was a very serious handicap all through the remaining period.

❚ On that point of whether Dulles succeeded in achieving restraint by creating an atmosphere of risk, we know today, from the official North Vietnamese history published in 1965, that the prospect of American intervention did concern the Communists deeply and gave them pause after Dien Bien Phu and Geneva. That history conceded that it would have brought an imbalance of power—as they put it—unfavorable to them. Geneva gave birth to one of the more durable myths of the Vietnam war: that the temporary partition of the country was little more than a confidence trick, which had deprived Ho Chi Minh's guerilla army of the rightful prize of total victory in *all* Vietnam after Dien Bien Phu.

Dien Bien Phu was not the comprehensive and decisive military victory it is so often termed. It did not give the Communists a dominating military position at this time. In 1970 the official history of the Vietnamese Communist Party published in Hanoi was cryptic but revealing of the time after Dien Bien Phu. It said: 'The revolutionary forces at this time were not strong enough to liberate the whole country. The enemy was defeated but was not finally subdued.' So while the Vietnamese Communists undoubtedly didn't like the concession that they had made at Russian and Chinese insistence over the timing of elections, there is no reason to suppose they would have done better to fight on, still less that this is what they would have wished. There is supporting evidence in his memoirs from Khrushchev who says that at this time after eight years of fighting the 'partisans' were near exhaustion and were relying on the Geneva conference to produce a cease-fire which would enable them to hold on to their conquests that they had made in the struggle against the French. So while it is true of course that Dien Bien Phu had proved a political and psychological reverse which broke France's will to carry on, there were clearly limits to the rapidity with which the victorious Communists could expand their control.

Ho Chi Minh was certainly not nearly so strong in the South. Pham Van Dong, later Prime Minister, the Communist negotiator at Geneva, agreed that they could claim the allegiance there of not more than one-third of the population.

So, the myth that the Communist revolution had been halted on the verge of complete success and that the French would have been expelled from the north and most of the south of the country within a year can hardly be sustained. There was a non-Communist Vietnam with a future yet to play for and decide. Dulles had won a pause of two years before elections were supposed to decide it. He sent out to Vietnam one of the legendary figures of this period of American involvement—an Air Force General, Ed Lansdale, who had won a reputation for skilful political warfare in the Philippines against the Hukbalahap rebellion. Lansdale's personality and activities were the material on which some of the most widely known books about Vietnam were written—including Graham Greene's *The Quiet American*. As the French quit the field in Vietnam, it was Lansdale who began to imprint an American personality below the seventeenth parallel.

Lansdale: I got a message telling me to go over to Vietnam immediately, and it gave some citations for the funding for my trip out there. At the end of that it said 'God bless you'. The military people that received that message, and sent it to me, said: 'We never saw anything like that before in a set of orders.' I said: 'I don't know who put that on there but it sure doesn't sound like I'm going to a nice assignment.'

Charlton: This was before the Geneva Agreement?

Lansdale: This was before it was signed.

Charlton: So Dien Bien Phu had fallen.

Lansdale: It fell, and this was right after that, very shortly after that.

Charlton: Dulles personally spoke to you, didn't he, and sent you out to Vietnam?

Lansdale: Yes. I asked the Secretary of State what I was to do there, and he said 'Do what you did in the Philippines'. I said: 'Well, I worked with the *people* in the Philippines, and in Vietnam the people running things there are the French right now, and a French colonial administration that I don't think I want to go out and help succeed. I don't want to see any nation go under Communist domination, but I don't much care for colonial regimes either.' So, he said to go out and help the people, and that's essentially what my mission was.

Charlton: After the fall of Dien Bien Phu the Communists, the Vietminh, led by Giap and Ho Chi Minh, had yet to consolidate their authority over the North. The great battle had taken place, the French had lost: but the French were still in control, weren't they?

Lansdale: They were up in Hanoi, and they were in control of the Red River Delta at the time.

Charlton: Now, what was the role of your mission, which was a secret mission, wasn't it? What was its role? How was it defined for you?

Lansdale: The only definition that I ever had was to help the Vietnamese people. I had a dual role of trying to help a military force, a national military force, the Vietnamese army, in any way that I could, to do battle with enemy guerilla forces. On the political side to help the Vietnamese administration within a social organization to work for the Vietnamese people. When I arrived in Vietnam there were many people, millions of people who were trying to stay aloof from the conflict, which was of course taking place in their own surroundings, their own land, their own block in the city. The people trying to stay away from the conflict said they wanted neither side, the French nor the Communist side at the time. That they, the aloof people, were the true nationalists, and this was another type of war. So I became allied with what I saw as a nationalist affair.

Charlton: Since the publication of what we now know as *The Pentagon Papers*, there is this phrase which has come under close scrutiny in your report which you sent back to the American Government, and these may have been your own words—I'd like to know if they are—that you talked about your mission's task being to beat the Geneva timetable and the Communist takeover in the North. How are we to interpret that? What were you trying to do?

Lansdale: I know that was my concept, so those might well be my 'orders'. I saw the timetable that had been set up in Geneva as being too short a time period for a government in the South to go at a very leisurely pace or to stay in its present organization and let political guerilla forces come into the South and fix up things around the districts and province perimeters and areas and dominate them. So, when there would be a plebiscite they could rig the ballot boxes and the voting and make sure that they won there. The Vietnamese government in the South was highly disorganized. It had no trained

executives, and I felt that we had to get people trained and in position.
Charlton: Can you give us an idea of the time that was left to you after the fall of Dien Bien Phu in Hanoi before you had to leave it and what, essentially, you tried to do? And what it was you achieved?
Lansdale: In the Hanoi area I had come to know some of the political leaders of parties and groups who were non-Communists, who were fighting as best they could against the Communists up there and who had known from the Geneva Accords that they would be leaving the North, who asked me for help then, and leaving stay-behinds, if you will. Their stay-behinds in this case were hand-picked people of their party whose loyalties they felt certain of, who would either pass information on or collect information, or take political actions, psychological actions, harassing actions—harassing being to slow down the workings of a government by making things not work. I helped in doing this advising them, putting people in, of not mixing intelligence clerks with action types of operations—that is secret actions—but suggesting a number of things that they might do, seeing that they got any training that was available at all for paramilitary type of operations.
Charlton: What sort of things were they?
Lansdale: Slowing down transportation. The head of the transportation company suggested himself that he was being forced to turn over all transportation, and personally despised having to do such a thing, actually pointed out things that might be done, which were done. But others in the form of propaganda, if you will, of putting out orders, putting out proclamations, even putting out suggestions looking as if they had come from the new leaders in the city, the Communist side...
Charlton: Black propaganda.
Lansdale: Black propaganda—to the people. Such things as shopkeepers to go through and make an inventory. Certain things were to be declared because they were going to be taxed by the enemy when they took over. That gave them an idea that maybe they shouldn't stay there and do business with the enemy. To increase the loads on bureaucracy and on red tape and add to it; and all of the little tricks that I'm certain that I don't have to go into for people in your audience. They're well known in all wars and all contests.
Charlton: The descriptions of what your Mission was up to in this period between 1954 and 1956 has been seized upon by radical critics of what the United States was doing at this time as throwing some doubt upon the genuineness of the exodus of the Catholic refugees

from the North to the South. Were parts of your activities to prepare the way for this exodus and in fact to encourage it?

Lansdale: One of the things that happened in an exodus of the nature of the one that took place from North Vietnam is pulling up of a people who have a passionate love of home, far more than an American in a restless country such as ours. These were people whose homes meant practically everything to them, along with their worship of their ancestors and so on. This is where their ancestors had lived, this is where their family had very deep roots into the ground. Most of the propaganda if you will, information work, that I did in the North was to cause these people to look at what they knew from having seen the enemy, and at themselves. If they were saying well I'll do it tomorrow or something, I merely upped the schedule and have them do it today and make up their minds and leave.

Charlton: Do you believe that when you went out there with this brief, and the money and support with which to do it, that Dulles viewed it as a positive attempt to take over from the French in giving support to a Vietnamese nationalism which was non-Communist; or were you there as a sort of trial run to see whether anything like that could be established on which the United States government could base its policy?

Lansdale: I can't be entirely definite on this. Secretary Dulles told me that why he was sending me was that I had been successful in the Philippines where I'd worked to strengthen the Philippines' own laws and to make them operate for the people, as it stated, and had kept the American action and so forth within Philippine limits. I think he must have seen some sort of a void coming up politically with the French pulling out, with a vote coming up—a plebiscite that quite obviously was going to give the rule to the Communist side. I think at the time he was just hoping that the Vietnamese side would become a viable type of national government and group and so on. Say France withdrew from there, which they'd promised to do and they were thinking of Vietnam being part of the French Union, and I think he was going along with that, but wanted to get the colonial administration out of there and have something supplant it that would work. I found that Diem when he came in—and in the very early days of Diem there, the first six months, eight months—was a highly popular person. He was even grabbed by people and ridden on their shoulders—he was that welcome and getting around most places and talking with the people who lived there. They all had wonderful things to say about Diem, and not so wonderful about Ho Chi Minh.

Charlton: But how does this square with what Dulles saw: a plebiscite coming up in Vietnam which the Communists would win? What you mean is, and this has often been misunderstood, hasn't it, that Ho Chi Minh and the Communists would win against Bao Dai, the old puppet emperor, but that was not what you regarded as a proper test of public opinion.

Lansdale: Yes, I think so. But I think the political estimate on that came out of the foreign service professionals, who were out there observing the thing.

Charlton: Not shared by you?

Lansdale: I didn't believe that, once I'd saw what was happening with Diem. I started hearing of Uncle Ho right away from the people and he was very well known: he wasn't always very well liked, but he was better known than the Prime Ministers were in the early government when I got out there, at the time of Geneva and just before. But that was a caretaker government of technicians and they weren't people of political charisma and so on.

Charlton: Surely your own efforts in North Vietnam were dwarfed by the enormity of the Communist victory at Dien Bien Phu—the defeat of the colonial power by a peasant army? Didn't that overwhelm everything else?

Lansdale: I'm sure it did, yes. It certainly overwhelmed the image of the white man out in Asia at the time just for the reasons you've stated. A native peasant army overcoming a professional army from Europe was a very dominant feature.

Charlton: Your task was to frustrate the Communist takeover in the North to any extent that you could while trying to consolidate an alternative in the South?

Lansdale: No. I was thinking originally that the plebiscite was going to take place, though we had a very short time to construct anything at all in the South that the people could feel an allegiance to, enough to vote for it instead of the Communist side. When we started work on that almost all of the executive posts out in the countryside that kept the government running were French who were leaving. So this was at the time of Geneva, but they were going to leave before the vote could take place. So there'd be no way of running things for the Saigon government out in the countryside where the voting would take place. So people had to be picked then to go out there, who were Vietnamese who would stay on, who could learn their jobs and learn

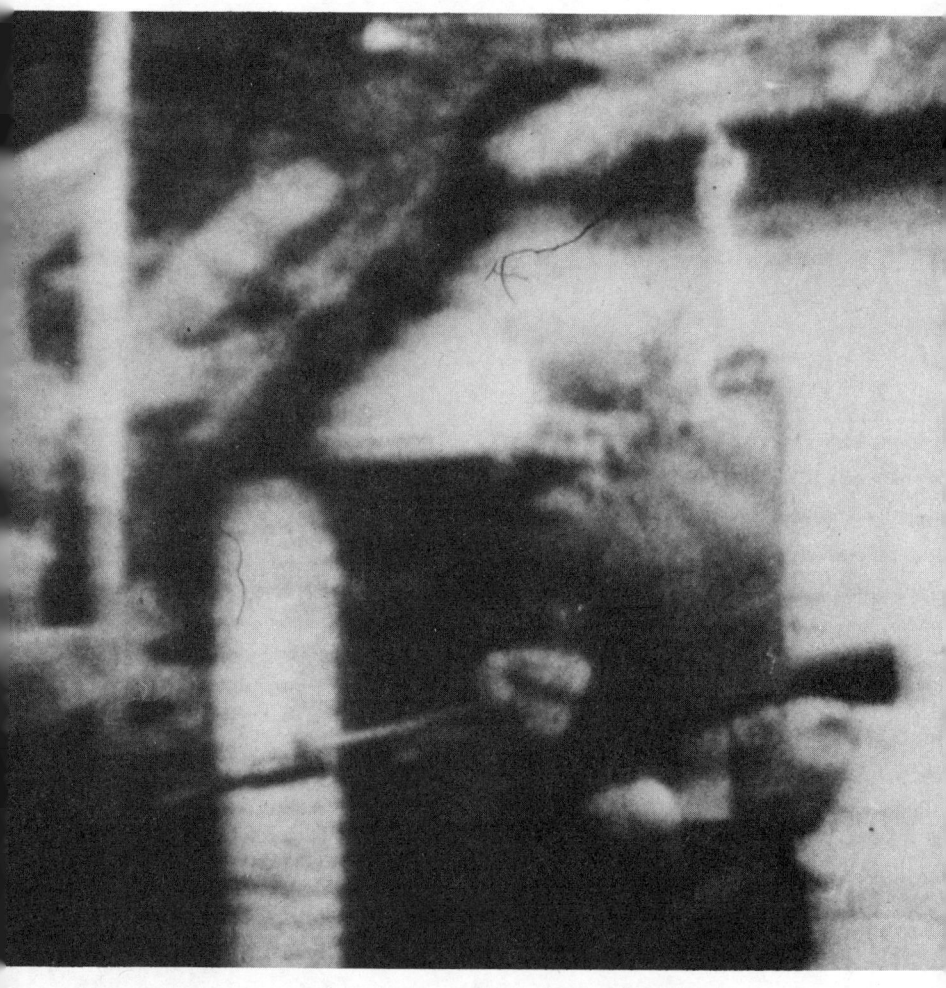

Figure 3. American Marine sets fire to the thatched roof of a hut (CBS)

Figure 4. Summary execution of a Vietcong prisoner by Brigadier General Nguyen Ngoc Loan, South Vietnam's Chief of Police, 1 February 1968 (Associated Press)

how to run a government post, you see. It takes time and experience.

▎The constituent parts from which Ed Lansdale and others were attempting to assemble an American-supported non-Communist state were, first of all, the main rice bowl of Indo-China in the Mekong Delta and a population of southerners who were generally of a more leisurely disposition than the energetic Tonkinese of the North. There was a complexity (in European terms like the Balkans) in the loyalty of this population to religious sects which had feudal troops. Of first importance was the ingredient of the refugees from the North, the exodus of those who had chosen *not* to live in the Communist-controlled zone. These were in particular the Catholics and members of the French-trained armed forces. After the Geneva Accords, almost one million came south—among them a young pilot who would one day be Prime Minister of South Vietnam, Nguen Cao Ky.

Ky: Dien Bien Phu happened when I was still in training in France. When I came back, the country was already divided. I was the last to fly the plane to Haiphong, to bring the last Vietnamese refugees to the South. I had nothing to do with what happened to my country at that time. A million Vietnamese left the North and went to the South, including my own mother and my family. So when I came back I came to Saigon instead of Hanoi.

▎Tran Van Don was another from the North who had fought against the successful Communist armies and chosen to go to the South, and would one day be one of South Vietnam's senior generals, with a political following of his own.

Don: We did not sign the Agreement, and we didn't recognize the political agreement made by the French. That was why we didn't want to open a general election with the other side, except if they agreed in that time to change the policy towards the South and inside South Vietnam after the 1954 Geneva Agreement. What we had to do was—if we were to keep the South free from the North—to organize our Vietnamese armed forces. Unfortunately the French at that time were trying to leave the country, to pull out their troops. The Americans were coming, and there was a transition period. It was very difficult for us to reorganize our armed forces and be able to face the very important armed forces from the North.

Charlton: After Dien Bien Phu, what encouraged you to think that you could establish a non-Communist government with popular support?

Don: We believed that after Dien Bien Phu the other side would try to launch some aggression to the South. That is why we tried to develop our armed forces.

Charlton: That I understand: there was an immediate need for armed strength in order to establish a non-Communist alternative. But how do you answer the point about popular support, a mandate from the people? Why were you encouraged to think that the people wanted to resist the Communists?

Don: I believe that at that time the people would like to do it because after the Geneva Agreement almost one million Vietnamese people left the North of Vietnam—I mean, left the country where the Communist leaders took over the control—to go to the South, and showed we didn't want to live under Communist regime.

The elections in Vietnam, which under the Geneva Agreement should have taken place within two years after the cease-fire—which meant not later than July 1956—were never held. By that time any interpretation of 'free' elections, in letter and in spirit, was a condition which could no longer be met. Ho Thong Minh, Defense Minister in Diem's government a few months later, has recorded in exile in Paris his recollections of the possibility of free elections in the North.

Minh [translation]: That depends on what you mean by 'free'. At least in the whole of South-East Asia I think that, first of all, the word 'elections' doesn't have the same meaning as it does here; and next, the word 'free' doesn't have the same meaning either. I think that the North had a firm hold on the population and that consequently the North could give any interpretation it wanted to a popular vote. So the question only arose for the South. As far as the South was concerned at that time, naturally in the regions that had been occupied for some time by the Vietminh—as they were called at the time—the population was against the Vietminh.

If elections had taken place in the South, what did Ho Thong Minh think—from his evidence on the spot at the time—would have been the result?

Minh: Many observers were of the opinion that if they had taken place, the North would have won. I also thought so, because the

North had a firm grip on the population; in the South where people as yet had no experience of Communism, they'd thought Communism would do something for the peasants; there were only a few pockets in the center of Vietnam, at Nha Trang, in particular, they alone had tasted a little of the Communist regime and they voted against it. In the main, though, the population was probably going to vote in favor of the Communists. That is why our idea was to try and consolidate the South and then to renegotiate with the North with a Southern State and a Northern State if you like, or South Zone and North Zone, to redefine the conditions in which future elections could be held between the two zones. And, we were widening, if possible, the terms of the Geneva Agreement on this specific point, while at the same time, of course, respecting the spirit of the Geneva Agreement.

The fact that elections did not take place was to become one of the most difficult issues for the United States to defend in their public policy, in the light of their early pronouncements that Ho Chi Minh might well have been the victor if they were held too early for the non-Communist elements to organize effectively. Although he had recently left the government at this time Dean Rusk took a personal interest in this question of elections.

Rusk: I tried to look up the record on that after I became Secretary of State and found very little in the official records, such as cables to our Embassy in Saigon and things like that. But I think one could make an argument that those elections should have been held, but I think those who would make that argument ought to blush just a little bit if they talk about free elections because there was no possibility of free elections either in North Vietnam or in South Vietnam in 1955 or 1956.

Charlton: Nevertheless, misnomer as it may have been, that's what the Geneva Agreement provided for, elections. And of course the charge against the United States is that in opposing them, or encouraging Diem in particular to oppose them, you were deliberately stepping round the provisions of that agreement.

Rusk: Well you know, remember the same time the Soviets were utterly opposed to free elections in Germany, utterly opposed to free elections in Korea. So the question must have arisen that why should we accommodate them in one spot if they wouldn't accommodate us in these other places. In other words, did we give them what they

wanted, and just say 'too bad chaps' if they refused to give us what we wanted in areas of equal or more importance to us?
Charlton: But again, can I say that that appears to reinforce the argument that Vietnam up till this time had still been considered in the general world design and strategy of the United States rather than the particular problem of Vietnam itself.
Rusk: I think that's true.

The man whom at one time it was thought Kennedy would choose as Secretary of State instead of Dean Rusk and who was later to become a focus for political opposition to the war in Vietnam was Senator William Fulbright. For many American liberals the issue of elections is seen as something of a stain on the American conscience. But how did it appear at the time to Fulbright?

Fulbright: In Congress we were not really concerned about it particularly. We had had no previous engagement in South-East Asia; and this particular Accord came at the same time as the height of the McCarthy period as we called it in Congress. Joe McCarthy, member of the Senate, was of daily importance to all senators because he was extremely active and was attacking senators along with everybody else. The development of what I would call practically a paranoia about Communism arose at that time. Mr Dulles, actually he didn't sign it. But if I recall correctly he verbally said he wouldn't do anything to thwart them. I think it was a verbal statement that he left, and left his representative, General Bedell Smith, who I believe said we would undertake not to destroy them. But we did go then and create SEATO, and it would appear in the light of history that we did take measures to prevent the implementation of the Geneva Accords.

This is a mistaken judgment, in my opinion, as to what is our interest, and the mistake is inherent in this highly emotional attitude that developed with regard to Communism and in accord with the principles of the Truman Doctrine that everywhere we would meet any challenge from the Communists. It was a great mistake of judgment not to recognize this in 1949, but I understand it because the atmosphere that had arisen as a result of Stalin's difficult period set our minds in that direction. Here we were in this deadly confrontation with the Russians, and we thought it was our duty to thwart them everywhere, not discriminatingly in the sense of Western Europe or Japan, but everywhere. That I think contributed to the attitude in South-East Asia.

▌ For Dulles, who did not accept that Ho Chi Minh was acting as a free and independent agent, China was the influence which was extending and had to be contained if all the dominoes were not ultimately to fall. The 'loss' of China as it was called continued to reverberate, and the vindictive McCarthy period had removed a certain balance of informed advice and perspectives in making American policy in Asia. One of its victims was Professor John Fairbank of Harvard.

Fairbank: The 'loss' of China is, of course, a laughable phrase, and yet I think it is worth using because it symbolizes the shock to the Americans. You have to picture the American public in the nineteenth century and even down to the twentieth century as a people with a large element of religion still. Throughout a hundred years they had had missions in China as part of the church work. Now this means that every year in the first part of this century there would be several hundred missionaries touring the country on home leave, sabbaticals, probably speaking every day to some group about China and our cause in China.

It conditioned the Americans to feel that the Christianizing and the progress of China was of concern to us. A rather possessive kind of attitude developed I think, and in a church community of great stability and with people of leadership capacity, like Henry Luce, this idea of our interest in China became very strong and settled. So when China went Communist it seemed like a real subversion of everything right. The Nazis started the Americans on the crusade against evil. After World War II, the Nazis having disappeared, the same picture of evil emanated from Stalin: he killed many millions of people apparently. So the totalitarianism that we were fighting in World War II easily shifted over into a struggle against totalitarian Russia. Totalitarianism was a frequent word of the 1940s and 1950s.

So then, when the Chinese Revolution became a Communist Revolution—for reasons that made great sense in China—this seemed like a further stage in the march of evil. The Americans who had fought it in the Nazis and opposed it in Stalinism naturally responded to the bugle call to oppose it in China, just a knee-jerk reaction, automatic almost. In other words, it was ideologically globalized and became a great crusade. The American mind had never encompassed the history of China or Japan, least of all Vietnam; we'd never even heard of the place before. In the case of Vietnam we had no returned missionaries, we had no tradition of contact, we had no people who had come back and told the church faithful about the nice Vietnamese.

Missions in Vietnam were French and Catholic, they didn't touch the Americans. American business was non-existent there, kept out by the French. We had a few consular officers; all they had to do was speak French. We had nobody who could speak Vietnamese. The country was absolutely blank on the whole subject of Vietnam; and therefore the more easily could we impose upon it the ideas that we had in mind about the cold war, and the necessity of fighting the evil of Communism. There was nothing to stand in the way realistically of this ideological push.

❚ Had there been sufficient evidence available in advance of the Sino-Soviet split of the late nineteen-fifties on which to base an alternative foreign policy in Asia; or had the McCarthy period deprived American policy of the informed advice necessary to make such judgments?

Fairbank: I think the British people that I know, from very early never believed that the Chinese were going to be under Russian dictation. They knew a little too much about China; and the Americans who knew that of course had been put out of business, the American Foreign Service having been decimated and the people who were not discharged being sent off to Labrador or somewhere. We had nobody in charge in Washington who really had the background. I think that we had Foreign Service Officers quite capable of calling the tune on history and China, and even in Vietnam by analogy to China. They were put out of business.

❚ The other principal influence on the specific problem in Vietnam was Korea, where the many months of protracted negotiations while the fighting itself had intensified—in conformity with the Communist tenet of 'fighting to negotiate'—had induced the Americans to suspect that the Communists were seeking a free hand in Vietnam while achieving stalemate in Korea. Korea had also established the precedent of a divided state where the opposing ideologies could draw a line on the map and a line in the mind and retire behind them to compete but co-exist. How did the Americans draw the parallels with Korea?

Rusk: Not a close parallel between the two geographic positions, but clearly a sense that how we reacted under our security treaty in South-East Asia (SEATO) would have some bearing on how we would be expected to react in other security treaties, particularly in NATO. The issue to many of us was to do with the fidelity of the United States to its mutual security treaties. Now if that should evaporate or seriously erode then I think we can anticipate very great dangers appearing again.

> For William Colby, shortly to be CIA station chief in Saigon, the parallel with Korea had implications for policy on the ground in South Vietnam.

Colby: I think that our military clearly thought in terms of Korea. And consequently our whole military assistance program was basically aimed at strengthening the South Vietnamese army, to meet an army attack. I think the political people in our embassy looked more towards a purely political solution. They thought that if the government would be good, would be open to all opposition currents, would not be authoritarian, that out of this would come a consensus, and a political cohesion, which would freeze the Communists out. I think the Intelligence approach was that neither of those was the answer. The real answer was again to start at the local level, to build up self-defense in the villages and hamlets. From that build a new social structure, a new political base. And that was the way that really has more analogies to the Malaysian experience than anything.

> On the political front in South Vietnam the personality who was to become the focus for the creation of a new and independent non-Communist state was Ngo Dinh Diem, a Catholic mandarin from an important family in the traditional Vietnamese imperial capital of Hué. Diem had been a significant political figure for many years. He had resigned from the first national government of Anam in 1933 when Indo-China was a French possession. He had been offered the Prime Ministership of the country several times in the intervening years by the Emperor, Bao Dai, and he had refused. He was a vehement nationalist with a public record of opposition to French colonial tutelage; and he was an outspoken anti-Communist. Unlike Ho Chi Minh who had spent nearly thirty years outside his country when he returned to lead the revolution in 1944 cloaked in the aliases of a professional revolutionary, Diem was well known and widely

credited with a reputation for virtue and courage. What were the conditions in South Vietnam as Diem returned to Vietnam from seclusion in a Maryknoll fathers seminary in the United States?

Minh [translation]: I must say that when I was a minister after Dien Bien Phu, on the whole, the climate was calm in the South. There was something of a respite. And this respite could also have come from the fact that North Vietnam was expecting elections rather than a confrontation, even a political one. Besides, from a military point of view, it wasn't possible for them to march, you know. But in any case, as we have been able to see, Communism could only win by military means. Only by military means, not by political. It was fairly difficult to conquer the South politically.

Diem as a declared anti-Communist and staunch opponent of the French had impeccable credentials for American support, given their own convictions that it was colonialism which was the reason for the Communist advances in South-East Asia. Senator Mike Mansfield, himself a Catholic and later majority leader in the United States Senate, recalls the first American meetings with Diem.

Mansfield: He came to the United States around 1951 or 1952 I believe, and I met him along with Senator John F. Kennedy at a reception. I was impressed with him then and I was impressed with him all the time he was in power in Vietnam. I think he wanted to do the right thing. I think he was undercut by some of his own people and not given the support he should have been given by the United States government. It wasn't a question of religion—the fact that we were all Catholics was just coincidental—but I had made many trips to South Vietnam. I was personally aware of what Diem was trying to achieve, his methods, his procedures; I felt he was on the right track.
Charlton: But what were the characteristics of Diem and what was his appeal as you saw it, that entitled him to your support?
Mansfield: Independence, integrity, a man who had one goal in mind and that was the whole independence of his country, a man who was willing to accept American help but only under certain conditions. A man who was taken in I think too much by some Americans and a man who paid the price eventually because of that.
Charlton: What do you mean he was taken in too much by some Americans?

CREATING A STATE—SOUTH VIETNAM

Mansfield: I think he trusted some Americans too much, and I think they took advantage of him.

Charlton: What influence did the French have, do you believe, in promoting Diem as a candidate who would attract non-Communist support in Vietnam?

Mansfield: They never liked Diem, they never trusted him. If they took him they only took him because they had no other choice. They were inclined to stay with the Emperor. He wasn't much of a ruler, and they were trying to work with their puppets in Vietnam, Vietnamese. They couldn't span the gap and there was no other choice but Diem when the time came. So the French didn't do anything out of the goodness of their hearts, but out of necessity.

The day Diem arrived in Saigon in 1954 the ubiquitous Quiet American was among the crowds.

Lansdale: We were all invited to come down to the airport to greet him, that is all of the foreign community leaders. I started off for the airport, saw immense throngs on the sidewalk and decided I would watch the people rather than the man arriving and see what their reaction was as they saw him. I stopped and waited with the people on the sidewalk—a very long wait of hours, and finally sirens in the distance and a limousine all closed up with outriders and police, motorcycle police, came along and zipped by the people. They were all ready to cheer and holding their kids up to see him, and, zing, he went right by and they were terribly disappointed at not having a chance to cheer and so on.

I felt if this was going to be the leader on our side 'God help us', because he had no instincts at all of politics and the people he was going to lead. So I jotted down some notes on how to be a Prime Minister of Vietnam at that moment, and saw the Ambassador, and said I'd like to show these to this man. The Ambassador said alright, if you make sure that he doesn't think these are official US views, but are strictly your own. I said, 'I'll do that'.

At the Palace people were running around. There wasn't a receptionist, it didn't seem to be organized in any way. I asked someone who was carrying a bundle of papers along the hall: I said, there's a new Prime Minister around and where is his office please? He said you go upstairs and at the head of the stairs you ask the man in the room there and he'll show you. So I went upstairs, there was a little room with a door open off to the left and a man sitting at a desk there and I asked for the Prime Minister, and he said 'Well that's me'. I told him about watching him come into Saigon, and the disappointment of the people, and the fact that I had my own personal ideas of some of the things that a Prime Minister might do. I said all of these ideas were generated from my time out among Vietnamese, and I thought this was what his own people were looking for. With that I sat down and gave him the papers, and we became close friends afterwards. He even liked some of the ideas and started asking me to come in and see him on concepts of things that foreigners had told him about. We finally came to see each other almost daily.

▌Sir Robert Thompson takes the assessment of Diem onto consideration of the broader problem of helping South Vietnam become a state in its own right.

Thompson: President Diem himself was a great nationalist. His brother had been killed by Ho Chi Minh's forces in 1945, also a leading nationalist, and Diem was absolutely untainted by any working with the French at this time and was to the Vietnamese a hero.
Charlton: Why do you think it was that the Americans often appeared to be maneuvered onto ground that they certainly didn't wish to choose, as appearing to be a substitute for the French colonial power themselves?
Thompson: I think this was partly caused by the resources situation. After all, South Vietnam in 1954 had gone through the whole of World War II under Japanese occupation and so on, then right through the first Indo-China war; the place was in a mess. It lacked government, it lacked a whole administrative system to run it, it was economically barely existing on sort of subsistence agriculture. Fortunately it is a great rice-producing area, and at least people didn't quite starve.

But there were simply no resources there; and the resources, therefore, had to come from the outside and had to come in quite large quantities. This automatically gave the Americans a very dominant role politically and economically in South Vietnam, before they were really involved militarily, in merely enabling their government to survive at all.

▌Diem had taken over as the head of the non-Communist half of Vietnam. American aid had switched from the French directly to the

Vietnamese. The Communists controlled the North. Diem set out to organize and install his rival authority to Ho Chi Minh in the South.

What were the American objectives at the end of the nineteen-fifties? Was the creation of a state in South Vietnam viable as a possible alternative to a Communist advance?

Colby: Yes, I thought that clearly the Diem Government was succeeding. There's no question about it. It was succeeding in the development program, the economy was moving ahead by leaps and bounds. The educational programs, the public health programs, all of these were essentially succeeding. And given another five years, there's no question about it, the appeal of Communism would be nil.

Charlton: And how successful in your view had the Communists been in implanting an organization in the South?

Colby: They had some, what we call professionally, 'stay-behinds'. They had some assets in the South, you might say. But the chief thing they had was about 50,000 young people whom they had moved north in 1954, when the 900,000 refugees had moved south. And these young people had been trained, had been disciplined, were good loyal party members, and began to reinfiltrate the South in about 1960. And this was the real key that a serious political and guerilla effort was commencing, because these were the activators, the organizers, the leaders of the apparatus, which would conduct this kind of an insurgency struggle. I still thought at that time that that was manageable, that that kind of a problem could probably be outrun by a vigorous political development, vigorous effort by the South.

As the incidents grew in number, we in CIA did begin a few programs of arming local villagers, helping people to establish their own defense capabilities. We talked with the Vietnamese government a great deal about this. And out of these experiments and out of our conversations came eventually the so-called strategic hamlet program which reflected the view of the government that a whole new social base had to be established for an independent non-Communist Vietnam. Diem was as impatient with the ex-colonial toadies as he was with the Communists, because he thought that both of them represented something foreign to a real nationalism, to a real Vietnam; and that the process then was to start at the village-hamlet microcosm, develop the new leadership and the new philosophy and sense of unity out of that base rather than operating through the French-trained bureaucracy.

We have already seen how anti-colonialism was a consistent and vigorous theme in American policy making. After Geneva, as the French withdrew, the United States no longer influenced events through the intermediary of the colonial power France. Therefore they were back where they were during that brief period in 1944 and 1945 when they talked directly to the Vietnamese.

The aid given for a period to France to fight Ho Chi Minh's revolution was now channelled straight to the Vietnamese in the South.

America's relationship to events in Vietnam was now a more personal and intimate one; it presented the chance to the Americans to help create something in their own image as a vigorous alternative to Communist advance. Enthusiastic in support and anxious for Diem's success, they found that chance harder to resist. The nineteen-fifties proved to be a point of no return.

The breathing space for President Diem to create a state proved to be shortlived. The Communists, who had drawn their breath in the North, were ready to advance once more. They began an insurgency which arose in the countryside in the South. They erupted into Laos where the North Vietnamese in even less equivocal violation of the Geneva Agreement took control. This created a new international crisis in the dying days of the Eisenhower Administration as it gave way to the Presidency of John F. Kennedy.

The New Frontiersmen hold the line

Let every nation know, whether it wishes us well or ill, that we shall pay any price, bear any burden, meet any hardship, support any friend, oppose any foe, to ensure the survival and the success of liberty.

John Kennedy addressed those words to the world at large and to the American people in particular, as he stood bare-headed in the biting cold of Washington in January on his inauguration day in 1961.

It was a speech purpled with rhetorical flourishes. Its call for youthful inspiration, its vigor and its confidence caught the imagination. After the lethargy of the Eisenhower years the world was on the move again. Westward look the land was bright! Gathered round the young President was a shining meritocracy of glandular, energetic, successful, already distinguished younger Americans—the men of the New Frontier. One of them was Professor Adam Yarmolinsky, like Kennedy himself from Harvard and who having served as special assistant to the Secretary of Defense in the Pentagon, was appointed deputy director of the President's anti-poverty task force. Kennedy's declaration set the context for America's responses to challenge in the sixties. What significance did his speech have for the armed forces of the United States?

Yarmolinsky: Clearly it's awfully difficult to realize that at the beginning of the 1960s the military were regarded with a lot less suspicion and concern—and opposition if you will—in the sort of political and opinion-making circles in the United States than they are today. I suppose that to begin with there was a kind of hangover from World War II and there was still a good deal of the cold war psychology that prevailed, hangover if you will from the Korean War. I believe we are not only sadder but wiser now. It wasn't that Kennedy had a notion that he would use the military to impose some kind of American hegemony or condominium on the world; but rather that we were the great defender and that the way we defended the rest of the world was primarily not through the use of military power but through the 'deterrent effect' of our military power. Now the notion that the rest of the world might not want to be defended quite that way was something that we discovered to our shame and agony in Vietnam, was an idea that just wasn't particularly current at least in the circles that I moved in in Washington and the circles I suppose that Kennedy took his advice from.

Charlton: But would you agree that the terms of the Kennedy inaugural, if literally interpreted—'let every nation know that we will go anywhere and pay any price'—and presumably he meant them in this respect to be so, did give a very positive role to the military, that they had to be prepared to back that commitment?

Yarmolinsky: Yes; after all Kennedy in his election campaign had made a great deal of his role as a military hero and that is one of the standard electoral qualifications in this country which you don't find nearly so much in Britain, and it *was* a factor. I need not remind you that all of us in the Kennedy campaign wore the PT boat tie clip, that was a great symbol.

Charlton: Of Kennedy's own time in the Navy, in that famous patrol boat. [Yes.] But the implication of the inaugural was that the armed forces would have a very positive commitment to fulfil, it meant increased military budgets. Was that also implicit?

Yarmolinsky: No it was not implicit. While military budgets did increase in the first few years of the Kennedy Administration, I would argue that they increased not in order to implement either aggressive ambitions or notions of a larger role for the military, but rather to make up for neglect in areas that the previous administration had let go by, and these were largely areas that had to do with the effective defensive or deterrent posture of the military rather than with the ability to respond positively or aggressively to foreign policy needs. The Green Berets have had a good deal of attention in the story, but the budgetary cost of the Green Berets was probably invisible.

Charlton: But they became, didn't they, a great symbol of the New Frontier itself?

Yarmolinsky: They became a symbol of the New Frontier. They were very unpopular within the military. They never made themselves accepted. I think that the realization that the rather frightening Dulles doctrine of massive retaliation was no longer practical, as well as being morally unacceptable, led to a kind of swing of the pendulum to the other extreme: we were not going to be in the awful business of creating Hiroshimas and Nagasakis in support of our foreign policy objectives. In fact, all we were going to have to do was send one of our Green Berets out into the woods to do battle with one of their crack guerilla fighters and they would have a clean fight, and the best man would win and they would both get together and start curing all the villagers of smallpox. It was that kind of almost euphoria.

Charlton: There was nothing in being, or implicit, in the New Frontiersmen that they brought with them not just a commitment but some sort of philosophy, embryonic as it may have been, of counter-revolution?

Yarmolinsky: No, absolutely not. As a matter of fact one of the early and I think one of the most important developments was when President Kennedy sent his brother Bobby on a trip round the world, through the less developed world, and Bobby came back and reported that although he and the President and people around them saw the United States as a young nation, 'vibrant and progressive and innovative', we were seen by the rising young leadership in these countries as kind of status quo, allied with repressive elements. He reported to his brother 'this is no way for us to be', because he was Bobby Kennedy. The two of them set up something with the innocuous name The Interdepartmental Youth Committee, which was really something to get the State Department off its duff and get us involved in working with the non-Communist, radical, revolutionary sometimes, elements in these countries, the elements that would be rising to power. And this had nothing to do with military activity.

▎While the self-confidence of the New Frontiersmen—like Adam Yarmolinsky—was a common ingredient it wasn't unleavened. George Ball was rather older and more experienced and more reserved and cautious about what the young President had said in that inaugural address.

Ball: I thought at the time that what he was really doing was translating the Truman Doctrine as it had been originally formulated into rather grandiloquent prose. And it seemed to me that he was therefore perpetuating the fundamental vice of the Truman Doctrine which was that it was open ended, as it was worded—although it was aimed at a very specific situation at the time.

▎Ball, who whilst Undersecretary of State in the State Department was the number two to Dean Rusk, had been closely involved with French politicians in the post-war development of Europe. His caution was reinforced by a more intimate knowledge of the consequences of the French experience in Indo-China. He was to become the first high ranking Cassandra within the Kennedy Administration as his original wariness became open, and expressed doubts about America's ability to keep the commitment a limited one.

The day before Kennedy's inauguration when he'd met Eisenhower, the outgoing President had administered the first shock of office to Kennedy.

Eisenhower, more or less out of the blue, had told Kennedy that he might have to go to war possibly unilaterally because of the irruption of Communist advances, including Russian intervention in Laos: otherwise—he said—the whole area would go. Professor Yarmolinsky remarked that the very first briefing he received in his new job in the Pentagon as the new administration took over was, as he said, 'when someone stood up and started telling us about a battle on the Plain of Jars'. What impact did this sudden presentment of danger and a threat to be met have on Kennedy?

Ball: I think it made a very big impact on Kennedy. After all, Kennedy was not all that experienced. I think there's been rather an assumption that he had a far more profound comprehension of the power factors in the world than, indeed, he did have, certainly at that time.
Charlton: Would you say that the Vietnam argument at this time was purely peripheral in view of all these other things that were happening, the Berlin crisis for instance?
Ball: Very much of a peripheral interest I think at that time. I certainly regarded it as such, and I think most of the people did. The significant thing—and it seems hard to understand now—is that outside of my own doubts and fears there was no challenge to the fundamental thesis that we had to go forward and had to do what we had to do. I think very few believed what I was saying, that this held the danger of engaging us on the Asian continent in a war which we couldn't win.

The New Frontiersmen brought with them to government an advocacy and interest in guerilla warfare, and that one of the essential options to nuclear conflict was an ability to fight small wars to deter aggression. An archetypal New Frontiersman in this respect, and a rather breathless evangelist for an ability to deal with insurgency, was Roger Hilsman, appointed Director of Intelligence and Research at the

State Department and later Assistant Secretary of State, Far Eastern Affairs.

Hilsman: Laos was the front burner. This was where everything was erupting, this is where the Soviets had introduced airforces. There were people in the American government who were advocating—this is no longer a secret I'm sure—SEATO Plan 5, which was a massive introduction of SEATO troops which was to go from Hué in Vietnam all the way across to Vientiane in Laos. So Laos was the issue. Now if you will recapture these days, Kennedy's first phase was a hawk phase. There is a press conference which is on TV tape where he has three maps showing the progressive Communist incursions into Laos. He talks in a very hawkish manner. He uses the traditional diplomatic language, that if this continues the United States will have to look to its own national interest, which is a threat of intervention. A *very* hawkish thing.

Then came the Bay of Pigs where Kennedy, you know, was stupid. He let himself be led around by the nose, by the CIA and by the top military. Immediately after the Bay of Pigs, he telephoned Averell Harriman and said, 'One of the lessons I have drawn from this terrible experience is that we must have a political solution in Laos and not a military solution', in fact, he used the words South-East Asia; and then he sent Averell to Geneva to negotiate the neutralization of Laos in 1962. Now this is the phase where people like myself probably had the greatest influence.

Charlton: Can you put a year on this? What time are we talking about?

Hilsman: We are talking about the summer of 1961. We're talking about the Vienna meeting, you see. The one thing that Khrushchev and Kennedy agreed to in Vienna, was that Laos was not worth a war. They quarrelled on every other issue, but on that issue they agreed to neutralize Laos. Kennedy then called Harriman and reported to him what happened at Vienna, and said 'I've learned this lesson from the Bay of Pigs'. So we neutralized Laos you see.

Charlton: The point is the Russians did not deliver ...

Hilsman: No. There's another point to be made. Later—in 1968—Harriman told me that he asked the North Vietnamese why they did not honor the clause of the 1962 Geneva Agreement about Laos. There was a clause in it that said neither side will use any third country as a passageway, which meant the Ho Chi Minh Trails. The North Vietnamese said, 'Well look, we will respect any agreement that we reach voluntarily, but we will not honor an agreement that is forced down our throats by the Russians'. And that's literally the words that they used to Harriman. We then shifted to Vietnam and we came into the counter-insurgency thing and in which our advice to Kennedy was: 'Don't bomb, don't use artillery, enlist the people, let the people fight, let the Vietnamese people fight the guerillas.'

| Hilsman emphatically rejects one interpretation of Kennedy's commitment to South-East Asia—that the fiasco over the Bay of Pigs in Cuba in the spring of 1961, led him to make a compensatory and muscular response in South-East Asia. Hilsman argues that the opposite was the case: despite what Eisenhower had said to him about the possible need to go to war over Laos, after the Bay of Pigs Kennedy was sufficiently shaken to dismiss that possibility altogether and to accept in Laos an imperfect and unenforceable agreement. So the President would wait and see what happened in Vietnam. Then, even though it might not be the place, would be the time to make a stand.

Kennedy's Ambassador in Saigon at this time was a career diplomat, Frederick 'Fritz' Nolting. What did he think of the whole concept—as the State Department had it—of planning for South-East Asia?

Nolting: The American government, in general really, did not view the whole Indo-China peninsula as one strategic area as it should have done. I think on the contrary they looked at the map drawn in 1954 and decided that these were different countries: Cambodia, Laos, North and South Vietnam; and they planned in terms of relations with different countries.
Charlton: Whereas the Communists of course saw it as unitary?
Nolting: The Communists saw it as a unit—particularly Hanoi—and they were much wiser to do so. This came out particularly when the Laotian treaty was signed in 1962 after a year of negotiations in Geneva; and that left open the access to some of the vital areas of South Vietnam.

We in the Embassy in Saigon became increasingly worried about the lack of safeguards under the treaty, and so did the Diem government which was a party to the negotiations in Geneva. So did the Thai government for that matter. As a consequence of the lack of safeguards in the Agreements on Laos signed in 1962, the 40,000 or so North Vietnamese troops in the Eastern provinces of Laos stayed there; and the Ho Chi Minh Trail became what some have called 'the Harriman Memorial Highway'.

As Ambassador Nolting foresaw, the lack of adequate safeguards in Harriman's Laos Agreements and their subsequent breakdown would add enormously to the difficulty of resisting the Communist insurgency in South Vietnam. Yet all subsequent American decisions were taken in the knowledge that this must be so.

Dean Rusk was now Secretary of State, the most senior political figure in the Cabinet.

Rusk: The only piece of specific advice which President Eisenhower gave to Mr Kennedy on the day before inauguration was that he put troops in Laos. He said: 'with others if possible, alone if necessary'. He said that he had not done it himself because he thought that decision had to be made by a President who was going to be there for a longer period. So the first year and a half of the Kennedy years we concentrated pretty heavily on Laos and the more we looked at it the more we felt that Laotians were generally a rather gentle and civilized people with very little interest in killing each other. When only Laotians were on the battlefield a few bangs made a terrific battle, there were very few casualties. It was only when the North Vietnamese came in with shock troops that there was any serious fighting. So we felt that the best solution there would be to get everybody out of Laos—ourselves, the North Vietnamese, the French, everybody.
Charlton: To neutralize it?
Rusk: And let the Laotians manage and mismanage their own affairs. Then create a kind of island of peace there if possible between North Vietnam and (say) Thailand and South Vietnam. And so we worked very hard on the Laos Accords in 1962, but we didn't get any compliance with them.
Charlton: Why were the Russians unable to enforce the withdrawal by the North Vietnamese, which was implicit in those agreements?
Rusk: In retrospect I suppose it was because they already were in some kind of competition with Peking for influence in Hanoi and they just didn't. Whether they wanted to or not I don't know; but if they had wanted to press the North Vietnamese I think they did not want to do so to the point of driving them into the arms of Peking. There was a point where the rivalry between Moscow and Peking might have worked to our disadvantage.

Charlton: Yes, the Russians couldn't deliver.

Rusk: The British and the Russians were co-Chairmen at the Geneva Conference [of 1954] and we hoped very much that the two co-Chairmen would succeed in reconvening the Geneva Conference for the purpose of looking at compliance with the Geneva Accords but we could never get any interest out of the Russian side.

Charlton: You must be aware that cynics called the Ho Chi Minh trail the Averell Harriman Memorial Highway as a result of the breakdown of the Laos Agreement: it made South Vietnam almost indefensible.

Rusk: Well again you see the Laos Accords were good if we could have gotten compliance with them. The same old story we have had over and over again.

Charlton: Shouldn't it have forced you to reconsider your whole involvement in South Vietnam? Militarily South Vietnam itself became a much more difficult proposition didn't it because those agreements broke down?

Rusk: Oh yes, that long frontier between Laos and South Vietnam greatly increased the difficulties.

The most influential *military* advice Kennedy had at this period was coming to him from General Maxwell Taylor, who in 1961 was the most glamorous and distinguished of American soldiers with the experience of high command. He spoke several languages, could quote in Greek and generally deeply impressed Kennedy as an 'intellectual' soldier. The President brought Taylor out of semi-retirement in New York into the White House as his military adviser, and specifically to investigate the Bay of Pigs incident. We shall hear from General Taylor substantially later, but here he offers a most interesting gloss on what Roger Hilsman told us of Kennedy's reaction to the 'fiasco' on the Cuban beaches.

Taylor: The Bay of Pigs fiasco was behind the very rough treatment the President received from Khrushchev who was certainly looking this young man over in their Vienna meeting. The President always referred to it as a sombre experience, as I'm sure it was. By the time I got into the White House to be an adviser on military affairs—and also on Vietnam affairs in so far as military aspects were present—it was very clear to me that he had the feeling 'I must not fail again—I must not fail again'. Laos, of course, in the summer of 1961 loomed much larger in the Presidential mind than did Vietnam which was relatively quiet; whereas Laos was obviously in danger of going some place up or down. There was considerable pressure, from the Pentagon at least, to use military force there. The Bay of Pigs made him very, very cautious, and I encouraged him in that caution. I thought he was entirely right. The last thing in the world I could imagine wanting to do was to get American forces involved inland to try to help Laos.

In 1961, Kennedy's first year in office, South Vietnam was only in the wings of American strategic policy and, in this most exacting year for the inexperienced President, other issues held the center of the stage: the Bay of Pigs, Khrushchev's hectoring treatment of him at the Vienna summit, the Berlin Wall. One who was closely concerned with the wider strategic balance was Dean Acheson's son-in-law, William Bundy. He had been ten years with the CIA. He was a convinced and active Kennedy supporter and accepted appointment as Deputy Assistant Secretary of Defense for International Security Affairs in the Pentagon.

Bundy: The theory of containment was still the dominant way of thinking. We didn't use the term particularly in Asia: curiously it never was used in any government paper that I'm aware of; but it was essentially what we were doing. We were seeking to prevent the Chinese version of Communism from expanding in the area of East Asia.
Charlton: It is interesting to look at the historical calendar. Coincidentally with very important strategic decisions taken by the Kennedy Administration in Indo-China, they appear with the Sino-Soviet split purely in terms of known dates. What bearing did the separation between China and Russia have on decisions at the time? Or were they not apparent to you at the time?
Bundy: Some people would have begun to spot the Sino-Soviet split as early as 1958. I remember I was then in the business, and I thought their behavior over the Middle East crisis that year, and over the Quemoy crisis, was a first indication that all wasn't quite well between them. 1960, the Soviet Party Congress—and again much more definitively in the 1961 Party Congress—the extent of the split became clear to anyone; and it was not doubted in Washington. It's important to note that in the fall of 1961 when Kennedy decided to send in advisers to Indo-China and to take a major step in further committing the United States there, that this was at a time when the

Berlin crisis was still at a very active point. Kennedy told James Reston [of *The New York Times*] subsequently that the effect on the Soviet belief in American firmness was a significant part of the reason that he decided to go ahead in Indo-China. And I'm inclined to credit that although it doesn't appear in so many words in the records of deliberations at that time.

Charlton: But it will doubtless be represented that the Sino-Soviet split had, in fact, removed one of the principal arguments for containment from that time onwards, Communism was containing itself in that sense.

Bundy: Yes and no. Because you might then say it wasn't a single threat but you could still see the possibility of the Chinese being a threat in their own area. Certainly as one travelled around the periphery of Asia, in the late fifties and early sixties it was very widely felt throughout South-East Asia that China's sheer mass meant that sooner or later China would move into the area seeking to establish a relatively gentle form of hegemony if you will, certainly gentle as compared to what the Soviets had done in Eastern Europe; that the Chinese would be expanding sooner or later. In other words, the Chinese were viewed as a major threat in Asian terms, even though nobody any longer thought that they were operating in close cahoots with the Russians.

Charlton: On the other hand, the principal impulses for the commitment in South-East Asia were coming not from the Chinese—that's a long-term perspective—but from the aggressiveness of Soviet policy at the time over Berlin, and the brutality of Kennedy's meeting with Khrushchev in Vienna for example.

Bundy: That is true of 1961. The point I'm trying to get at is that there was a change in the view of the source of the threat. In 1961 it was definitely the Soviet threat. Then you went ahead to the Cuba missile crisis [of 1962] and then to the easing of tensions with the Soviet Union in the summer of 1963, the signing of the Limited Test Ban Treaty and so on, and at that point the feeling of Russia as an overpowering menace tended to recede. You can actually see this not only in the official reasoning, but in the public opinion polls in the United States at this time.

But concurrently, the belief in the Chinese as a threat tended to rise. The two curves crossed, as people who think in terms of graphs like to put it, and the idea of China as a menace grew particularly from the time of the Sino-Indian conflict in the fall of 1962 which seemed (and I think exaggeratedly) an example of the Chinese being ready to move hard in peripheral areas. Then you had the Chinese moves to associate themselves with Indonesia, which was then under Sukarno and was threatening Malaysia. You had a lot of threatening noises out of China, and an apparent building of ties with Indonesia, with Pakistan, with Cambodia, that seemed to indicate that the Chinese might be a more threatening nation. At any rate this was a belief held in Washington, held in academic circles in this country, held as far as I could tell by most of China's observers of the period.

Charlton: If you had to nominate a single thing out of this whole context of probe and test of American will and resolve—by, particularly, a Soviet policy and by the appreciation of a possible threat from China in the long term—if you had to nominate one thing which gave weight and credence to the Taylor/Rostow proposals as they came back to Kennedy from Vietnam, what would you nominate, which one?

Bundy: The fall of 1961? I think it was the sense that you had to stand firm in this area, that otherwise the idea of Communism as the wave of the future would have a very great effect. The nations of the area felt very threatened. It was then in a Soviet guise, but the Soviets then loomed very strong. That would be what I would regard as the line of reasoning. There was no single dramatic event that led to it.

It is not possible to divorce America's involvement in Vietnam from consideration of strategic factors. But the history of that involvement discloses a consistent confusion of aims and purposes. So what therefore were the instructions the new Kennedy Administration gave to Ambassador Fritz Nolting when he first went to Saigon in 1961?

Nolting: I should perhaps begin by saying that I was brought over from my post in NATO in Paris in the spring of 1961 when the Kennedy Administration was just forming itself and working out its policies for various areas. My briefing in Washington, between Paris and Saigon, was rather brief. I had meanwhile consulted a number of people in Europe, when I knew about this appointment—in France and in London—people knowledgeable about South-East Asia and Vietnam in particular. But the briefing in Washington consisted really of attendance at task force meetings which were organized in Washington to try to advise the President on policies to be pursued in Vietnam. Those meetings perhaps lasted ten days, a week to ten days. Pretty solid briefing meetings, with discussions of the various alternatives of US policy. Out of that came a recommendation by the task force to the Kennedy Administration, and that recommendation approved by President Kennedy really was my instructions.

Charlton: But, do you feel you went out there to continue a policy already in being, or to give that policy a new emphasis and if so, what was it?

Nolting: I think to give the policy a new emphasis. To continue the Eisenhower policy of supporting the South Vietnamese through their elected government short of the commitment of American combat forces. To do this in a stepped-up way, in view of the increasing violence of the Vietcong which had begun the year before in 1960 or maybe as early as 1959. To do it through various means, economic help, political support, intelligence gathering, particularly the supply of weapons to South Vietnamese forces, and through a training system by the US military consisting not only of logistics problems and use and imports to South Vietnam, but in the use of those weapons and in training and training camps. So, in order to do this, the instructions put a great emphasis on building a bridge of confidence between the US mission and the government of South Vietnam, which was the Diem government, which had been in office as you recall some six years then, and had just been re-elected.

Charlton: So there was no question, when you went, of your making a personal assessment of Diem's position in the country; that had been decided before you went, and unequivocally he was the man you were to support?

Nolting: Well, no. It had been decided tentatively that he was the best bet, and that he was worthy of support. But I recall vividly talking with President Kennedy about my mission and instructions and he said in effect that the success of this increased American effort to support Vietnam depended on Diem and he wanted my frank appraisal of him. After my arrival in Saigon I was very open-minded on this question for a number of months because I thought it was a crucial question. I ended up feeling that this man was honest, that he was dedicated, that he had the best chances of rallying the nationalist spirit of the non-Communist South Vietnamese of anyone on the political scene. While he had his shortcomings, which were a stubborn streak, a tremendous overdose of verbosity and he wasn't a good administrator (he tried to do it all himself), he was not a dictator in the sense of Western concepts. I mean he wasn't a cruel person, he wasn't an autocrat in the Western sense. He was autocratic and paternalistic in the mandarin sense, which is quite different. In my judgment Diem was a dedicated, responsible leader. He had wide

support among the peasants of South Vietnam. This support was based on his reputation for honesty and justice, and his hard work for his people.
Charlton: But would you agree that the new emphasis of the policy that you took to Saigon was a stepping-up, as you put it, of the American commitment in arms and aid and advice; and did that limit the autonomy that Diem had been exercising, did it limit the capacity of the South Vietnamese government to act?
Nolting: No, on the contrary. That point is very important. My instructions were *not* to take over any control but to try to build up mutual confidence so that our advice would be taken seriously; but the responsibility for the actions was clearly left in the hands of the Vietnamese government.

Of the many milestones which mark various stages of the American entry into Vietnam, and the later humiliating exit, a special significance naturally attaches to some. President Kennedy began the process which progressively committed America more deeply when he acted on some of the recommendations of a special study in October 1961. It was that mission, the Taylor/Rostow mission already referred to, which was sent out to report to the President on what should be done in South Vietnam. It was headed by General Maxwell Taylor and by Professor Walt Rostow. Taylor was one of the few who was not a complete stranger to Vietnam. Once, during the Korean armistice, he went down to look at Saigon in the period following the Geneva agreements of 1954 and on the outskirts of the city he had seen the thousands of refugees in their camps who came to the South when the North fell to the Communists. He got some feel then for the terrain, and had also got the feel of intrigue among the officials and ministers around President Diem. Now some six years later the Taylor/Rostow findings persuaded Kennedy to act.

Taylor: On 1 July very shortly after I came to the White House in 1961 as the President's military representative, some of his advisers—I think Rostow was one of them—started needling him to get Taylor to go to Saigon and tell him what needed to be done. This was the result of several very unfavorable reports from Vietnam that brought home I think to the White House for the first time that we'd been too much concerned about Laos. So the thought was: 'Let's take a harder look at what's happening in Vietnam which we haven't dismissed, but nonetheless we have neglected.' I resisted the trip all during the summer, saying I'd be very glad to go, or at least I would obey the President very happily, knowing that the situation in Saigon was a can of worms. But first I must be told what was the policy of our government, because my mission was not to go out there to recommend a new policy, but to get the current policy working. So all through the summer, we had a series of useful discussions, which made these people get together and focus on the problems. The Administration was still very new, and they sat there day after day on the subject of what to do, what we wanted over there and what kind of instructions to give me. And it ended with my getting an instruction in a letter from the President which made it very clear that I was to go out there for the purpose of examining the situation, recommending ways to facilitate the attainment of our objectives in South Vietnam and to make them more feasible than they appeared to be under the present circumstances.

Charlton: You've mentioned yourself the difficulty you had before you went, getting a clear idea of what the policy was, and no-one can be more painfully aware than you that this was one of the principal criticisms of the American involvement. Depending which American you asked, you always got a different answer as to what the aims and objectives were in Vietnam! So, can I ask you to say, not in the light of revised opinion perhaps, but what at that time you believed the aims and objectives of the American involvement were?

Taylor: If you read the [National Security Council] policy statement of May 1961 it was just as clear as it had been I thought since Eisenhower's time, and it remained equally clear with both Kennedy and Johnson! I don't know that President Nixon ever made a statement in exactly the same terms. We were there for two purposes: one was to defeat the effort of North Vietnam to impose a Communist state on an unwilling South Vietnam; and secondly to allow South Vietnam to choose its own government and so on.

Charlton: You've told us what your instructions were, on the Taylor/ Rostow mission. What were your recommendations?

Taylor: First, the overall one was that we must give the Vietnamese the feeling that a new relationship was being established, a very close relationship of comradeship and increased support from the United States for Vietnam; and the steps to be taken under that rubric would be first a major increase in the advisory personnel, and stressing—not exclusively but very strongly—the intelligence field. On my trip I had found very quickly that the information we were getting back in

Washington was highly unreliable. What happens in a bureaucracy like Washington is that you send out some economic question wanting all the data at once—for example how much rice was grown in a given province in comparison with ten years ago—questions which would be very difficult if addressed to the most advanced government in the world. The result was that the Vietnamese had the embarrassing choice of saying 'sorry we don't know' or putting something together quickly as their best guess. So we found that when our people at the Embassy received such a request, they'd walk across the street with a Washington cable—all they could do—and give it to a Minister and politely request the answers. In due course they'd get the answers, and put them on the wire to Washington. There very gravely we were drawing charts and maps and putting computers to work on such data which being garbage going in, was garbage when it came out, and resulted in many misapprehensions in Washington.

Charlton: Your recommendation was that aid and the American presence should be increased?

Taylor: We proposed aid in various forms, for example in the intelligence field, and in the military field especially in light aviation. We felt that the helicopter and the light plane were probably the greatest technological aid that we could give. So both were stressed very heavily. Also to assist governmental administration we offered to send over specialists, technocrats you'd call them I suppose, to go into their ministries. Diem didn't like that idea. He didn't reject it, but it just never happened. Another thing we recommended (and Diem very reluctantly agreed to but never allowed to happen) was that we formed teams of Americans and Vietnamese specialists to go into every province and get some of the answers we needed. That would be the quickest way if we could really survey the provinces as a team. But Diem was very suspicious of the foreigner getting into his business, and hence never permitted the joint survey.

Charlton: Did you understand and sympathize with that attitude of Diem's at the time that you were in fact taking over?

Taylor: To a large degree. Of course I tried to persuade him to acquiesce so I would say: 'Yes, I can see your reluctance Mr President, but don't you realize that if we get the information in this form it'll be accepted and acted on much faster in Washington than if we send back requests supported by data which is proved to be inaccurate.' Well, he would say, yes. But still nothing would happen.

Our most controversial recommendation was the question of American troops. As for President Kennedy, I knew when I left the

White House, that the last thing he wanted from me was a recommendation to introduce American ground forces. I knew that, and I told him quite truthfully I had the same feeling. The first point of stop on our trip was Honolulu. All the military in Honolulu closest to the situation said we must get some American forces into Vietnam soon. By the time I got to Saigon the Vietcong had increased their strength during the last nine months. Laos appeared to be going down and from Saigon's point of view the settlement that we were making in Laos was a sell-out to the Communists, which discouraged them. Finally, they were having the greatest flood of the Mekong in a hundred years. Practically every place south of Saigon was just a muddy sea. So again everybody said to me: 'Let's get some American forces in; we need them very badly if only for morale purposes.' I very reluctantly agreed to try out the idea on Diem, because Diem earlier had asked for troops and could be presumed to favor it. I should have mentioned that the first time the President ever approached me on the subject of Vietnam in the summer of 1961, he gave me a letter from Diem asking for support for 60,000 more Vietnamese troops. 'Well,' I said, 'Mr President, I'll have to take a little time to reply.' I told him when I gave my report on 3 November: 'This is the answer to the question you gave me back in May.' The recommendation I gave was that we form a logistic task force composed largely of engineer, medical and signal troops, for the purpose of helping with the flood situation. This force would bring in only enough infantry to give protection to our logistic forces at work. And then when the flood subsided we could say: 'Well we've done our job and can now go home'—if indeed we had not got the favorable reaction which our local officials expected from this military presence. Considering how the situation developed I might have been wise to recommend the 8,000 combat troops as was later attributed to me. In fact I never recommended any number, merely the dispatch of a logistic task force capable of certain tasks.

Charlton: Did you recognize at the time in your own mind that by those recommendations, if not for combat troops then for a large and visible American presence, that you had in fact crossed the Rubicon, that you had altered the nature of the commitment giving Diem what he needed to win his own war, involved America in a new way and had run the risk of being seen to supplant the French as a colonial presence?

Taylor: My defense would have been if one were needed that I didn't think my proposition necessarily implied all that! Had I known what

the future held the better course would have been to introduce a strong American combat force right then, and see whether that wouldn't deter the enemy when they saw that indeed the United States was ready to fight for this place if necessary.
Charlton: Do you also agree that the mere presence of that force made it more difficult, and limited the capacity of the government of South Vietnam, to act?
Taylor: Oh no, a few thousand troops largely composed of engineers armed with bulldozers and the equipment necessary to clean up after a flood would have had no such effect. Actually the number of advisers that resulted from my recommendation amounted to many more men in uniform. Again, I didn't know how many advisers my recommendations supplied. There were certain functions that needed to be done, and I recommended we send the necessary numbers to perform these functions, leaving it to the Embassy to recommend the exact numbers and justify them. Well, I was amazed by the final figures. The total number eventually came to around 17,000 advisory personnel, far more than anything I'd thought would ever have been necessary. But they were all needed as events proved.
Charlton: Which of your recommendations on that mission were not accepted?
Taylor: Actually they were all accepted in a certain sense. None was rejected, put it that way, but President Kennedy viewed the military force about the same way that President Diem viewed the joint missions to the provinces. He didn't like it, so it was delayed for review after review. The Joint Chiefs didn't like it because the force wasn't big enough. So really there was nobody very keen about it, and it just dropped away.

The Taylor/Rostow mission in autumn 1961 changed the American commitment in Vietnam. Taylor recommended American troops as a task force be sent to South Vietnam and felt that the deterioration in the South could not be stopped without them. The compromise was to send military advisers and support units. How was this report, then highly secret, received by America's representatives on the spot in Saigon?

Nolting: On the whole good. Sound in the sense that I think if we'd continued on that basis and had not been thrown off course, the improvement would have continued. I would not have expected a wholly satisfactory situation in South Vietnam for many years. But I think the chances were that that would have been a gradual improvement and a viable South Vietnamese state, assuming American material support but no military forces.

| Why was the Ambassador against military forces? Was it that he and his colleagues in Saigon were concerned that *any* increase in the American military presence would limit Diem's grip on his own people and ability and capacity to govern?

Nolting: I think that the prevailing opinion of most of us in the Mission was that unless the Vietnamese could pacify their own country and somehow put down the Vietcong, or win them over— and 'win them over' was the expression—under their own steam and with their own manpower, that an expeditionary force from any foreign country would not be successful in doing so; that this was an internal struggle that had to be won on an internal basis. Now it's true that there were great injections of support, material support and others to both sides; but I entirely agreed with President Diem, and discussed this many times, that if they couldn't do it with their own manpower and their own government, the victory would not be viable even if there was a short term military success. And so it was that point that influenced my reporting and my thinking more than any, I think.

| One of Nolting's colleagues in Saigon was William Colby, who had been the CIA station chief in Saigon since 1959. He was critical of the Taylor/Rostow mission.

Colby: I think that their solution of strengthening the government and to change politically was at fault in two respects. The strengthening came out to be military strengthening. The urging of change turned out to be: 'let the opposition have a role in the government'. Well, the problem really wasn't a military problem. It never was. But I once had a conversation with McGeorge Bundy outside the White House and I was urging him again and again, 'Now let's get back to the guerilla war'—this was in the mid-sixties—'that's the only important element of this thing, the guerilla problem and that's in the villages, that is at the lowest level. That's the kind of program we need.' We had had lots of policy papers which started off with the need to rally the involvement of the population in the battle at the local level, but then we never did anything about it. We sent helicopters, but we didn't send rifles for self-defense. We sent tanks but we didn't send shoes for the local home guard groups. This kind of an imbalance. McGeorge Bundy said: 'Well, you may be right, but you know the structure of the American government really won't permit you to do this.' We didn't have the machinery. We looked at things as either a military problem; or a problem of economic assistance, building dams and highways; or a political problem, which meant relationship with the political parties and the national assembly. There wasn't any mechanism to work on the village problem until we later developed one.

Now the CIA did start in the 1960/61 period with the precursors of the strategic hamlets. Then the government did put up a kind of jerry-built structure within the aid mission to support the strategic hamlets; but again there was a bifurcation. The economic assistance program would come through the aid, the military assistance would come through the military. There was never a combination of the two, military and economic-political, at that level.

The strategic hamlet program I think was basically a good idea. It had one major difference from the Malayan experience in that the Malayan new villages had barbed wire round the village to keep the people in and to control their exit, and the amount of food they would have, so as to keep them away from the Communists on the outside. The strategic hamlets in Vietnam, the stakes in the defense lines pointed outwards. The political thrust of that was the self-defense of the hamlet.

William Colby there identified what became a long cycle of conflict among the Americans in defining precisely their priorities, their aims and their purposes in Vietnam—which ultimately evaporated their will and resolve.

Although President Kennedy had not approved the Taylor/Rostow mission's equivocal recommendation about combat forces being sent, the American participation had been significantly increased. Three American Presidents had shrunk from committing the US to a larger involvement in Vietnam. What had made Kennedy take a further step? George Ball, in a personal exchange with Kennedy about this time, made a prophecy.

Ball: I don't think Kennedy had any real appreciation of the way in which the United States would be progressively drawn into a deeper and deeper involvement. I think under the terms of the Vietnam settlement in 1954 we had been limited to six hundred; and that was about what we had. Six or seven hundred. And it seemed to me that if we would begin to put more advisers in there that this would gradually involve us in a military contest and that it was a very deceptive kind of trap in which we might be falling. So I talked to first Secretary McNamara and his deputy Roswell Gilpatric and I told them of my apprehensions. I also told Secretary of State Dean Rusk of my apprehensions. I told Dean Rusk that I was going to talk to the President about it, and he said the President is as much entitled to your advice as to mine. So I did talk to President Kennedy, just the two of us one afternoon, and I said I was deeply concerned about this. I felt he would make a great mistake to accept the recommendations of the Taylor/Rostow Report and that if we started down that road that within five years' time we would have 300,000 men in the paddies and jungles of Vietnam, and we just couldn't find them again, and it was just impossible terrain in which to engage our forces.

He replied 'Well George, you're supposed to be one of the smartest guys in town, but you're just crazier than hell. That will never happen.' Now, what he meant by that is obviously a subject for some conjecture. He could have meant, which I suspect he did, 'I will never let it happen', or he could have meant, 'your analysis in the situation is wrong and that isn't the kind of process which is likely to occur'. I don't know which. There's been all kinds of argument of course since his death as to what he would have done had he not been killed. I will only remind you that at the time he was killed we had 16,500 men in Vietnam and there were two or three thousand more ready to go over. So that certainly the escalation was proceeding fairly rapidly at that point.

▎In American government there is a good deal of thinking out loud. The burden of ultimate decision lies only on the President. People got varying and conflicting impressions from Kennedy about the limits he was prepared to go to in South Vietnam.

The advice given to President Kennedy about Vietnam was not narrowly based. He had entrusted Taylor and Rostow with the official mission, but he sought and he got other opinions too. Taylor and Rostow had no sooner returned than the economist J. K. Galbraith (who'd been made Ambassador to India) was on his way to Saigon.

Galbraith: Nehru was visiting the President in November of 1961. At that juncture, Maxwell Taylor and Walt Rostow were just back and had submitted the Taylor/Rostow report. I went over one day —since I was busy educating myself and since I had reason to do so because of my relationship with Nehru who was also Foreign Minister, as you'll recall—I went over to read this report. I remember Walt Rostow saying that it was Top Secret, and I nonetheless picked it off his desk and said 'OK Walt, that means that I'm qualified to read it'. I was outraged by the thing. The idea of military involvement there horrified me. I had been in South Asia a bit, although not in Vietnam, so I knew something of the problems of carrying out a policy that distant from home. There was a particular proposal to send in troops disguised as flood control workers. The Mekong was in one of its periodic floods, and we could slip them in—this was Walt's proposal—really to defend South Vietnam, put down the insurrection, but they would be innocent flood control workers. I mean, I was wondering why in the world we didn't send them in in Boy Scout uniforms, it would be just as plausible.

So, I went to the President, and in this I had the advantage that we had grown up together and we were friends; there was no great formality in doing it. At this time, there had begun to develop in Washington a very healthy suspicion of the foreign policy establishment, a very healthy suspicion in the President's mind, something that had been very usefully cultivated by the Bay of Pigs abortion. And the President said 'Well, you go out and have a look.' So instead of going back to India, by way of London and Europe, I went back by way of Vietnam.

Charlton: Did you go to Saigon for the President because having seen the Taylor/Rostow report, you were appalled by it and you wished to influence the President and suggested that he send you? Or, did he seek your second opinion, and from people like you, as a result of his suspicions of Taylor/Rostow?

Galbraith: One doesn't know for sure, but I've always had a theory which was that the President did not like the Taylor/Rostow report although he didn't quite say so, and that he wanted me to go there so he could say: 'Well, Professor Rostow, he recommends this. But we've had another Professor there who is quite opposed to the whole idea,' that this gave just a slight margin of extra talking points against it. Now, this is purely a theory but this was my distinct impression at the time.

Charlton: What was the essence of your objection to that report?

Galbraith: Becoming militarily involved there. I did not think that we wanted to have troops there. I wasn't particularly persuaded by the strategic unwisdom. I just didn't think that we could guide a development of that country so far away and particularly by military means. The report that I wrote after I was there suggested that we keep our non-military advisers and that we keep the military (I don't think I proposed withdrawing the small military mission that we had), that we should continue any work of rural salvation and assistance that seemed useful, but that for us to be involved in succession to the French would be quite wrong. President Kennedy, when he asked me to go out there (and I don't want to build this mission up to anything more than it was) had no doubt as to the report he would get back from me. He knew that I was not blessed with an open mind on the subject.

Charlton: You saw a danger of America being seen to replace France as a colonial power in the eyes of the Vietnamese, did you?

Galbraith: Oh yes, but this was not a deeply perceptive point; this was something that one would have thought of immediately and that we would be the new colonial power there, sure. I have to say that my whole case at that time was against becoming involved militarily.

So, were the findings of the Taylor/Rostow mission to Vietnam an absolutely critical moment for the United States? A final word on this comes from Dean Rusk.

Rusk: They were an important moment, but I think the effort, well into 1965, was to try to put the South Vietnamese in a position to do this job largely themselves with considerable American assistance and with a number of American advisers. But it was not until the early part of 1965 that the North Vietnamese began to move the divisions and regiments of their regular army from North Vietnam to South Vietnam and presented President Johnson with a wholly different situation.

But it was with the Taylor/Rostow mission that a die had been cast. Kennedy's maxim 'Give Diem what he needs to win his own war' was no longer the detached support it had been. A considered decision had been taken to become more intimately involved by sending more Americans into the paddy fields as military advisers to help Diem resist the Communists. In Taylor's own words, because 'the Indians were coming through the windows'.

How at this time did the Americans form their assessments of the

THE NEW FRONTIERSMEN HOLD THE LINE

Catholic nationalist President they were supporting in South Vietnam, Ngo Dinh Diem? First some evidence of how Kennedy was viewing things by the end of 1962. A powerful political figure, Senator Mike Mansfield the Democratic majority leader in the Senate, went to Saigon and on his return submitted a written report to the President which was not well received. Mansfield, a Roman Catholic himself, had been disturbed to find Diem, whom he supported, becoming a recluse and his influence declining. Kennedy sent for Mansfield early in 1963.

Mansfield: He called me down and said he had changed his mind and that he wanted to begin withdrawing troops beginning the first of the following year, that would be in January 1964. He was very unhappy about the situation which had developed there and felt that even then with 16,000 troops we were in too deep.
Charlton: Is it fair to make the distinction at this time that troops in this particular instance were acting as advisers to the South Vietnamese forces, and while they were taking part in actions they were not doing so as organized fighting combat forces. Can you remember this conversation you had with Kennedy? What did he say at this time?
Mansfield: He felt that we'd made a mistake, that he was going to begin pulling out the troops on the first of the next year and he was very concerned and, I believe, mortified at how far we'd gone in.
Charlton: What do you think changed his mind about that?
Mansfield: Well, maybe he was more susceptible to the facts, rather than to the propaganda. Maybe he was listening to others besides the Pentagon. And maybe he was going back to his old thinking about Indo-China while he was a Senator and reviving some of the views he held then, which had been in abeyance in the meantime—he'd thought that the Vietnamese should become independent, he was against French colonial rule. He finally arrived at a decision, I believe, by means of which he thought that we had gone too far at that time, and the time to reverse things was in the immediate future.

It is significant if Kennedy was sufficiently uneasy about the commitment he had recently approved to be apparently deciding in his own mind that he had gone too far and wanted to pull back. But did he?

The then Secretary of State had heard of this conversation between Mike Mansfield and the President.

Rusk: Well, sometimes that story has taken the form of a statement by President Kennedy that he would take the troops out of Vietnam after the election of 1964, in 1965. I find it very hard to believe that President Kennedy wearing his hat of responsibility as President came to such a conclusion for one *unimportant* reason, and for one very *important* reason. I had hundreds of talks with President Kennedy about Vietnam and on no single occasion did he ever express to me any ideas on that line. That's the unimportant reason, but after all I was his Secretary of State.

The more important reason is that if he had decided in 1962 or 1963 that he would take the troops out after the election of 1964 sometime during 1965, then that would have been a suggestion that he would leave Americans in uniform in a combat situation for domestic political purposes and no President can do that. Now, President Kennedy was a man who liked to chew the fat and gossip with people and explore ideas; and I am not suggesting at all that Senator Mansfield was untruthful. But I am just saying that the President of the United States, in my judgment, did not reach any such conclusion in 1962 or 1963.

❙ The most obvious pitfall with the American involvement in Vietnam is to extract one event or sequence of events from the whole epoch. 1962 was the year of Cuba and nuclear brinkmanship with the Russians. Vietnam could not and did not receive single-minded attention. But the American government was uneasy. With their additional commitment to Diem they were impatient for results and more deeply sensitive to his performance. Ambassador Nolting characterizes the thrust and urgency which the men of the New Frontier were demanding.

Nolting: Very gung ho fellows, wanting to get things straightened up in a hurry, clean up the mess. We've got the power and we've got the know-how and we can do it. I remember on one occasion cautioning Bob McNamara that it was difficult, if not impossible, to put a Ford engine into a Vietnamese ox-cart.
Charlton: What did he say?
Nolting: He agreed, but he said: 'we can do it'. He agreed that it was difficult.

❙ Diem was the central figure for the Americans. Senator Mike Mansfield's trip was first hand evidence and from one who was disposed to be sympathetic.

Mansfield: I went to see President Diem. He was very withdrawn, very secluded. He was not the Diem I knew. So the only conclusion I could come to—it was at best a guess, an estimate—was that he had fallen under the influence of his brother and his [brother's] wife and they were taking over control.

Charlton: One explanation of that which has been given I think that he was becoming deeply suspicious of American intentions at this time, and would not speak openly to any Americans. Do you think he was being especially guarded, or was he somebody cut off completely from reality as you saw it?

Mansfield: I think he was gradually being cut off from reality.

Charlton: So would it be true to say that you shared the disillusionment of Diem that became more and more apparent in 1963? [Yes.] Well, did you support the decision to overthrow him in the sense that when the United States as an act of policy withdrew support from him and did not make that support conditional they at once made it clear that it was going to be given to the generals in South Vietnam as well?

Mansfield: Absolutely not.

Charlton: Now what was the basis of your decision?

Mansfield: Because I still had confidence in Diem, not in the generals and not in his brother. There was no settled figure among them, there was no man who could be called a soldier-statesman among them. We were getting off the right horse and getting on the wrong horses.

In May 1963 to accompany the developing insurgency of the Communists in the countryside there were suddenly major disturbances in Saigon. Militant Buddhists from among the religious majority in South Vietnam demonstrated against the authority of the Catholic President Diem. These events, and the way Diem asserted his authority, made Vietnam vault into the headlines in the United States almost for the first time [see fig. 2]. The New Frontiersmen were shaken.

Hilsman: I think Diem was accepted as a nationalist by enough of the South Vietnamese population for him to defeat the gangs and then some of the factions. The tragedy of Diem was that he then turned away from his nationalist thing. We had a person at the head of the Vietnamese government who at least had some command of nationalist sentiment, not total, but some, and we were urging them not to use artillery or air forces but to win the hearts and minds of the people and all that stuff. We had some hopes for a while. Then came the Buddhist crisis you see, where a Frenchified Catholic Vietnamese President began to beat up the Pagodas and kill Buddhist priests and Buddhist nuns. This horrified us and we said: 'Look, if you go on like this we are going to have to disavow you.' They did, and we did, and that brought on the coup. There were no secret machinations: it was all perfectly public.

But, beginning in May of 1963 with the Buddhist crisis, before I'd even shaved in the morning, I would get a call from Mr Kennedy—and the President was capable of four-letter words and he used them! He increasingly from May 1963 on as the Buddhist crisis progressed, became convinced that Diem and the whole elite couldn't do it. He began to instruct me, as Assistant Secretary for Far Eastern Affairs, to position ourselves to do in Vietnam what we had done in Laos, i.e. to negotiate the neutralization of Vietnam. He had made a decision on this. He did not make it public of course, but he had certainly communicated it to me as I say, in four-letter words, good earthy anglo-saxon four-letter words, and every time that I failed to do something he felt endangered this position, he let me know in very clear language.

Charlton: How would you define the neutralization of Vietnam, when Kennedy saw that Diem was failing?

Hilsman: Well, first of all if you will recall the time, in the fall of 1963, the maximum advisers we had in Vietnam when Kennedy died was 16,500. In a nation of twenty million people this means that most Vietnamese had never seen an American when Kennedy was killed. But before he was killed, he ordered the withdrawal of a thousand Americans.

This was a time when fundamentally conflicting assessments from South Vietnam began to swirl around the President. What was the CIA saying? William Colby was now back in Washington running the Vietnam desk.

Colby: Our position always was that Diem was about as good a leadership as you were going to get in Vietnam in this damn time. That America's main interest in Vietnam was not the small details of how it ran its internal government structure, but whether it was meeting the Communist challenge, that the strategic hamlet program was the proper strategy. Let's not be diverted from it. Let's support it. Our interests were that it got strong enough to fend off the Communists in that fashion. Now, there were other people in Washington who claimed that it was hopeless with Mr Diem, that the dislike for his authoritarian rule, the political opposition was so strong, that the Communists could not help but win in the long term with that kind of management. You know about the famous time in which President Kennedy sent two people out to Vietnam to come back and tell him what they found out after a week's visit. One, General Krulak, came back and he said he'd been to thirty provinces and he'd looked around the countryside and the war was going basically alright. There were problems but they were being solved and we were on the right strategy and it was making progress and so forth. The other one said he'd been to the three main cities, and he'd talked to the political people, and even the people within the government, the bureaucracy, and the unanimous opinion was that the war was hopeless. And President Kennedy asked whether the two gentlemen went to the same country.

Well, they did, and that was the key problem in Vietnam, that they did go to the same country, they looked at different things. Each one saw what he was looking for, came back and reported. The key question was never answered. Which one were we interested in? Were we interested in a perfect constitutional democracy in a small underdeveloped country in Asia, recently freed from a hundred years of colonial rule? Or were we interested in some kind of a structure that would prevent the further expansion of Communist control?

Colby believes that it was not realistic to demand instant democracy, and what was needed there was effective government.

George Ball, a senior government insider, thought the time had come for a hard line and drastic reappraisal of Diem. What was the reason for his disillusionment?

Ball: I became finally disillusioned with him when it appeared that Madam Nhu and her husband [Diem's brother] were in a position where they were dominating him to a very considerable extent. Where they had this whole affair of the attack on the Buddhists and the kind of indecent response on the part of the Nhu family, and a feeling that the United States couldn't tolerate staying close to an ally who was behaving in such a thoroughly detestable manner; we either had to get him to shape up or we had to withdraw, which I personally would have preferred to have done.

▌ George Ball's boss was Dean Rusk. How in Rusk's own mind did the State Department come to decide that President Diem was no longer entitled to American support and why?

Rusk: We never decided to get rid of him in the first place, but we could see clearly that he and his brother—perhaps his brother more than he—were pursuing policies that were bound to lead to the destruction of South Vietnam in relations with not only the Buddhists, but the students and others. We pressed him very hard in 1963 to change his policy. We urged him for example to send his brother off as Ambassador to Washington or London or Paris or some place. We put restrictions on our aid to Vietnam as a means of public pressure. The decision to overthrow him was made by the military there in Vietnam. At that time we only had a handful of Americans out there. We could not have supported him over against forces that were against him nor could we have overthrown him if he had had their support.

▌ The American government was so shaken by the Buddhist crisis that it brought home and replaced Ambassador Nolting. Notwithstanding what had happened, Nolting's advice about Diem remained unchanged:

Nolting: When I was ending my term on 15 August 1963 I did not feel that there was going to be a coup d'état, I did not feel that Diem was going to lose control. I felt that his government had suffered a setback but could recover, and I still felt that it was the best bet for South Vietnam and for the United States' interest for several reasons. First that the political situation in South Vietnam was not as bad as depicted, that is Diem had much more grass root support—or rice root support if I may use that term—and secondly that any *other* government could only be a military government, that the result of the military government would be to call on the United States for military forces. That was their way of thinking. They would naturally much rather have big, well-equipped armies, including American armies, than to have to fight it out themselves. Seeing that, I thought it was a horrible mistake to withdraw support from the Diem government.

▌ But Nolting's judgments from Saigon were no longer being accepted in Washington.

Hilsman: Kennedy would send people out there, you know, like myself or Mike Forrestal and others, and they would come back and say Nolting has become wedded to Diem. Localitis, we used to call it, you know. It's a condition which happens to British Ambassadors as well as American Ambassadors. They become the advocates of the local Government. Then you see Nolting went on leave and Bill Trueheart his deputy, his protégé, after a month of Nolting's leave, began to be anti-Diem. So it was almost unanimous.

▌ The stage was now set for what was barely perceived by the Americans at the time, but was soon apparently a momentous decision. American policy in South Vietnam so lately ringing with convictions and Presidentially supported epithets like 'Sink or swim with Ngo Dinh Diem' was about to go into what seemed at the time giddy reversal. William Bundy was then Kennedy's man in the Pentagon looking after international security affairs. I asked him whether the decision to withdraw support from Diem was a deeply thought out and considered action in the American government.

Bundy: Oh yes. I think the final decision to dissociate ourselves from Diem, the decision of late September and early October 1963, was carefully thought through, which doesn't of course mean that it wasn't open to grave question in hindsight. If you look at it in hindsight, you would say why didn't we think harder of pulling out, that really the generals wouldn't be any better, and that there was a major weakness at the core of the South Vietnamese structure and it simply wasn't worth supporting.
Charlton: What was your own attitude at the time?
Bundy: My own attitude was reasonably hopeful, that if there was to be a change in government it would be for the better; and I believed very strongly then in the existence of a really valid non-Communist nationalist feeling in the South, that they could pull themselves together, and in the degree of threat they then confronted which was supplied and directed from the North. I think the facts are perfectly clear on that. We thought that the threat could be handled; and that therefore they could dig themselves out. Then in the ensuing year and a half, year and two thirds, they went from one bad government to another, and they showed that they couldn't really seem to form a

decent government, so that it got progressively worse. But that's what I then believed.

Charlton: But when you say it was deeply and cohesively argued, do we infer from that that no great difference was seen between Diem as somebody that United States might support, and the generals? In other words that there was no great difference perceived in transferring support from Diem to the generals?

Bundy: Yes, that's true. We thought Diem would want to go on with the same policies. We just thought he'd lost his whole base of domestic support by his attacks on the Buddhists and the students, many of whom were the children of his own senior officials.

I remember particularly one senior official who came to Mr McNamara in late September when we were in Saigon and said this simply can't go on. Our feeling was that he'd completely lost touch with his people and that he was no longer an effective leader; but there was no understood or suspected or surmised difference of attitude as between him and the generals in their resistance to the guerillas and to North Vietnam.

Charlton: It was one thing to support a constructive nationalist who had had some success in South Vietnam in giving that state some cohesion. It was quite another actively to intervene in that state's affairs to withdraw support from Diem, and in fact procure the coup. That immediately changed the nature of involvement and, as has been suggested, it became an American war from that moment on; and I think this is the essential point I'd like to hear you on. Was that point closely argued and thrashed out before the decision was made?

Bundy: No, I don't recall it being argued at length. I think it was realized by all of us who were thinking about it, that this put us a notch deeper in, and we all approached it in that spirit. It was a very serious decision. It so happens that it wasn't argued at length. It's one of those things you can see more clearly in hindsight, and perhaps it should have been argued more. In fact, I don't believe it would have changed the decision.

▌ The fateful decision that Diem would have to go left unclear how it was to happen. It was to lead to his assassination following an offer of safe conduct.

The central instrument of the change of government in Saigon, with which the Americans signalled their desires and intentions to the generals in Diem's American-trained army, was the now famous telegram of 24 August 1963. We now hear the major participants in the drafting and sending of this telegram. It originated in the State Department where the initiative was taken by Averell Harriman, George Ball and Roger Hilsman.

Hilsman: The first thing that has to be said is that the famous telegram of 24 August produced nothing, nothing happened as a result of that cable.
Charlton: That was no fault of yours, you wanted it to happen.
Hilsman: No, no that is not true, that's not true. What we really wanted to do was for Diem to change his policy, send Nhu to be Ambassador to Paris. But not for a coup: that's what we wanted, but that is beside the point.
Charlton: Who drafted the telegram?
Hilsman: I drafted it.
Charlton: In response to what request?
Hilsman: In response to a request from the generals of Vietnam. You see what had happened was that the Voice of America picking up ordinary news things had announced that the Vietnamese Army had killed Buddhist priests and nuns. The generals came to us and said it was not the Vietnamese Army, it was Special Forces dressed in army uniforms and we demand that you deny this. Then the further thing they said was that we fear for our lives. If we find it necessary to take power and remove Diem what will you do? Well, we investigated it. We discovered that it was true, that it was not the Army but the Special Forces. And I drafted a telegram which said we will instruct the Voice of America to say that it was the Special Forces and not the Army; and if there is a coup we will examine the new Government on its own merits. Rusk then added the paragraphs saying that if there were an interim period of indecision we would endeavor to supply any anti-Communist forces through other channels than Saigon port.
Charlton: Had a decision been taken to withdraw support from Diem some time in advance of this, and you were waiting for this opportunity?
Hilsman: No, no, no. In fact, a decision to withdraw support from Diem was not made at that time. This was what we would call a contingency telegram.
Charlton: But it was implicit on the subject?
Hilsman: It was implicit.
Charlton: Why were you drafting such a cable of such enormous importance, as it seemed at the time, in response to a request from the South Vietnamese generals?

Hilsman: We had warned the President of South Vietnam that we heard rumors that he was going to beat up the Pagodas. We warned him that if he did it, we would denounce it. He did it, in the absence of our Ambassador. We got a telegram from our Acting Ambassador, saying the generals were saying that they feared for their lives, they might take power. If they did, what would be our attitude? We responded. One gets this kind of telegram about once a week, you know, from all over the world ...

Charlton: Now you have told us that you drafted the famous telegram and it was sent off round the circuit of the government for approval at various levels by the Defense Department, the State Department and so on. Now what happened to it when it was circulated that Saturday morning?

Hilsman: Well first of all, there were only two points in the cable. The first point was, alright, yes, we recognize now that it was not the Army who killed the priests, that beat up the Pagodas, but the Special Forces. We will make a public announcement saying so.

Charlton: Which was to save the honor of the South Vietnamese Army and the generals?

Hilsman: Exactly. The second point was a very standard thing, which happens almost every week, and that is if there were any change of government in South Vietnam we examine the new government on its own merits.

Charlton: And that would have been the formal and normal State Department response? So it came back to you in what form?

Hilsman: Well, what happened was that it went by secured communications to President Kennedy at Hyannisport; and to Secretary Rusk who was at the UN. It came back from Kennedy with no change, but it came back from Rusk ...

Charlton: Just let me stop you there. In other words Kennedy made no alterations to the telegram as you drafted it?

Hilsman: No.

Charlton: And he had seen it and approved it in that form?

Hilsman: That's right, yes. It came back from Rusk though with an additional paragraph, about which some of us had some reservations, but which said: if there is an interim period in which two factions are struggling we will endeavor to support all anti-Communist factions through other ports than Saigon. The implication being that if the generals revolted, and it wasn't immediately successful, we would attempt to supply the generals through Hué.

Charlton: And that was the crucial extra paragraph?

Hilsman: That was the crucial extra paragraph.
Charlton: And Rusk was wholly and personally responsible for that extra addition?
Hilsman: Yes.
Charlton: What happened then?
Hilsman: Averell Harriman and I went out and tried to find the acting Secretary, who was George Ball, who was on a golf course in the rain. We came back to his house and we got on the telephone, or George Ball got on the telephone.

▌ So George Ball was retrieved from the golf course by Harriman and Hilsman and brought indoors, to the telephone. Who did he talk to?

Ball: I telephoned the President, who was at Hyannisport. I read him the telegram. And he said, 'Well if you think it's alright, and Rusk and McNamara are for it', he said, 'alright go ahead.' So then I got hold of Rusk, and paraphrased it to him, because I thought we had an open line. And he in effect said, 'Well, if the President is prepared to go ahead, and you're prepared to go ahead, and you can get hold of Gilpatric' (McNamara I think was out of the country at the time but Gilpatric was his deputy) 'why, alright.' Well, somebody reached Gilpatric and he approved it. The telegram went out. I don't think the telegram made any real difference. The historians, I think, have put much too great weight on it, because the generals didn't reappear on the scene. They didn't organize themselves, they didn't get rid of Diem and the weeks went by and the weeks went by and the situation got worse and worse, and the President himself finally stated on national television, for the benefit of the Diem regime, for them to hear, that he was going to have to withdraw aid from Diem, as I recall, unless the Diem regime changed its attitude. And this was far more of a signal, coming directly from the President and in those much tougher terms than anything in the telegram, anything so far.
Charlton: But as you know, the popular version at this time was that there was a group, Harriman, Hilsman and yourself, inside the State Department, who perhaps saw this as the first opportunity to unseat Diem, a decision having been in fact made to do that at the first opportunity.
Ball: Well, I have never discussed the matter with—as I recall—with Harriman and Hilsman. I wasn't involving myself very much in the matter because I had a lot of other things to do with respect to other parts of the world. I'd rather left it in Rusk's hands at that time,

because this was an area of the world in which he was much more vitally interested than I was. I certainly was totally disquieted by the way the Diem regime was behaving. It was fine with me if the other Vietnamese wanted to substitute somebody for Diem that I thought would behave in a way that was much more compatible with our own ideas.

Charlton: Well, if not specifically by you, would you say that a decision had been made, to your knowledge, to drop Diem at the first opportunity, and this was it?

Ball: The decision made by Harriman? I don't know whether there'd been a decision. It could well be, but it wasn't anything that I discussed with them at the time, and I don't have direct personal knowledge.

Charlton: It's just that it came up in the weekend. It had the air of great haste about it.

Ball: Oh no, no. It came up in the weekend, because that's when the telegram was received.

The most senior cabinet member involved was the Secretary of State. Unlike many of the others contributing to this book, Rusk, when he left office years later, took no documents with him, had kept no diaries, and wrote no memoirs.

Rusk: A telegram went out in August from Washington while President Kennedy and Secretary McNamara and I, all three were out of town. It was cleared with us by telephone, but in the most guarded terms. When I was called about it I was told that the President already approved it. Well, what was my role at that point, you see? But when we all three got back to town we thought that it had been rather different than we would have sent ourselves had we been there.

Charlton: There was a draft in the morning and a revised version in the afternoon. Do you say that the President had approved both of those?

Rusk: I don't recall the two drafts. I mean, I don't recall that particular circumstance.

Charlton: Did you make an alteration yourself to any of those drafts?

Rusk: No, we simply pulled back from that telegram in our own conversations with Ambassador Lodge to make it clear that we were not going ourselves to become responsible for decisions as to whether or not a coup would be launched. After all during this entire period not only in Vietnam but in a good many other countries rumors of coup came almost every day and every week. So this itself was not all that unusual.

Charlton: My information is that a crucial paragraph in that telegram which went out from the State Department was added by you?

Rusk: Oh, I don't think so. I was out of town. It was discussed with me on the telephone.

Charlton: Yes, but did you add anything to it as a result of that discussion?

Rusk: I don't recall that I did.

Charlton: The crucial paragraph I am talking about which was subsequently interpreted as giving the green light to the generals to go ahead and make a coup involved the State Department making it clear that American aid and support would be supplied through alternative ports, or ports other than Saigon. That paragraph was added by you. Is that true?

Rusk: It might have been added by the State Department, but I just don't recall that paragraph at all. Certainly not; I don't recall myself as the author of it.

Charlton: But you approved it?

Rusk: I didn't have a text in front of me. It was cleared with me on the phone in rather general terms because we were on an open telephone line.

Charlton: Yes. I just wondered why the haste at this weekend. It was fair to suggest perhaps that you were looking for an opportunity, the first opportunity to make a change in policy and to move support away from Diem?

Rusk: It was after this telegram that we continued to try to work with President Diem to do something about his brother, and publicly cut back on our aid program as a means of pressure on President Diem. So this telegram was not the watershed, was not the dividing point.

▌What happened after the positive act of sending the telegram?

Ball: After the weekend, when Kennedy got back from Hyannisport, and Rusk was back, and particularly when the head of the CIA, John McCone, came back—he had been away too—McCone then began to say, 'Well this was a very bad mistake, we don't want to get rid of Diem, because we're not quite sure what we'll get'. There was a feeling that maybe we'd better try to undo it; and I think there was a telegram that went out that heavily qualified this. But I think this is really a kind of stillwater as far as history is concerned, because I don't think that this was what affected the decision. I think the decision, if it was strongly influenced by anything that occurred in Washington, was made after the President had himself said, on television, that this is 'becoming impossible', and that we're going to have to withdraw aid. I can't remember the exact language, but it was along this line.

Charlton: Which was an even stronger signal to the generals to get on with the coup?

Ball: Yes, a much stronger signal and this came up I think about two months later. The incident of the telegram occurred in August. I don't think that the actual coup occurred until November, something like that.

Charlton: Would you agree the effects of it whether it was the telegram, or the President's subsequent public statement that he was going to withdraw aid from Diem, and at the same time making it clear that aid would continue but to Diem's successors, the generals, would you agree the effects of that were disastrous?

Ball: I think it would have been disastrous to have left Diem there with the Nhus using him as though he were a puppet. They were bringing disgrace on the United States. They were creating a situation which was quite intolerable, which I think had it continued would have led to a very great continued disorder in Saigon. I don't at all accept the thesis that this was a disaster which changed the course of the war. I think it was the kind of situation which illustrated the fact that we should never have been deeply engaged with these people under any circumstances.

Charlton: It may not have changed the course of war, but changed the nature of America's involvement.

Ball: I think it was inevitable because, I think, Diem was losing control of the situation.

Charlton: The general criticism levelled at this period is that because America had intervened to the extent of, in fact, procuring the coup, that you made yourselves from that moment on responsible for the outcome of the war.

Ball: Oh, I think that's a grave rewriting of history, I don't accept that at all. I think that we found ourselves with an ally who was behaving in an outrageous fashion. Had he continued in power, I think, the situation would have become intolerable, and we might have had to withdraw completely.

Charlton: Which would have agreed with your own judgment?

Ball: It would have been fine with me, but I don't think we would have withdrawn. I think we probably would have had to go in ourselves and move in and assert greater power in any event.

❙ We must now go back a few weeks. Ambassador Nolting had been replaced in Saigon by Henry Cabot Lodge, a Republican, hardened in the cold war arena during his time as Ambassador to the United Nations under Eisenhower. He was a Republican patrician and therefore a symbol of bipartisan support for the American involvement in South Vietnam and a symbol too of the changing assessments of that involvement in Kennedy's government. Cabot Lodge was still unpacking his bags in Saigon when he received this famous telegram ordering him in effect to move towards the overthrow of Diem. What were his feelings?

Lodge: I was thunderstruck. I had been in Hawaii on Wednesday. I'd seen Mr Hilsman who was the Assistant Secretary for Far Eastern Affairs . . .
Charlton: And who drafted the telegram?
Lodge: I believe so. A number of senior officials were there. We had long sessions and covered everything and nobody ever said anything about a coup. Then I got on the plane for Tokyo and I was pulled out of bed in the middle of the night and told I had to get right down to Saigon because the police had gone into the Pagodas and were shooting at the worshippers.

So I got on down to Saigon on Friday and then Sunday came this telegram telling me to do whatever I could to overthrow Diem, and to, in effect, press the button. Well, I discovered there wasn't any button and that we weren't anything like as strong as we thought we were; and that the generals were very dubious about our capacity to keep a secret, keep our mouths shut, and that really nothing was going to happen. Then just as I was sitting down to write a telegram explaining to Washington that nothing was going to happen came the decision of Secretary Dean Rusk, who is a very sagacious man, cancelling the telegram for the coup. Now that has never received any publicity and I am grateful to the BBC for giving me a chance to give that cancellation some publicity because the usual thing is to assume that that telegram is still pending somewhere.
Charlton: On whose advice was it cancelled?
Lodge: Dean Rusk, who was Secretary of State. You don't need to go any higher than that.

Charlton: But, did perhaps some telegram asking for clarification of instructions go from you, something like that?

Lodge: I thought about asking for clarification of instructions and then I thought no, that I wouldn't do that. After all I was a man out of politics, I wasn't a career diplomat. I've been a Republican all my life in a Democratic administration; and people are always ready to suspect something less than complete loyalty and so on and I wanted to be loyal to President Kennedy and I wanted to carry out his orders. And I'd been in the Army enough to appreciate the importance of discipline and obedience and all that. So I decided no, I would not ask for clarification. I can read English, I could understand perfectly well what the telegram said, I thought it was very ill-advised; but I only had had twenty-four hours in the country and my opinion wasn't worth very much to me or anybody else. So I said 'I'm going to try to carry it out'.

Charlton: What was the likely reason for that telegram being sent in that atmosphere at that time, at a weekend when none of the signatories to it appeared to have appreciated that they hadn't all been consulted? It seems to have been a very hasty thing. The President was rung up at his beachside home in Hyannisport and said if it's OK with Dean Rusk it's OK by me. It looks rather a hastily conceived thing. With what motives do you think, and by whom?

Lodge: Well, I just think people get carried away. I think people get carried away in all countries, I don't mean to say the Americans are the only ones who get carried away, but in the State Department you had men who had devoted a large part of their lives to this thing, they were on it day and night and they'd got worked up and I think it was all done in the spirit of sincerity. That doesn't make it any less reprehensible.

Charlton: Do you think that a group in the State Department opposed to Diem seized their opportunity that weekend in a quite deliberate way?

Lodge: Well, that's the obvious explanation, that there was a group that had been working on this question for a long time and they were emotionally involved and very sincere.

Charlton: And opposed to Diem, of course?

Lodge: And opposed to Diem and they felt the time had come. The situation had gotten so bad. Diem was going to such extremes. The people in the United States were indignant at the way he was treating the Buddhists and so on. This was the time to do something, this was the time to strike. I think an honest man can differ as to whether it would have been a good thing to have gotten him out had they been able to do it, but I can see how an honorable person can think that that was a good thing to do.

Charlton: How quickly did it become apparent to you in Saigon that the overthrow of Diem was perhaps *the* crucial turning point for the Americans in Vietnam, that it changed the character of the war?

Lodge: It was *a* turning point.

For the alternative to Diem the Americans—and Henry Cabot Lodge their Ambassador in particular—were looking to his generals. One of the trio of leaders of this coup was Tran Van Don, who was perhaps in closest contact with the CIA in Saigon. Diem had earlier survived an immature and ineffective attempt to dislodge him back in 1960. General Don says the colonels involved at that time had had contacts with American intelligence. And this time the Vietnamese generals were fully conscious of soundings by the CIA on the possibility of moving to get rid of Diem. Ambassador Lodge had found the Vietnamese generals reluctant to make that move. Why were they?

Don: Because I didn't trust anyone. I am sorry to say, but I didn't trust any American, you know. The problem came because we knew what happened in 1960. I met Cabot Lodge once a few days before the coup; and I never mentioned about the coup. I said something can be changed, something must be changed. We would like to do it ourselves, and I ask you Mr Ambassador that must be a Vietnamese affair.

Charlton: What finally therefore decided you to launch the coup? There was quite a long delay before it actually happened.

Don: To make coup you need to have all the good factors on your side to success, you know, and you need to approach some military leaders also. They are very important. When we were ready, and when for the last time I met President Diem and Mr Nhu, I met them and asked them if they would like to change the policy. If they changed the policy I would say that the coup would never happen. Unfortunately they didn't want to change. The fact was the day of the coup at 2.00 in the afternoon Ngo Dinh Diem called me on the telephone. He asked me a question: 'What are you doing?' I couldn't answer that we are making a coup; but I said: 'Mr President, yesterday I came to your office. We have given to you two months ago a petition from the generals asking you to study and change the policy.

You answered me yesterday that you have nothing to change because everything is all right now.' Mr Diem answered to me: 'Yesterday I spoke with you; but today I was ready to announce some reform and a new government.' And I said to Diem: 'Why didn't you tell it yesterday to me? It is too late now. All troops are moving to the capital.'

Charlton: What influence in the timing of the coup was played by the American cables making it clear to you that American aid was not conditional, that the aid which had been given to Diem was going to be available to you as well? Was that the final factor that decided you to go ahead?

Don: Several weeks before we had approached the Americans to ask them, for example, if they had a coup, do you support after that the new regime? The answers came from Lodge to his CIA men, 'Yes'. That was a good factor. And the timing was 1 November because we were ready, and in that time Mr Nhu, who was the main assistant to Diem, was planning to make a false coup for arresting the supposed protestors.

Charlton: Including yourself?

Don: He didn't know who. He would like to make a false coup to arrest all the protestors, you know, because if there was a coup all people who like to be in the coup will follow the coup. I mean at that time that is a very good opportunity for the government to arrest all these people. And the coup was called when Nhu gave orders to the general who was in charge of the capital. He has all troops on hand, and he gives them the order to make a false coup. They call it operation Bravo 1. When General Ton That Dinh report to the group of the generals that he was ordered to make a coup, we ordered him to make a second operation called Bravo 2. It was the real coup. That is all.

Charlton: If you so mistrusted the Americans, and the CIA in particular it would seem, how were you able to put your trust in the confirmation that aid would be continued to Diem's successors, that is to say, those who led the coup? What was it and what authority finally convinced you to go ahead?

Don: It was the time to do it because of the political situation, the internal situation. There were many demonstrations. Monks were arrested and there were many demonstrations outside and it was time to do something even if the American side didn't approve it because in that time they were afraid that the coup will fail.

Charlton: On the other hand you did take one American into your confidence.

Don: No. I just promised to Lodge to call him when the coup will start. 'I will call you to be there close to me because you have to follow the coup. That's all. You have to report what happens.'
Charlton: My information is that you informed Conein [of the CIA] several hours before.
Don: No, I just called him 15 minutes before.
Charlton: When you say the Americans came to you and said: 'Yes, it will be alright, aid will be continued' on what authority were they saying that? Were you told that that came from the President himself for example, that Kennedy had said this?
Don: No, we didn't ask from President himself. We just asked the Americans, will you support: but we didn't mention about aid too. When Cabot Lodge asked me, the only time I met him before the coup, four days before the coup, he asked me, do you need something. I said no, we don't need anything. We don't need anything. We have got enough arms here, we have got enough things now, what we need is more hours and spirit to do it and so on. What we need is after that to get your support. I said support, I said nothing about aid.
Charlton: No, support was the vital thing. You were assured that the regime would be supported. But on what authority were you assured? Did you believe the President had given that assurance? Kennedy had made a speech publicly talking about the desirability of changes in personnel.
Don: That is right. I remember the terms.
Charlton: Yes, and how did you interpret that?
Don: That he would support any change, any change.
Charlton: The change of personnel being Diem himself. On whose orders was President Diem killed?
Don: That is a very delicate question. I can say to you that Americans were *not* involved in the death of Mr Diem and Mr Nhu. That is my only answer.
Charlton: It's widely believed that General Duong Van Minh, one of your co-conspirators, gave the order.
Don: People say it.
Charlton: Do you agree with that?
Don: He was the boss in that time.

General Tran Van Don did not dissent when I interpreted his answer as meaning yes. The Americans were shocked at Diem's assassination. He was supposed to have safe conduct. But they had encouraged the circumstances which led to it and which perhaps made it inevitable. They had inspired the overthrow of the constitutional head of a state whose creation they had insisted on and whose cause they were championing. The consequences of that responsibility were to deepen the American involvement in Vietnam.

But within three weeks another death was to blot out the memory and obscure the consequences of this one. John Kennedy was himself assassinated. Fear and a feeling of instability gripped America. Affairs at home for the Americans overwhelmed all else. For Kennedy's successor, Lyndon Johnson, Vietnam was a runaway crisis and a responsibility he inherited.

5
Trying to win with LBJ

John Kennedy was murdered in Dallas on 22 November 1963. The Vice President, Lyndon Johnson, succeeded at a time when the United States was deeply shaken, and feelings of fear and instability began to pervade the country. America started to immerse itself deeply in introspective examination.

So the first charge upon Lyndon Johnson and his first consideration as President had to be the restoration of a sense of security and continuity. A Presidential election—Kennedy had in fact been campaigning in Texas for his second term—was less than twelve months away. And, while inside America everything seemed different, outside little had changed.

Vietnam, for Lyndon Johnson, was a commitment he had inherited. He was in this, as in all respects at first, little more than the executor of his predecessor's will. On the very day he was assassinated, in a speech in Dallas, Kennedy made this reference to Vietnam:

We should realize what a burden and responsibility the people of the United States have borne for so many years ... Without the United States South Vietnam would collapse overnight.

The Americans had both desired and inspired the coup which overthrew Diem. A military junta was now in power and, at the time of Diem's and Kennedy's deaths, 16,000 American advisers were lying out in the heat and the rain of the rice paddies, training and exhorting the South Vietnamese army to match the efforts of the Communist guerillas. The overthrow of Diem had changed both in nature and degree therefore the American involvement in Vietnam. To the extent that they were responsible *for* it the Americans were responsible too for the consequences *of* it. In this sense, by the time Lyndon Johnson took the oath of office, Vietnam had already become an American war. Lyndon Johnson took command when the United States had switched its political allegiance in South Vietnam to the generals and was looking to this new meritocracy it was trying to create for the more effective pursuit of the goal of an independent non-Communist state. On the spot in Saigon though, the Americans were soon rueful at the nature of the change which had been wrought. Government leaders came and went, as they said, 'as though caught in revolving doors'.

Still fresh in memory was the slogan of the Kennedy government, 'Sink or swim with Ngo Dinh Diem'. As has been said, from sinking with him it now looked as though they were proceeding to sink without him. General Maxwell Taylor had been one of Kennedy's senior advisers. In 1964 Lyndon Johnson sent him out to Saigon as Ambassador with full powers and responsibility for America's advice to the South Vietnamese government on political as well as military affairs. What did he find when he got there?

Taylor: 1963 was the critical year when we pulled the rung from under Diem and created the chaos that took place thereafter. I inherited the mess which grew out of the Diem assassination and the frustrating experience of having to deal with five different sets of province governors, five different sets of cabinet ministers, many changes of the senior military command, in this period of time. I would say that was the lowest point in our effort until the very collapse in 1975. So my task was that of the Dutch boy with the leaking dyke, sticking in his thumb to plug the thing up and hold it together.

I would say that the American representation that I inherited as Ambassador was about that which had grown out of my recommendations in 1961. It had taken about a year and a half or something like that to get the people in place, trained and so on. The overthrow of Diem was the best news that Hanoi ever got because Diem typified the stubborn resistance of the South. So there the leaders immediately said 'Well, this is fine, let's get going to exploit this'. So they started the first big influx of the larger tactical units, in contrast to individual reinforcements of the North Vietnamese who were advising the Vietcong in the guerilla movement. So there was a very clear and evident change on the part of Hanoi at that time; whereas the response in the South had been simply more chaos, more turmoil and no progress. Actually there was retrogression, I would say, in the effectiveness of government both in political and military terms.

General Taylor used that familiar metaphor about inundation to describe the stage the insurgency had got to in the countryside, while newly sponsored political leadership was indulging in a series of adolescent coups that brought an almost intoxicating turnover in governments. One gets a strong hint of how goaded the Americans felt by lack of success and how they were seeking to change the terms of a struggle which were being dictated all the time by the Communists.

Under the circumstances, and with that attitude of mind, the time was rapidly approaching when the Americans would seek the salvation of the cause by demanding their own more forceful intervention. In reaching that decision all turned on the nature of the conflict itself. To what extent that was understood is a matter for argument without end. Sir Robert Thompson was a persistent advocate of limiting the aim and the cost in Vietnam at a time when the Americans were about to expand both.

Thompson: Mao has said that the strategy of insurgency warfare is to use the villages to encircle the towns. In other words to gain gradual control in the rural areas so that you gradually push the government back into those towns defending these urban areas and defending the communications between them, while the guerilla forces gain control of the enormous rural population base and the rural economy on which in fact the whole country depends. But I think the strategy is much higher than that, that is the strategy on the ground. The real strategy can be defined in terms of time, space and cost. If guerilla forces gain control of rural areas in the way I've described, it is going to take the government a long time to regain them. In fact, almost as long probably as it took the guerillas to get into the position which they are at any given moment. So that you are faced with a five to ten year war. Therefore you've got to have the political and psychological means to fight a long war, you've got to have the economy of effort that enables you to do that. When I talk about economy of effort think in these terms—that if you have a bridge in the rural areas and you put twenty men to guard that bridge, fully armed, and they sit there for two years and nothing happens, and then on the one night something does happen they are caught sleeping, the bridge is destroyed and they are killed and their arms are lost. Think of that in terms of cost right over the period. I want to come on to the second point about space in these rural areas, that if you've got time on your side, it's because you're holding this space in the territory of the rural areas.

Also you're holding space in another sense altogether; and that is your subversion, your ideology, your penetration, intimidation, terrorism, any instrument which you like to use, is penetrating into the government secure base areas—so that a government is not certain whether it can rely on everyone who is supposed to be on its side or is even part of its own forces. In this sense you've got a tremendous space to deal with. Anyone can understand, for example, that if you have a rebellion which is merely, say, in a large country, one small tribe in one given area of the country, well of course you can deal with that with no problem at all.

But if you've got a rebellion that is stretching right out so that you have everything from the hand grenade in a bar in the capital city to attacks on police stations in remote rural areas, the government has got enormous space to cover in its defense of these vital areas and of its people. Now this is imposing very high costs against comparatively low costs on the guerilla side, and you get what I think is finally the real key to this strategy, that the cost of the guerilla forces which is indefinitely acceptable is imposing costs on the government which are not indefinitely acceptable. At that point, even though the guerillas have not won a single military battle, they are winning the war.

Charlton: And therefore that makes clear that an absolutely fundamental objective of any antidote to a successful guerilla campaign must be to undertake it on the same basis as a protracted commitment at a cost you can endure?

Thompson: Yes, I have defined that in rather a nasty way, in that if you can have stable peace, I don't see why you can't have stable war. But if you are dealing with protracted war you have got on your side to be able to fight what I call a stable war, which means that you can stand the cost indefinitely of holding that protracted war through economy of effort, through the measures that you are taking; and psychologically people seeing that this is right, that this is working. Politically that starts to give you the political support to carry it on, economically that it does not cost too much. You've so designed your forces, so designed your commands, that you get an economy of effort.

Charlton: Do you believe that the Communists with their ideology had a superior method of analysis and adaptation which was insufficiently understood for a long time in Vietnam, at least for long enough for them to have won and maintained the strategic initiative throughout that conflict?

Thompson: I am not sure that analysis is quite the right word from the point of view of their ideology. Frequently their ideology led them into wrong analysis, because under their ideology it was naturally assumed that all the people would automatically support them, which of course was far from true. Let me just take the example of the Tet offensive where in 1968, where when they came into the towns they thought that all the people of the towns would automatically rise up in their support, whereas in fact it had exactly the opposite effect. So their analysis was not always right. But where I found that their analysis was extremely good was in their analysis of the governmental difficulties and later of the American difficulties in fighting a war of this nature.

I think also you have to understand that after the experience of World War II and particularly after Korea which was a straightforward invasion across the 38th parallel and very much a conventional war, and coupled also with the fact that to be faced with a war like this was really difficult for the United States to adjust to. In fact they never really did adjust. I'm a great believer in the fact that one of the great problems with these enormous American institutions like the State Department, the Defense Department, the CIA even and US AID and so on, that it was very hard for the bureaucracies and the staffs and the headquarters staffs to be flexible in their approach to a war of this type. They had to use what they'd got, they had to use the men who were trained for something different. Therefore there was always a tendency to fight the war you wanted to fight rather than fight the war that you'd got.

| After Kennedy's death, President Johnson's task was to pull America together.

The President gave himself the same objective in South Vietnam—to pull it out of the chaos. Johnson had hurled himself upon the task of the Presidency as if to devour its burden and overwhelm its difficulties with his own enthusiasms and ideals. He launched a program for the Great Society, an expanding latter day vision which would recreate Roosevelt's New Deal. The prospect of a universal American largesse would be available to all. And this was how Johnson's own forceful personality first began to impress itself on Vietnam and he offered and sought to apply the programs of the Great Society to Vietnam as well. Walt Rostow, from the beginning one of the principal policy advisers on Vietnam to Kennedy, was still so with Johnson—he became special assistant in the White House on National Security Affairs. Later, in 1974, he summed up that viewpoint to a student audience in Texas.

Rostow: Ultimately, President Johnson's view of Asia was closely related to his view of the race problem and of social reform in the

United States. I remember his telling me once of the visit to his little office outside the Oval Office where he saw visitors in private, of a Senator, whom I shall not name, who, arguing against his position on Vietnam, leaned over and put his hand on the President's knee and said, 'But Lyndon, they're not our kind of people'. President Johnson said that in thinking about that statement and responding to it, he realized how deeply he did disagree because he felt they were our kind of people in Vietnam and in Asia. They were people who wanted for their children what we wanted. And they wanted their children to grow up healthy, to have an education, to be the very best they could be, given their God-given talents. They wanted for their country independence and a right to shape their own destinies. And he felt deeply that Asians were as important to us in these terms as Europeans or peoples of the Middle East. This, I believe, was the critical difference in the leadership of the United States when the costs of the war in Vietnam increased and the debate about Vietnam became intense.

And so it was that American aid which had put Europe on its feet after the war, began to pour into Vietnam. Johnson wanted schools built there, roads made, and wanted to try and do on the Mekong what America itself had done in the Tennessee Valley during Roosevelt's New Deal.

Aid came ashore in indigestible quantities to rally morale and stiffen the will to resist the inexorable pressure from the Communists —coming from the North and in the countryside. Lyndon Johnson, who'd spent a political lifetime of successful personal diplomacy, always seeking accommodation, forever avoiding the necessity for choice if it promised confrontation, was for the first time faced with an opponent whom he could not sit in the same room with and, as he was fond of saying, 'reason together'. A non-Communist South Vietnam was not negotiable.

In 1964, as General Maxwell Taylor remarked, there had been a big increase in the number of guerillas infiltrated into South Vietnam out of North Vietnam through the sanctuaries along the open nine hundred mile border with Cambodia and Laos. And with the Saigon Government so unstable, the Americans on the spot were clearly trying to do something which would somehow turn the tables and allow them to break out of a cycle in which they always seemed to be dancing to the tune of the Communists, to initiatives held by the other side.

Taylor: This was the situation all the way through, because of the fact we had resolved to stay within the confines of South Vietnam.
Charlton: So how did you see the possibility of breaking out of that?
Taylor: Well. The only new thing available in the military field was to put pressure on Hanoi by using the air program.
Charlton: By bombing the North?
Taylor: By bombing the North, which initially I had wanted to tie to the terrorist actions committed against American installations. The latter was an interesting new development. For reasons I couldn't understand the Vietcong for years never directly attacked the Americans in South Vietnam, not until the attack on the Bien Hoa airfield in November 1964 which was the first act and that occurred about two days before election time in the US. I went back to the office and told my deputy Alex Johnson, 'Well, here's one that's going to bounce in Washington. Here is a case of a clear change of enemy tactics: they're now targeting our people in the war.' We had no tactical units in Vietnam as we were still on the advisory basis. But nonetheless, Bien Hoa was essentially an American field, and we had some heavy planes on it. Hence the attack was a significant change in events. Hence I recommended a reprisal attack at once against a field in North Vietnam. It was rejected as it probably should have been but I thought it time to have the President think about reprisal.

The next incident of this kind was on Christmas Eve when I was bringing Bob Hope from the Saigon airfield to his hotel just about a block away from the Brinks Hotel, a billet of the American officers. Just as we arrived, terrorists blew up the Brinks, setting it on fire. Flames were rising and fire department engines were screaming round the square. Bob turned to me and said, 'This is the warmest reception I've ever received'. Again I recommended a reprisal to Washington but didn't get it! And then about three weeks later the attack on Pleiku airbase occurred. It just happened that McGeorge Bundy was visiting Vietnam at the time. I told him what had happened, and showed him my cable to Washington which I was about to send, again recommending reprisal. I suggested we call up Washington and tell them it was on the way. We talked by telephone to Cy Vance in Washington, and then forwarded the cable which resulted in the first use of our air power in South Vietnam against a North Vietnamese target.

▌The pressure had been growing on Johnson as Commander-in-

Chief to agree to bombing as an expression of American determination and will to support the Saigon government and to convince Saigon that that was indeed the case and so improve their determination in turn. A new word was gaining wider currency—'escalation'. Until the attacks on American personnel in their barracks in South Vietnam these recommendations had been refused by Johnson. But in August 1964, three months before the events of which General Taylor spoke, an incident took place in the Gulf of Tonkin which was to provide subsequently the political pretext for retaliatory air strikes, and later an enormous expansion of America's involvement in the war.

Two American destroyer patrols—code-named 'de Soto'—sailing close to the North Vietnamese coast in the Gulf of Tonkin were attacked. The strongest disbelief apparently attaches to whether the second of these attacks did in fact take place, as we shall hear. George Ball was the number two man in the State Department to Dean Rusk.

Ball: At that time there's no question that many of the people who were associated with the war saw the necessity of bombing as the only instrument that might really be persuasive on the North Vietnamese, and therefore were looking for any excuse to initiate bombing.
Charlton: And this may have been the incident that those people were waiting for.
Ball: That's right. Well, it was: the 'de Soto' patrols, the sending of a destroyer up the Tonkin Gulf was primarily for provocation.
Charlton: To provoke such a response in order to pave the way for a bombing campaign?
Ball: I think so. I mean it had an intelligence objective. But let me say, I don't want to overstate this, the reason the destroyer was sent up was to show the flag, to indicate that we didn't recognize any other force in the Gulf; and there was *some* intelligence objective. But on the other hand I think there was a feeling that if the destroyer got into some trouble, that would provide the provocation we needed.
Charlton: Now one is relying largely on gossip here to support what you've just been saying, that the Gulf of Tonkin Resolution was in fact drafted some two months earlier—so the gossip says—in preparation for this.
Ball: Yes, I think that's probably right. I mean not in its final form, but there was a document I suspect kicking around. I think I probably was aware of something of the sort.

Charlton: Yes. I mean how is one to treat that sort of thing? Is that legitimate contingency planning or does that suggest a degree of deepening conspiracy within the government to bring about certain new directions in the war?

Ball: Well, I think that there was a feeling on the part of the President that he had to get a new grant of power from the Congress, that some overt act of aggression might justify it, and if such an act of aggression occurred then he wanted to be ready so he could use that opportunity to get the kind of support from the Congress so that he wouldn't be acting alone. It was a desire in other words to rally the Congress in support of the war. I doubt whether you could call it a conspiracy. I find that rather too strong a word. I think it was a tactical opportunity that they were looking for.

Charlton: Yes. It seems to me the important thing is that all the time the dissent in the United States was heightening or deepening.

Ball: Not so much at that time. It was just really beginning. I think that what the President was more concerned with was that there was a kind of lukewarm support for the war, and he had a feeling that if he were going to take the measures which the military were telling him were going to have to be taken if we were going to win the war, that he had to be sure of his ground and get a much firmer support. The Tonkin Gulf Resolution was that kind of expression of support from the Congress which he felt he needed.

Charlton: Now by this time you were beginning to play—and Johnson uses the phrase in his memoirs—the role of Devil's Advocate within the government. You were revealing opposition, as I think he says, on many issues to the way policy was being conducted particularly on this one. But before we get to the President himself, your principal opponent it has been suggested at this time was McNamara. Can you give us some idea of the character of the arguments that you had with McNamara? A portrait is painted of you, for example, rather alone, opposing the thing all the time; and McNamara refuting you with great vigor with facts and figures all the time which you couldn't call on. Is that fair? Can you just describe this period?

Ball: One has to understand McNamara's own responsibilities. He was the Secretary of Defense and he had the responsibility for the conduct of the war. Now as long as the war was going on, he wanted it conducted effectively. To conduct it effectively he felt that some escalation was necessary. He was very good in resisting the more exorbitant demands of the military. If he had taken the demands of the military in terms in which they were presented to him, the sky-rocket would have gone up far faster than it did. But he held back, and constantly was under enormous pressure. So, I don't want to create the impression that he was, you know, a jingo or out to make the war larger than it need be. I think he honestly felt that escalation was necessary; and I was standing in the way.

By the autumn of 1964, therefore, with Ball putting down on paper to the President those arguments which challenged most of the assumptions of the Vietnam policy, the first open and declared rift had appeared within the American government—but was being contained within it. 1964 was election year. The opinion polls showed that two-thirds of the American people took little interest in Vietnam or what was happening there. While Johnson was under heavy pressure to authorize bombing to rally South Vietnam and convince the North Vietnamese of American resolve, he was reluctant to do anything which would disturb the apparent detachment of so large a majority of Americans; and with an election coming he held his hand. Johnson's Republican adversary, Barry Goldwater, was critical of half-measures in Vietnam which conformed, at that time, with the military doctrine of graduated response and called for a strategy for victory which included bombing the North to force the Communists to the conference table.

The incident in the Gulf of Tonkin in August gave the President an opportunity to convince Hanoi of American resolve and to show that where America was directly challenged he would act decisively. Within twelve hours he had authorized a reprisal air raid against the North, and within two days he went to the Congress of the United States and asked them to vote on the Tonkin Gulf Resolution. This resolution asked the Congress, in these words, 'to approve and support the determination of the President as Commander-in-Chief to take all the necessary measures to repel any armed attack against the forces of the United States and to prevent further aggression. The United States regards Vietnam as vital to its national interest and to world peace, and security inside Asia.' The Congress passed this resolution in August 1964 by a vast majority. There were only two lonely votes against it out of a possible five hundred or so.

When Lyndon Johnson took the decision in the following year to send American combat troops to South Vietnam he regarded this resolution as having given him sufficient a mandate. The Tonkin Gulf Resolution was steered through the shoals of Congress by the chairman of the Senate Foreign Relations Committee, Senator William Fulbright. In March 1964, six months before this, President Johnson had had a conversation with Fulbright about Vietnam. He was saying that while it was under heavy strain the policy bequeathed to him by Kennedy, of supplying the South Vietnamese with training and supplies, had not yet failed. The President proposed to carry on with more of the same. If that proved insufficient to prevent South Vietnam going under, then a very tough decision would have to be made, either to put troops in or withdraw and, as he said, let the dominoes fall. He invited Fulbright to meditate upon that prospect. But then within two years of the Tonkin Gulf Resolution being passed and with thousands of American soldiers going to join an expeditionary force ten thousand miles away from the White House, William Fulbright became a focus as chairman of the Foreign Relations Committee for opposition to expanding the war.

Fulbright: I took the position, when we finally became interested in the 1960s, that this was really a civil war in Vietnam as to who would control this colony freed from the control of France. But we didn't really intervene in a substantial and serious way until Johnson came in. I didn't know enough about it to be concerned about it, or to have any reason to disagree with what the President proposed. No-one on the Committee took Vietnam seriously really until the Johnson period. It looked like a sideshow, I mean a very insignificant sideshow, compared to Europe or Japan.
Charlton: And that goes for the rest of Congress, not just your own committee?
Fulbright: Exactly. So when the President came along: 'I think I'll send'—whatever it was—'ten or fifteen thousand people out there', it didn't occur to us to take that very seriously. We had far more than that, I think two to three hundred thousand in Germany.
Charlton: What view did you take at the time of the Gulf of Tonkin Resolution?
Fulbright: Well when the President presented it and described the events that he alleged took place at the Gulf of Tonkin, I had no reason to question him. I don't normally assume a President lies to you; and certainly not Johnson, because I'd known him well and he never had in any serious way that I can remember. So I accepted the theory of that resolution, and the fact of the two different incidents. The theory of the resolution, as presented, was this was the way to avoid and to stop the war, not to prosecute a war. If we showed unity,

and the Congress supported the President in his action in the attack upon the ships in the harbor—you know, after the second incident—to this little country of only whatever it was, fifteen million people, peasants, the United States was determined, and if we showed determination, they would stop, and they would have a settlement, and this was the way to end the war.

Charlton: Now, I'm not quite clear how you suggested that Johnson was lying to you at that time.

Fulbright: He lied about the incident. That is, this enabled him to get it through quickly without debate. He said this had occurred. He said this attack, this unprovoked attack upon our ships on the high seas, could not go unpunished.

Charlton: This was the second attack?

Fulbright: That's right, and that we should respond quickly, and this would show them our determination and therefore they would stop. The whole fighting would stop if they knew we were determined to follow through. 'We bloodied their noses', was the way he put it. 'They know we can destroy them.' Mr Rostow was at the same time preaching the idea of surgical bombing. These people would give up if we would just bomb them in a serious way, and they could see what we could do. Then they would stop. He sold it on the idea this was the way to keep from any real engagement.

Charlton: So you believe the President lied to you on two grounds: the second incident did not take place; and also that his motive was in fact to change the nature of the war from a limited to a more open ended one.

Fulbright: It now appears to be true. This resolution was used by him afterwards to always justify the war.

Charlton: Nevertheless you were the chairman of the Foreign Relations Committee, and floor manager. What arguments did you use in recommending the resolution to the Senate for approval?

Fulbright: One of the arguments was that he had no intention of becoming involved in the war—I mean sending troops and doing what he did—because I was sure he was not to change our policy which up to then was non-intervention, which he was at that time advocating in his campaign for the Presidency.

Until the later nineteen-sixties American Presidents all enjoyed the support of the Congress for the policy of global containment which was the legacy left to the United States by the outcome of World War II. The exceptions involved undeclared wars in Korea and

Vietnam—and in particular Vietnam where there was no clear purpose or prospect of decisive victory. It was a war therefore alien to the American temperament and which had many ingredients to make its unpopularity almost pre-ordained.

The Gulf of Tonkin Resolution was bitterly to divide the Executive and the Congress. Within two years of its having been passed, and Johnson having invoked it as Commander-in-Chief to land an expeditionary force on the mainland of Asia, the President had another fight on his hands. This was the one waged against the Vietnam policy by Senator Fulbright in the Senate, where for so many years Lyndon Johnson had been master of all its sensitivities and grand manipulator of all its coalitions. Fulbright (and Mansfield the majority leader] claim that the President betrayed them over the Gulf of Tonkin.

Dean Rusk who spent many hours in severe public examination on Capitol Hill over the Vietnam policy as Secretary of State is adamant they were not betrayed.

Rusk: Anyone who suggests that I ever went to a committee of Congress or to a group of Senators and thought one thing and told them another is simply mis-stating the facts that never occurred. Some of them were embarrassed by the fact that they had voted for the Tonkin Gulf Resolution and tried to find a way to retreat from it. Senator Fulbright was ready to say quite frankly: 'I made a mistake.' Well, that's all right. I have no objection to that. But this notion that they were fooled is nonsense. If you will look at the Congressional Record and look at the colloquy on the Senate floor, the questions put to Senator Fulbright by Senators and his answers to them, his answers were almost identical to the then views of President Johnson. But it was many months after the Gulf of Tonkin Resolution that we saw the divisions and regiments of the regular army of North Vietnam invading South Vietnam, and that created a very different situation than the one we hoped for in August 1964.

Charlton: But the wording certainly seems to support the President's view: it did give him very wide discretionary powers.

Rusk: Well, the Tonkin Gulf Resolution was an exercise of the war powers of Congress.

Charlton: And yet one also is very impressed with the Senators who still seem to be convinced that they were given the impression that a much more limited intention was made or intended when it came to implementing those words despite the wording given to them.

Rusk: In 1966 Senator Morse, a man for whom I had a high regard but who was an opponent throughout, made a motion to rescind the Tonkin Gulf Resolution. He only had the support of five Senators, four besides himself, in 1966. It's my personal view that Senators ought to vote, and that the Executive branch of the government has a right to rely upon the way they vote without all the whining around the edges. Let them bring the matter up and vote on it so we will know where they stand.

Charlton: It's a proper time to ask you about negotiations, the possibility of a negotiated settlement. You were under fairly consistent pressure from former allies at this time that the United States was not perhaps daring enough to negotiate. In your view was a non-Communist South Vietnam ever negotiable?

Rusk: Not as far as the North Vietnamese were concerned, no.

Charlton: Did you ever have any response to the limited air strikes against the North in 1964 following the Gulf of Tonkin?

Rusk: No; we found Hanoi was very adamant about negotiations and in that they were apparently fully backed up by Peking. You see there were times when we tried to bring this matter before the United Nations but both Hanoi and Peking said that this was not the business of the United Nations and this caused a good many delegates of the UN to say 'Alright then, let's not bring it up, let's use other machinery'.

Charlton: But you never had the numbers of the UN to bring it up, did you, effectively?

Rusk: There were times when we did not have enough votes in the UN Security Council to put it on the agenda but that was a matter of counting noses behind the scenes. But when we turned to the use of the Geneva machinery they wouldn't use that either. So, then there were all sorts of direct and indirect contacts trying to explore this thing further but in retrospect my guess is that Hanoi never had an incentive to negotiate because up until well into 1967 I think they thought that they could achieve what they wanted by military means. But beginning sometime in 1967 I think they realized that if they just hung on that they would win it on the political front even though they could not win it at that time on a military front.

Charlton: In terms of the growing movement of dissent in the United States?

Rusk: Sure yes, and they were right in that judgment.

Charlton: This is crucial, isn't it? Why do you think it was always difficult and perhaps impossible for you to convince American public opinion that it was worth doing at all? All the time it seems to me you were being maneuvered onto ground you didn't wish to occupy. It was never your policy to have a million troops in Vietnam. It was never your policy to bomb the North. It was never your policy to duplicate the methods used by the Communists in South Vietnam for example in some of the pacification techniques. So from this moment on it does seem to me that increasingly you were at war with your own public opinion. Why do you think that was?

Rusk: With considerable sections of our public opinion. In terms of the change that made the difference, I think that that change came perhaps in the first few months of 1968 when people at the grass roots came to the conclusion that if we couldn't tell them when this conflict was going to end we might as well chuck it. Now, we couldn't tell them when it was going to end.

Charlton: When you say 'people at the grass roots' did you feel that you knew who they were?

Rusk: Well, I'm from the grass roots myself and we heard from a lot of them and you get this kind of a reaction from Senators and Congressmen, local political leaders, Governors and others, who reflected this expression, this change in point of view. But there were other considerations. For example we never made any effort to create a war psychology in the United States during the Vietnam affair. We didn't have military parades through cities. We didn't have beautiful movie stars out selling war bonds in factories and things like that as we did during World War II. We felt that in a nuclear world it is just too dangerous for an entire people to get too angry and we deliberately played this down. We tried to do in cold blood perhaps what can only be done in hot blood, when sacrifices of this order are involved. At least that's a problem that people have to think of if any such thing, God forbid, should come up again.

Charlton: But as you say the problem really was at the grass roots, that you couldn't tell how or when it was going to end. That was essential to the whole thing wasn't it? Weren't you in the position of having to deceive your public opinion as to the open-endedness of the commitment? One is very struck for example by what *The Pentagon Papers* show in McGeorge Bundy's memorandum at this time about the commitment of American troops, that nothing must be done to make this appear as anything but consistent with existing policy, which one knew that it no longer was. That the commitment had changed from a limited one to a much more open-ended one.

Rusk: That depends on what you mean by policy. Policy was to try to prevent South Vietnam from being overrun by the North. Then if it takes say 50,000 men the policy is the same. If it takes 400,000 men the scale or the effort changes but not the objective in view.

Charlton: But the nature of the commitment that Kennedy had gone to Vietnam with, to give Diem (for example) what he needed to win his own war, had quite obviously changed, hadn't it? It was now no longer a limited commitment. It was even an American war.

Rusk: But the escalation came from the North Vietnamese before it came from the American side. Look, we waited five years of North Vietnamese infiltration and penetration before we bombed North Vietnam at all. Now it was not until the North Vietnamese divisions and regiments of the Regular Army entered South Vietnam in early 1965 that we began any significant build-up of forces beyond the levels that President Kennedy had put in there. This word 'escalation' had been reserved by the news media for the United States side of it. They didn't look at the North Vietnamese side.

▍That is to run ahead. To return to 1964: in that year William Bundy moved to the State Department and became Assistant Secretary for East Asian and Pacific Affairs. How did he view the Gulf of Tonkin affair?

Bundy: Let me say at the outset, that contrary to some of the interpretations that people in *The New York Times* placed at the time of the publication of *The Pentagon Papers*, the Tonkin Gulf incident was totally unexpected and unpremeditated on the part of the Johnson Administration.

Charlton: Which one are we talking about? There were two.

Bundy: Well, either one, 2 August or 4 August whichever you wish. Actually I'd gone off on vacation then, and I have in my files—this is not a secret paper, it was a paper that I wrote with another fellow in which we said we were now assuming that we would go through the election campaign on the present course, that we would say maybe we would have to do something at some point; but that we would not confront that decision during this period, that we would go on not changing the actions we were taking, which were confined to South Vietnam. We were expecting to ride out the next few months on course. We didn't expect any incident to arise; and therefore when the North Vietnamese (as we believed was definitely the case) attacked our destroyers on the 2nd and again on the 4th, we thought they were in effect spoiling for a fight, and that you had to respond to that.

Charlton: What do you say to those who do believe that that second incident was engineered, contrived in order to make it possible for you to carry out the next and only available option as you saw it—the policy of bombing the North?

Bundy: Absolutely not. The first thing I did in the afternoon when we were getting resports of the second attack was to ask for the intelligence reading on it. The people whom I trusted said the evidence seemed to us beyond any doubt. That evidence has come out since in subsequent Senate hearings, including intercepted orders to a North Vietnamese unit to attack. Subsequently, there's been some question whether those orders weren't copying old messages from two days before, but there's no question they were intercepted in the proper sequence and at the proper times on 4 August. When you added those to the eye-witness reports—you wouldn't have believed the sailors who said they saw torpedoes and this kind of thing, on a dark night: anybody who knew the Navy knew that that couldn't be wholly relied upon, and there was no damage to our ships on the night of 4 August. But when you combine the reports of being fired on with the interception of what appeared to be clear-cut attack orders, then it didn't seem to be any doubt about the case. There was no contrivance about this. The men who made those decisions believed absolutely firmly that the attack had taken place.

Charlton: On the other hand, that second incident was consistent with your objectives that it was going to be necessary to bomb the North in order to weaken the will of North Vietnam, to get it to abandon its support of the war in the South?

Bundy: No, as a matter of fact it didn't fit with our plans at all, to be perfectly blunt about it. We didn't think the situation had deteriorated to the point where we had to consider stronger action on the way things lay in South Vietnam. And in political terms, as it turned out, Johnson probably did gain by his prompt and measured response, by his one-shot response and then not going further into a real bombing policy at that point. But nobody could have foreseen that. One would have said that he was in danger of losing his whole basis of argument against Goldwater in the campaign. In short nobody would have planned this, nobody did plan it. It was totally unexpected and the response was entirely on the level.

▌ President Johnson won the election of 1964 in a landslide. The bombing of North Vietnam had begun in the autumn after these first attacks on American personnel and installations. By July 1965 however, his senior advisers were telling Johnson that in itself the bombing was not enough to arrest the decline and fall of South Vietnam. They suggested to him three options: first to withdraw; second to go on at the present level which would make the position weaker and leave until later the choice of withdrawal or the emergency landing of an expeditionary force too late probably to do any good; and the third option was the prompt and substantial expansion of military pressure against the Communist guerillas in South Vietnam. Johnson chose the third. It called for a massive commitment of two hundred thousand troops. Despite themselves the Americans were re-enacting the role the French had played fourteen years before.

Taylor: The fear which we always had, even at the outset, was: 'We don't want to take this war over, we want to do just those things the Vietnamese can't do for themselves'. Now this turned out to be very difficult when our military forces arrived, because these units would come there, and their commanders, for only six months or so, all anxious to accomplish something. And there was every tendency to push the little brown men to one side: 'Let us go do it.' And we erred many times in allowing that to go too far.

Charlton: When you had your long conversations with Lyndon Johnson about the sending in of American combat forces the objective must have been to win a military victory. What advice did you give?

Taylor: I objected very strongly to the speed in which Washington was trying to throw forces in once the President had decided to land American combat forces, mainly on the ground that General Westmoreland was not ready to accommodate them yet. South Vietnam was an undeveloped country and a tremendous lot of preparation had to be made. The President had decided early in the game that whatever the field commander said he really needed and that Joint Chiefs approved, *he* would approve. So in that sense the sending in of additional military forces became hardly automatic since they always had to be approved—but nonetheless you knew what the Presidential answer was if the Joint Chiefs indicated Westmoreland wanted more troops and that he was ready to receive them (in other words if he had accommodation for them): we would send the troops. Incidentally, the President was very much worried about Da Nang because there was a tremendous base there. South Vietnam was run out of Da Nang, and he was getting very worried about it because of the increased weakness of Vietnamese forces under this pressure which was coming in from the North. So we had first a battalion as I recall, and then I think two or three battalions at sea just out of sight, floating off Da Nang ready to go in. You had both advantages of having forces available while still not deploying them on the ground.

So there was very little debate on subsequent increments once that basic decision had been made. It was clear that Washington was going to put in the necessary forces to re-establish the situation in South Vietnam. Hence the thought was: 'Let's get enough in there fast.' The way to suffer heavy casualties is to have long-drawn-out, indecisive operations in range of enemy weapons where he can kill off your troops little by little. The way to avoid that is to go straight at the heart of the enemy with ample force to get it over with. Bear in mind that this was not a one-sided war that we were conducting. It was a bilateral war, and Hanoi was pouring everything they could down the Ho Chi Minh Trail with the obvious intention of taking over the northern part of South Vietnam.

Kennedy had not wanted to lose the war, but had balked at sending combat troops to South Vietnam. Lyndon Johnson, who had voted against an American airstrike to save the French garrison at Dien Bien Phu ten years before this, was now faced as President with a different choice. He either had to lose the war and be seen to lose it; or he had to send troops. The shift from bombing to an expeditionary force of combat troops without the further approval of Congress undoubtedly helped to sow the whirlwind of hostile protest in the United States.

Johnson's priority was to launch the Great Society. He was encouraged by America's vast wealth and his faith in its limitless capacities to ensure that the United States could have both guns and butter. He believed to go to the Congress would mean a formal declaration of war. The Congress would force a choice between the Great Society to which he was summoning the nation, and the war; and he was in little doubt that the Great Society would be the casualty. He also believed that a prolonged and open debate at a critical stage of the conflict in South Vietnam would undermine the principal thrust of the policy which was to let all know—in particular Hanoi, Moscow and Peking—that America would underwrite and uphold its guarantees once given. Lyndon Johnson therefore tried to win in Vietnam, and to win quickly; and all his political skills were exercised to camouflage the fact that he was conducting not just an undeclared but an expanding war. If it had never been American policy at the outset to have (as it would become) half a million troops in Vietnam; if at the outset it hadn't been envisaged that there would be intensive bombing of North Vietnam; if that had not been the original policy what then had happened?

Bundy: Beginning in February 1965, it did become American policy to conduct a very measured—we hoped carefully controlled—program of bombing; and at that time we hoped that that would cause the North Vietnamese to be prepared to pull back and negotiate. We didn't think the threat within South Vietnam on the ground was so serious that the South Vietnamese ground forces couldn't continue to handle it. But we did get into a deliberate policy of a scale of bombing, which was later very much exceeded when we went into what might be called an all-out limited war. Now on the question of policy on ground forces, it's true when we made the decision to enlarge the American ground forces (the big decision was July 1965) to 175,000 I think initially, we didn't have any such figure as 500,000 in mind. We did think it might go as high as 250 to 300,000 if I recall correctly, but on that ball park. We didn't think that it would be in any way necessary to go higher than that. It was only after we'd seen how very effective the North Vietnamese could be in getting their forces down, and how much it took in the mathematics of guerilla war to counter any guerilla force, that we gradually found ourselves forced to go higher and higher. But you're quite right. There was not a decision: we will send a half million men. Circumstances stretched it much further than anybody then foresaw, and obviously that was an error in our foresight.

Charlton: In other words the aim of limited commitment had in fact changed. I wonder if I might press you on this concept of 'all-out limited war'. You were in fact, by introducing American ground forces weren't you, engaged in an open-ended commitment?

Bundy: That's true. It was essentially open-ended. If it got worse you were by then ninety-nine percent likely to raise the ante yourself. So it was open-ended. We didn't then envisage that it would take anything like half a million men.

Charlton: What did you feel about the need to conceal the fact that this was an open-ended commitment, because if you hadn't concealed it, you would have provoked a sharp debate within the US, which if it had happened (and had led as one must have supposed it would have, to open division) would have, of course, destroyed the basis of your strategy, which was to convince the North Vietnamese of your unyielding will and resolution. So, how did you approach that central dilemma when it came to dealing openly with public opinion in the United States?

Bundy: Well let me say that at my level, I always assumed that there would be very full Presidential statements and Congressional action. And the key period to look at there is July 1965 where the initial course of action recommended by Secretary of Defense McNamara to the President called for the calling-up of reserves, which required Congressional action; and called for a very heavy immediate supplemental financial appropriation to meet the costs of the war. Then in a very dramatic way that I wasn't party to, and after there'd been consultation with some of the Congressional leaders—I particularly recall Gerald Ford being in the room in his capacity as House minority leader—President Johnson changed the signals and opted for the lowest possible key Presidential announcement, and opted for not presenting the course to the Congress, and so on.

Charlton: Was that honest?

Bundy: Well, it depends on your view. It was certainly in my judgment at least as honest as many things that Franklin Roosevelt did in the course of 1941. The trouble was that this turned out badly, and therefore looks much worse in history.

But if you look at the factors affecting President Johnson at that point—let me say what the calculations were and I've talked to a number of people on it. You had the Great Society measures. There were about (say) ten or a dozen of the major authorizing bills that set up new programs. About six of these had been passed by the Congress and another six were still to go, and what I'm sure he calculated—and this was very much kept to himself so I can't say this is a historical matter, but it fits with everything that other participants would put together—that you were going to lose the chance to pass at least three or four of these if Congress tied itself up for five or six weeks. It would also give a weak impression to the North Vietnamese. That was true: but we never doubted that in the end the Congress would overwhelmingly support this policy. Public opinion polls were in support of it. The Congress was in support of it.

Charlton: Did you have the opportunity of suggesting to the President that the time had come, because of the measure of necessary deception—whatever we call it—dictated by the circumstances of this commitment, that he should in fact go back to Congress and seek some reaffirmation of America's aims and involvement?

Bundy: As it got worse, there certainly were points at which one wished there had been something more explicit than the Gulf of Tonkin Resolution. It was so much a matter of degree. I didn't, as I say, feel that the members of Congress were in any sense basically deceived. I just thought it would have been sounder—and this is mostly hindsight, I have to say—it would have been sounder to have the great debate, get it over with and thereby be able to say: 'Congress, you looked at this, you supported it,' and so on. Now there again, though, I have to say I didn't urge that, and that was a mistake I'm sure on my part. I think the President's decision would have been the same (up through 1966 at any rate, and this is the key period) because it was then we were making all the major commitments.

He was trying to have his domestic program and get the funding for it; and if he had come out with a very strong 'We are now at war' statement, I don't think there is any doubt that a key segment in the leadership in the Congress would have said: 'Very well, you can have your war, but you can't have the money you want for your Great Society as well'.

Charlton: How concerned were you by the conflict in aim? That this was where the military and political objectives of pacification got out of sympathy, that the methods you were forced to pursue as you saw it, the introduction of firepower and of mobile warfare of a very destructive kind, would progressively alienate you, not just from the population in Vietnam but from your own domestic opinion?

Bundy: Certainly many of us saw the possibility that they would have considerable negative effects in terms of the reactions of the South Vietnamese people. One could see this happen in other wars and other circumstances where you had to use this much firepower. The same time the North Vietnamese, by introducing their regular forces which began in late 1964 at the latest, made it harder and harder not to have a considerable component of that sort. So it was always a question of finding the right mix and I think we did overdo the military side of it. I don't think we ever had an adequately marshalled civilian side to the whole thing. I don't think we had an effective war governing mechanism in Washington at any time: and we were dependent on how it worked out in the field, and I think the natural tendencies were carried out in the field; the military tended to do their thing which is to fight wars with equipment and machinery.

This became a totally disproportionate share of it, and this was one of the mistakes.

> If the commitment had now—as has been argued—become more open-ended with the call for escalation, what were the limits as Johnson himself saw them? Walt Rostow, his special assistant in the White House at the time, spoke of this in 1974.

Rostow: He was determined to maintain the independence of South-East Asia, as our commitments as a nation and his view of the importance of the area demanded. And he was determined to do this in ways which would minimize the likelihood of a larger war involving either the Soviet Union or China. To this end he was extremely careful about the forms that American military action took. I have no doubt that he and some of his advisers remembered the manner in which we had stumbled into a quite substantial military engagement in the Korean War with the Chinese. He felt that in the world of the 1960s this would be vastly more dangerous and carry with it much greater possibilities of a nuclear war. Therefore, he conducted what you might call an intermediate or moderate policy, in which we used our forces inside South Vietnam. We *bombed* North Vietnam, but with great care to avoid hitting Soviet and other vessels in Haiphong Harbor; and he did not permit US forces to move into North Vietnam or indeed into Laos. This view was unpopular in the country. If you study the public opinion polls, you will find that systematically the public view was that we should apply more military power against North Vietnam. That was the majority view in the country and the majority view in the Congress. I felt that there were things we could and should do that would shorten the war that would not bring on a larger engagement with either the Soviet Union or China. I felt that to fight a battle from inside South Vietnam, using only air power against the North, would involve a prolonged and difficult war and an indecisive one. I took this view from some knowledge of other guerilla wars and the extreme difficulty of ending them if there was an open frontier. I felt that we ought either to do one or both of two things: to put our forces, a couple of US divisions, to cut the Ho Chi Minh Trail (or trails, as it's not a single trail) in Laos and go into North Vietnam as far north as Vinh, which was still a good long distance from Hanoi, Haiphong and from the Chinese frontier. Moving in there would block a good many of the infiltration trails, and we would hold a piece of territory against North Vietnamese withdrawal from Laos, Cambodia and South Vietnam. President Johnson was aware of that view. I did not spread it around the government. I did not spread it into the press. It was a view I held honestly. I felt the President should know it. On the other hand, I was conscious of what Secretary Rusk used to say. He used to say: you or I could make a recommendation to the President and advise him to do something and say these will be the consequences; and if we are wrong we can call up and say 'Sorry sir, our judgment was wrong' and we could resign and disappear. But he, the President, must stay with the consequences of his decisions and with history.

So that while I took a somewhat different view about the safe limits for the use of American military power, I quite confidently accepted President Johnson's judgment and strongly supported him to the end.

For three years, from 1965 until 1968, General Westmoreland, the commander on the ground in Vietnam, sought a military victory in South Vietnam in the sense that he tried to destroy the fighting capacity of the Communists. At the same time bombing of the North intensified, to force the North Vietnamese to abandon their attempt to take over the South. General Westmoreland's strategy and the protest movement against the war in America will be the subject of a separate chapter.

In the first war to be seen on television in the intimacy of the private home, the bombing in particular stirred powerful political reactions, engendered by the image of a super power punishing a small country. The disproportion of means began to lead to a discrediting of the ends.

Thompson: When the bombing campaign first started, it was retaliatory. It was because of certain actions taken by the Vietcong in the South against American installations and also against South Vietnamese. And President Johnson more or less turned round and said: 'If you do those against us, we cannot do the same thing against you because we do not have the ground forces in the North, but we will use the assets which we do have which is an airforce.' A perfectly legitimate thing to say. Now, if he had kept the bombing campaign down to retaliatory action, I think he would have been in a much stronger psychological and political position because what he would have been saying to Ho Chi Minh and the North Vietnamese politbureau was: 'If you do this we will reply with that.' Every time that they did something nasty in the South, then the Americans would reply with a bombing raid on the North, on a specific objective; and I think that would have been a perfectly legitimate way of carrying it on. What happened, of course, was that having started the bombing under this concept, it then changed into an actual bombing campaign, attempting to destroy the North's capability of carrying on the war in the South. In other words, attacking the communications, attacking the supply depots. In that respect, it made the mistake of being very, very gradual—it escalated very, very slowly.

At this period of course it was the bombing campaigns of the type of World War II—in other words, they were free bomb falls in the sense that it was the pilot aiming with ordinary bombing instruments, not entirely accurate. Very hard to hit a lot of these small bridges. In fact there was one small bridge there, the Thanh Hoa bridge, that had over 800 sorties flown against it. Somewhere between 50 and 100 American aircraft were lost against that particular bridge, and it was never hit. It was not only not effective, it was counterproductive in that it gave this impression of being David defending against Goliath.

If you are going to use that power, it must be effective; and if it's effective and it achieves its result quickly, then people will accept it.

Charlton: But in political terms it brought the Americans to the conference table, would you agree, rather than the North Vietnamese?

Thompson: Oh yes. This, of course, became one of the aims of the bombing campaign. That you only had to keep the pressure up a bit more, you got all these phrases like 'five minutes more' and so on, and 'they will come to the conference table'. I was saying all the time: 'I'm sorry, but it's bringing *you* to the conference table, not the North Vietnamese.'

Charlton: And it did in the end.

Thompson: It did in the end.

▌ Once Lyndon Johnson had committed 'his boys', as he called them, to the ground war, they had his total support and all his vast energies behind them. We have General Taylor's word for it that few were more 'hawkish' about prosecuting the war in Vietnam than the President. George Ball was one of his trusted confidants, but opponents.

Ball: Well, he was a Texan and he had a bit of the Alamo spirit. He kept repeating something that unhappily Mr Nixon was to say many times since: 'I'm not going to be the first American President to lose a war.'

Charlton: In fact, Dennis Brogan, the British historian, somewhere says that no society on earth has perhaps thought victory to be so inevitable as the Americans.

Ball: Well, that was the assumption always, I want to be quite fair to President Johnson because I think he has been misunderstood: I think he had graver doubts about the war than several other people around him, and in fact he was my best friend while I was urging this kind of opposite course. On several occasions, at the end of one of these very heated arguments when we would really get very worked up about this, and I would be standing by myself and saying: 'I don't think the Secretary of State or the Secretary of Defense is giving you good advice at all, I think this is catastrophic if you go down this road,' and so on: at the end of the day, the President would put his arm on my shoulder in a rather intimate manner that he always had and say: 'George, I can't tell you how grateful I am to you for disagreeing with me'.

By 1968 and three years of search and destroy operations conducted by General Westmoreland, the Communist guerillas had taken disproportionately vast casualties, sometimes in the ratio of six or ten to one. Nevertheless their will to go on appeared unbroken.

In 1967 perhaps the most important American domino, and one inside the government, had begun to waver and would later fall: McNamara, the Secretary of Defense. His disenchantment became known suddenly and dramatically. He was being overwhelmed by doubts. In preparing *The Pentagon Papers* he asked his staff to provide answers to one hundred questions about the war in Vietnam, and was querying the low ratio of weapons captured to killed and deducing from that the probability of large civilian casualties. 'McNamara's gone dovish on me', President Johnson was saying in the White House. McNamara's war was now Johnson's war.

These were the three years in which America had chosen to express success in a statistical orgy of body counts, some thousands of square miles of forests defoliated to lay open and expose through the dense jungle canopy the sanctuaries and supply routes used by the guerillas, and talking of millions of tons of bombs dropped. Both sides had committed atrocities. The Communists conducted a long and systematic campaign of murder of government officials. When the Communists briefly occupied the imperial capital of Hué in 1968 they massacred hundreds of people after summary drum-head courts-martial, and buried many alive. For the Americans the corrosive acid of the nature of the war in which their enemy was so often unrevealed had induced breakdowns in discipline like the horror of My Lai.

By 1968 General Westmoreland was fighting far from the population centers near the borders of Cambodia and Laos, and on the demilitarized zone at the 17th parallel. He was claiming victory in sight and envisaging being able to lower the number of American troops. This confident hope was suddenly reduced to dust. In February the Communists launched their Tet offensive, and by appearing within the ring now being held by Westmoreland on the frontiers of South Vietnam and attacking forty provincial towns and cities they in effect overthrew the assumptions of the American Vietnam policy.

Within four weeks Lyndon Johnson had to face in the Presidential primary in New Hampshire the first personal political test since his landslide win at the polls in 1964. New Hampshire showed an extremely powerful swing against the war policy. Four days later Robert Kennedy announced that he would be a candidate for the Presidency.

I run because I am convinced that this country is on a perilous course and because I have such strong feelings about what must be done and I feel that I'm obliged to do all I can. I run to seek new policies, policies to end the bloodshed in Vietnam, and in our cities. Policies to close the gap that now exists between black and white; between rich and poor; between young and old, in this country and around the rest of the world. I run for Presidency because I want the Democratic Party and the United States of America to stand for hope instead of despair, for reconciliation of man, instead of the growing risk of world war. I run because it is now unmistakably clear that we can change these disastrous, divisive policies only by changing the men who are now making them. But the reality of recent events in Vietnam has been glossed over with illusions.

This double blow to Lyndon Johnson, coming on top of the reverse in Vietnam, probably reinforced his dramatic decision which he announced to the American people and the world on 31 March 1968:

I am taking the first step to de-escalate the conflict. We are reducing, substantially reducing, the present level of hostilities. And we are doing so unilaterally and at once. Tonight, I have ordered our aircraft and our naval vessels to make no attacks on North Vietnam except in the area north of the demilitarized zone where the continuing enemy build-up directly threatens allied forward positions and where the movements of their troops and supplies are clearly related to that threat. Even this very limited bombing in the North could come to an early end if our restraint is matched by restraint in Hanoi. I shall not seek and I will not accept the nomination of my party for another term as your President. But let men everywhere know, however, that a strong and a confident and a vigilant America stands ready tonight to defend an honorable cause, whatever the price, whatever the virtue, whatever the sacrifice that duty may require.

So by withdrawing himself from the campaign for re-election, coupled with largely ending the bombing, Lyndon Johnson considered that the best hopes of negotiations and a scaling-down of the involvement in Vietnam would lie in the hands of a new team and a successor. Paul Warnke, Assistant Secretary of Defense for International Security Affairs in the Pentagon at the time—and appointed by President Carter as his negotiator on arms control—explained how the bitter turn-around in American policy was argued and presented after Tet. Warnke was and is a close associate of Clark Clifford, the man Johnson made Secretary of Defense to replace McNamara, and who is supposed to have persuaded Johnson to yield.

Warnke: I think you have to recognize the Tet offensive did two things. In the first place it very seriously eroded the strength of the Vietcong and the North Vietnamese, but at the same time it just destroyed the entire myth that had existed about the fact that the United States position in Vietnam was being well established, and that eventually victory was going to be secure. So that the military aspects of the Tet offensive were entirely favorable for our side but the psychological consequences of Tet made our eventual withdrawal from Vietnam inevitable; and it was at that particular time [1 March 1968] that Mr Clifford became Secretary of Defense.
Charlton: Was it a revelation to you, Tet? Did it destroy the myth to you?
Warnke: No it did not. You see, you have to recognize that we in the Office of International Security Affairs were taking a very pessimistic view as to the war. It seemed to us that what we were looking at was

an increasingly successful American occupation of Vietnam, but that unless you were prepared to face an indefinite American military occupation of Vietnam you weren't getting any place. I think that the people in my shop believed there was no sort of a base of support in South Vietnam that ensured its continuity and its viability, after an American military withdrawal.

Charlton: Did you have a very difficult time personally in the Pentagon because of that position? Did you declare it openly?

Warnke: There was no question about where we stood, none whatsoever. There was I think a considerable body of support in the American government for exactly the same position that we were stating. There were numbers of people in the State Department. There were numbers of people in the Defense Department who took a similarly jaundiced view of the entire pursuit. There was substantial support for getting extricated from what was increasingly a debilitating kind of experience.

Charlton: So along came the Tet offensive. Now immediately after it there was an immediate conflict of interpretation as to the significance of it. It was being claimed very quickly as a great military victory. What opportunities did you therefore have to present it in a quite different light, as the basis of an authoritative position and advice for the President?

Warnke: Well, it was about at that point that Mr Clifford became Secretary for Defense. And even before he formally took office, he was appointed as head of a task force by President Johnson to evaluate the situation, and respond specifically to a request that was made by General Westmoreland for something like 206,000 additional troops.

It seemed to me that it posed the issue very clearly, that you could not at that point have put in 206,000 additional troops without going on a genuine war footing. You would have had to admit that you were fighting a war. It would have required I think a tax increase. It would have required the mobilization of the reserves. It was an opportunity at that point to decide just what we were doing, and what the chances were that it was eventually going to be in the American interest. And you also have to recognize that at this point there were two different positions among those who wanted to have 206,000 more troops there. I think that President Johnson was genuinely frightened. I think he thought that there was a chance of military defeat, and that he thought of this request as being almost a panicky request for reinforcements, that what Westmoreland was saying in effect was that: 'I'm in trouble here, and I need more troops, or else we're apt to lose.' Now that was *not* General Westmoreland's attitude at all.

I think one of the things that began to make Mr Clifford feel that a thorough reassessment of the American position was overdue, was a cable that came in from General Westmoreland which indicated that he was on the offensive all over the country and was beginning to capitalize on the heavy losses that the other side had incurred. Now this was a very different kind of a viewpoint than that which he had been given by President Johnson. I think at that point Clifford recognized that what Westmoreland and the military were talking about was an all-out effort to secure a military victory. That really posed the issue very clearly, because if you felt that a military victory was unfeasible—because even if you secured it you still had nothing except an occupied Vietnam—then it made no sense at all to send more troops over seeking a will-o'-the-wisp.

Charlton: Clifford began to ask the questions in a quite different way? Now what was the question that he asked which no one had asked up to this time?

Warnke: The basic question was: how do you go about securing military victory, under the circumstances of Vietnam, if now we give you another 206,000 troops? (I'd like to say that that means that you beat the enemy in every battle.) How do you go about ending the war, how do you go about capturing the flag? I think he forced people to think in those kind of concrete terms. You see the problem in Vietnam was, as I say, that what we were trying to do was to impose a particular type of rule on a resistant country. And that required occupation, just as we occupied Japan and wrote their constitution.

President Johnson was the man that had to make the decision, and there was a considerable battle that went on for the President's mind and heart during that period of time. I wouldn't say that he was a lonely figure (I think sometimes he tended to dramatize himself in that particular role) but he did have very substantial support. His National Security Adviser was telling him every day that he was right, he should persevere; and I think that Secretary Rusk remained resolute during this entire period of time.

Charlton: How did you interpret his decision not to run again in 1968?

Warnke: I interpreted it as being really almost an underscoring of his recognition of the fact that he had to do something about Vietnam; and whatever he had to do about it was going to be unpopular.

Charlton: But the interpretation you placed upon it was that this was America getting out of the war?

Warnke: I wasn't sure. I wasn't sure where the President was going to go after that time. You have to recognize that what was in fact said in the speech of 31 March was inconclusive. That basically he didn't announce any sort of a change in American objectives.

As a matter of fact some of the statements he made indicated that he considered the objectives to be unchanged. He didn't announce that this was putting a lid on the number of troops that we were going to send there, he made no commitments in that respect. The only really positive thing that he did was to pull back the bombing, and quite frankly I did not think that was going to be enough to get the North Vietnamese to respond. I thought we were going to have to stop the bombing in North Vietnam totally and unconditionally before the North Vietnamese would accept a movement towards negotiations. Once we had taken an affirmative step towards negotiations that probably meant we were going to be headed in the right direction.

▌A more intimate and personal epitaph for the last days of Lyndon Johnson's Presidency comes from George Ball, who recalls meetings with the President in the days after Tet when even Johnson's great resolve and energy were driven away.

Ball: He called a meeting of the so-called senior advisers or wise men or whatever, a bunch of superannuated characters who had been in the government at one time or another—not necessarily his administration but in earlier administrations—people like Dean Acheson, Jack McCloy and so on. This had happened several times, and I had been present at these meetings several times and the same thing had always occurred. That is, everyone had been for going full speed ahead, except me. But I'd made the same arguments there that I had made within the government, even though I was outside of it, but at this meeting something happened that was quite extraordinary. This was immediately after the Tet offensive and the group assembled in the evening before meeting with the President. We heard two briefings, and they were very discouraging about the effect of the Tet offensive, and what it had done to set the whole cause back in Vietnam.

Charlton: They were not military briefings, I take it?

Ball: One was a military briefing and one was a civilian briefing. One was a briefing by Colby. They were very good. The next day the group met. They were considering a request from Westmoreland for, I don't know, 75,000 more troops or something of the sort. Secretary Clifford was there, and he was for limiting the response to a much smaller number, and he was beginning to develop grave doubts about the whole thing. So we had an argument in the morning, and again I repeated my usual arguments, and I found much more tendency to agree with me there than had happened up to then. So we decided that McGeorge Bundy would be sort of the spokesman for the group. We then assembled in the Cabinet Room and the President wanted to hear our advice to him.

And McGeorge Bundy led off saying that the group had met and that he had something he wanted to tell the President which he thought he would never say to him, that he now agreed with George Ball and this was the general sentiment of the group. And we went around, and it wasn't unanimous by any means; but there was a strong advice to the President: 'Look, this thing is hopeless, you'd better begin to de-escalate and get out'. And this was the first time he'd ever heard anything of this kind, he could hardly believe his ears. I think he was very shocked. He was clearly disturbed and he kept asking probing questions. He really couldn't believe it. Here were people like Dean Acheson and Douglas Dillon, people of that kind who had been pretty stalwart up until then.

Charlton: It's an interesting comment on what one supposes the Presidency of the United States to be. Is it a collective thing in which decisions are taken collectively? Or at that time were all the burdens of this enormous decision on one man?

Ball: They still are. I mean this is the nature of the government. The burdens are on this one man. It is not a collective government. I mean, this is one thing that may be hard to be understood in the UK; but it's a fundamental distinction. The President makes the decisions.

6
Gulliver in Lilliput

▌General William Westmoreland, whom everyone called 'Westy', was the commander of American forces and the land war in Vietnam from 1964 until 1968. This whole chapter is his personal account of that time.

In it the United States, by committing its own troops and the firepower and mobility of its superbly equipped divisions trained for a war on the plains of Western Europe, tried to win the war in South Vietnam by a technological knock-out. This was the strategy known as 'search and destroy'. One single American division had over 400 helicopters, which could pick up and set down in places many miles apart a whole battalion of combat soldiers several times a day. Each infantryman was armed with a rifle which could fire many hundred rounds a minute. This spectacular mobility and firepower would, it was hoped, nullify the advantages of time and space enjoyed by the Communists, who attacked at times and places of their own choosing and could come and go across an open frontier nine hundred miles long. Westmoreland was given command of the war on the ground in June 1964, after a brief period as deputy to the commander of the American Military Mission in Saigon, General Harkins. The so far limited American commitment, which restricted their involvement to advisers in the field, was about to change substantially.

Following the overthrow of President Diem, the series of successive adolescent coups by the military junta was producing political chaos, and the Communists were making rapid gains. Westmoreland's own appointment was a symbol of the change. He was now no longer an adviser: he was commander of the land war, and before long he would have half a million American soldiers in South Vietnam. General Westmoreland had fought his first combat in Tunisia in 1943; and later in Germany he was a junior member of an elite group of dashing American paratroop commanders who then and later were destined for high distinction—Ridgeway, Maxwell Taylor, Gavin. By the time the Korean War came he was a general, commanding airborne divisions.

There was an inevitability about his progress which raised no eyebrows when the Americans chose him as the best general they had to try and stop the rot in Vietnam. No one called Westy brilliant, but he was forceful, decent, poised, dependable; and as things got messier and messier in Vietnam, with his rugged, clean cut, good looks he stood as a reassuring symbol of American intentions. In television's first war, image was important for politicians and soldiers alike. Westmoreland was a soldier of his time and had been to the Harvard Business School, the better to comprehend and manage and organize the complex army placed in his hands.

As commander of the fighting troops he formed a personal understanding with President Johnson, who after the political failure in Vietnam brought him home to become Chief of Staff of the Army. Now retired, he has tried unsuccessfully to become Governor of his home state, South Carolina, for the Republicans. He has published a book of memoirs—*A Soldier Reports*.[1]

By the time General Westmoreland went to Vietnam to command the land war he had the knowledge that the Communists had shown great resolve and tenacity in more than twenty years of fighting and that all efforts to defeat their insurgency had failed. I asked him therefore in view of this if he remembered in what frame of mind he took up this formidable task.

Westmoreland: I had been a student of insurgency warfare and had watched very closely the developments in Vietnam and had an intuitive feeling that eventually I was going to end up there; and I turned out to be right. Very much ringing in my ears and the ears of all officers at that time, and I would say not only in the military but in the State Department, was Mr Kennedy's very emotional and stirring inaugural address: we'll 'bear any burden and meet any hardships, support any friend, oppose any foe, to ensure the survival and success of liberty'. So, although the genesis of our commitments started with the Truman Doctrine in 1947, Mr Eisenhower, through Mr Dulles, propounded the strategy of containment. Mr Kennedy gave another dimension to this commitment. It was idealistic and an emotional commitment.

Charlton: And that impressed you at the time?

Westmoreland: It not only impressed me, I think it impressed all my colleagues too, and we felt pretty good about going to Vietnam to fight for such an idealistic principle. Of course, I hoped that the so-

[1] Doubleday, Garden City, NY, 1976.

called insurgency could be stemmed, without the commitment of major US forces, through the use of advisers; and that the Vietnamese could be rallied, they could be trained and their backs could be stiffened to the point where they could ultimately prevail over the Hanoi regime. But when I first arrived in Vietnam I frankly was astonished at the state of affairs. As you remember, Diem was overthrown and unfortunately assassinated on 1 November 1963. Our country made a grievous mistake, particularly Mr Kennedy's administration, in getting involved, not only in encouraging the South Vietnamese to overthrow Diem, but participating in that effort. And I think morally that pretty well locked us into Vietnam, because there was no leadership standing in the wing to take over.

Charlton: Do you accept incidentally that because the United States had been instrumental in the overthrow of Diem that you had saddled yourself with responsibility for the outcome of the war in effect, that that was the significance of Diem's overthrow?

Westmoreland: Of course as a soldier I went there with a sense of mission, and as a matter of fact the entire United States team, to include the civilians as well as the military, had a sense of mission. We were not policy makers, we were people sent there to carry out national policy; and in no time do I ever remember during my four and a half years in Vietnam any discussion in the mission council, chaired by the Ambassador, any thought of pulling out.

Charlton: You said that Kennedy made a great mistake over the overthrow of Diem and I wonder whether you thought then (as you appear to do now) that the significance of the coup was that from then on really you were saddled with the outcome of the war? It was an American war from then on, because of that intervention?

Westmoreland: I didn't think in terms of any alternative other than the achievement of success. I was shocked at the overthrow of Diem and the fact that Diem was killed. (I was not in Vietnam at that time, I did not arrive until January of 1964.) I inherited this political chaos. I described it as a situation so nebulous, it was almost like trying to push spaghetti. From day to day we didn't have a governmental apparatus to work with and that *per se* forced us to get more involved in trying to stabilize the situation, politically and economically as well as militarily, more than any other thing. If there'd been a constituted government there with some strength of course I don't believe we would have got involved.

Charlton: Did you at the time appreciate, would you say, the significance of the change between Diem and the generals? You make the obvious point that it led to chaos; but can you say that you appreciated and understood at the time that its real significance was that the war was being Americanized, that by as an act of policy overthrowing Diem it became an American war, in a sense that it hadn't been up till that time?

Westmoreland: I think that was a turning point without question; and that the aftermath of the successful effort to overthrow Diem inevitably got the Americans more deeply involved.

Charlton: What encouraged you, General, to think that South Vietnam was militarily defensible—in view of the fact that the failure of the Laos Agreements negotiated by Averell Harriman in 1961/62 had left you with a task of immense difficulty, in that you had a flank completely open throughout the war?

Westmoreland: The military fully recognized that. On the other hand, as I said before we were people with a sense of mission. We were not policy makers and we were going to do our best to make good our commitment. Now, our strategy of course was not to unify the two Vietnams by force, it was not to invade North Vietnam, it was not to *defeat* the North Vietnamese army. It was to put pressure on the enemy which would transmit a message to the leadership in Hanoi—that they could not win, and it would be to their advantage either to tacitly accept a divided Vietnam, or to engage in negotiations. Now that was our strategy and it was not an unreasonable strategy under the circumstances. But of course it was so poorly executed by virtue of unwise political decisions that it turned out to be a nonviable strategy.

Charlton: But it was never American policy to have half a million troops in Vietnam, was it? It was never American policy to bomb the North? How did that happen, if it was never policy?

Westmoreland: I don't think it was an avowed policy, but I don't think any reasonable person ruled this out. Certainly I didn't rule it out. But it was not surprising to me that ultimately we had to commit sizeable forces. I anticipated that early, hoping it wouldn't be necessary. I was very cautious in making a recommendation in 1965 to put in American forces. That's the last thing in the world I wanted to do. But it was either that or the country was going to be defeated militarily.

Charlton: So the strategy was the application of military strength on a gradual basis, step by step, by that pressure to try and persuade the North Vietnamese to give up their support and contribution to the insurgency in the South. And your hope was that they would give up long before the American commitment reached the level that it ultimately did?

Westmoreland: Precisely so. But coupled with that was a concerted effort to put some backbone into the Vietnamese, stabilize their government, improve the economy, open roads, and increase and improve the proficiency of the Vietnamese armed forces.

Charlton: Now you've made it clear that you thought that implicitly it had to be a pretty much open-ended commitment, while you hoped it wouldn't be. You give that impression. Yet the politicians were certainly not conveying that impression, were they, to the American public? Was that the principal difficulty as you see it at that time?

Westmoreland: This is an interesting question. In the spring of 1964 when I'd been selected to replace General Harkins after I'd been in the country for several months, I had a long talk with McNamara. I told Secretary McNamara—whom I'd sound relations with, and he's a man of considerable ability—that I couldn't see the end of this commitment, it was going to be a long-drawn-out affair, because it was a formidable task. It seemed to me that our success was going to depend in great degree on the staying power of the American people to support it, and I'd given quite a bit of thought to that. I recommended to the Administration they think in terms of a people-to-people program, to get the American people emotionally involved and better informed as to the real situation in South Vietnam with perhaps some emotional attachment to the South Vietnamese. Mr McNamara brushed this aside. He didn't explain to me why, but I later found out that this matter had been discussed in the policy making circles of our government at the highest echelon, and it was the fear of the Johnson Administration that if this became a matter of public debate, and the American people got emotionally aroused, the hawks might take over control; and by virtue of this a confrontation could ensue with the Chinese People's Republic. In other words, they were more afraid of stirring up the hawks than the doves, a very ironical development, but that was the reasoning. Therefore, a policy decision was made to keep the war 'low-key'.

This manifested itself in the college draft deferment policy. It manifested itself in the guns *and* butter policy, and by that I mean to pay for the cost of the war the public debt was increased, rather than taxes. As a result of this—contrary to Mr Kennedy's charge 'we'll bear any burden, pay any price'—the only ones that bore a burden, paid a price and made a sacrifice were those on the battlefields, who were mainly the poor man's sons, and their loved ones at home. The average American, the war didn't touch him; except he was exposed to the war through television and this of course was the first war that has ever been seen in the homes of America, or homes of any other nationality.

Charlton: Did you have the opportunity of putting this point of yours—that greater support among the American people had to be enlisted—did you have the opportunity of putting that directly to the President?

Westmoreland: No, because after I talked to Mr McNamara, and he was not receptive, I had plenty to occupy my time in South Vietnam. Actually this was a dimension of this war outside of my competence, and outside of my responsibility.

Charlton: But it was very much affecting your conduct of the war, because the dissent within the United States became a major element in the strategy for the conduct of the war.

Westmoreland: It certainly turned out that way. But I did not perceive that it would become the problem that it was. I perceived that it would become a problem, but the magnum of the problem far exceeded anything I'd anticipated.

Charlton: Let's go back to when the first of your troop requests of American combat troops were arriving in Vietnam. You had had your brush with McNamara at this time and were brushed aside, as you say, in your anticipation that American public opinion was not being properly alerted to the fact that it would have to support a much longer commitment and a more open-ended one than they were being told. Did you appreciate then, that the trouble really was that the Government couldn't tell the truth to the American people? It always had to announce that there was progress being made, because to do otherwise would not have convinced the North Vietnamese of the basic idea, which was that your commitment was an open-ended one and was meant to show readiness and your willingness to go on as long as needs be.

Westmoreland: There was progress being made during that time frame that was not great but it was present and we had every expectation that we could continue those trends, which we did. Things continued to improve as we gained know-how and got more resources in; and the Vietnamese gained more confidence all the way through 1967. Of course our successes in 1967 basically provoked the Tet offensive which was a reaction to our success, which is of course not uncommon on a battlefield. But, during those early days when US forces were brought in, we all hoped that the enemy would get this message that according to our strategy we were trying to transmit. Those early troops were associated with transmitting that message to the Northern leadership, but they were also designed to keep the South Vietnamese Government from collapsing. With the first troops that I brought in I secured the airfields, because we'd started the bombing campaign after the enemy shelled Pleiku and since our strategy at that time was dependent upon bombing the North—which was the only offensive element from a strategic standpoint. I had a responsibility for securing those airfields.

Charlton: When the troops came ashore, March/April 1965, the President gave instructions—as we know from *The Pentagon Papers*—that 'these preparations should minimize any appearance of sudden changes in policy'. McGeorge Bundy says the President's desire was that these changes should be understood as being gradual and wholly consistent with existing policy. Now was this honest? It may have been expedient, but was it honest?

Westmoreland: I won't pass judgment whether it was honest or not; but it was a manifestation of an avowed policy of playing the war 'low key', to use an American expression.

Charlton: But as you surely realized, and have told us that as you understood it, it was in fact a change in policy. The war was no longer of a limited nature, although you hoped it would be; but it ultimately passed from a limited commitment to an open-ended one.

Westmoreland: Well you're quite right, that's what developed. However, in all fairness to Presidents Kennedy and Johnson, they were victims of wishful thinking and many of their advisers were victims likewise. They felt that if they could surmount another hurdle, that the enemy would get the message and things would calm down.

Charlton: But in your talks with the President at this time—and you were to form rather a close relationship with him—did you not express to him disquiet about the way the war was being presented to public opinion, which you realized was going to become more and more important to you?

Westmoreland: Well, of course, you fully appreciate I was in Saigon, I spent very little time in Washington. I had very few contacts with the President. There's a myth which prevailed at that time and I suppose still does in some quarters, that the President was on the telephone with me every day. I never talked to the President from Saigon, never. I only talked to the White House once, and that's when they called me to get my appraisal of the first few hours of the

Tet offensive. Mr Johnson did call me back and the spring of 1967 he ordered me back to talk to the annual meeting of the Associated Press. Then, unbeknownst to me I was scheduled to talk to a joint session of Congress. Now that put me in center stage, and put me in a very awkward position; and frankly relayed a false message to the American people to the effect that I was in overall charge; I only had a part of the responsibility. My responsibility was confined to South Vietnam. I did not have the bombing campaign, which was under the Commander-in-Chief Pacific. I reported not only to the Commander-in-Chief Pacific in Hawaii, but also to the Ambassador for all purposes. The Ambassador specifically was vested with the responsibility for the political, psychological and economic facets of this war, which we categorized as 'nation-building'.

Charlton: In your book you say that the President should have gone back to the Congress and asked for some re-affirmation of support.

Westmoreland: It was the Gulf of Tonkin resolution that took place in August 1964 that gave the President the authority from the Congress of the United States to use whatever military forces were necessary to carry out our objective in South-East Asia. I point out in my book that one would have thought that the President and the leadership in the Congress would have asked for affirmation of the Gulf of Tonkin resolution every year. The policy of the Executive Branch and the policy of Legislative Branch progressively grew further and further and further apart, and of course this is ultimately what brought about the collapse of South Vietnam. Now in all fairness, one has to think in terms of the mood of the country at that time and I go back to something I said earlier—there was a great fear of the hawks by the Democratic administration and Mr Goldwater personified those hawks. Mr Goldwater in his Presidential campaign [in 1964] even talked about nuclear weapons. So there was a fear by the President, and by the Congressional leaders, that if this matter became a subject of national debate and the Congress of the United States was asked to affirm the Gulf of Tonkin resolution, a national debate would ensue, and that the hawks could get the upper hand and this could bring about a confrontation with Red China.

Charlton: But wouldn't you agree there was another aspect to that, perhaps? While the hawks may have been one side of it the other aspect was that to reveal what actually was happening—that the war was not limited but open-ended from this time on—would have provoked such a debate within the United States that it would have destroyed the strategy, which was to convince the North Vietnamese that America was ready, willing and able to fight a protracted war no matter what the cost?

Westmoreland: That is conceivable, but I don't think it was necessarily inevitable. In fact I don't think it would have been inevitable. I think if all the cards were laid on the table and became the subject of mass debate at that time, the American people would probably have closed ranks and would have supported a more aggressive strategy.

Charlton: By 1966 there was dissent within the government of a sharper kind. George Ball, the Undersecretary of State, was telling the President that it was a losing war. He said to him: 'No one can show that whites can win a civil war in the midst of a population which refuses its co-operation to the white forces.' He quoted examples which he thought served that point he was making.

Westmoreland: Well, of course, I'm not aware of Mr Ball saying that to the President, because I was not privy to discussions at that level of Government. But Mr Ball was wrong. The South Vietnamese did give us co-operation in the main. They were very receptive to our troops—far better than I thought would be the case. I had great trepidation in committing troops there in the first place, feeling that they could become persona non grata in the country that they were there to presumably save. But such was not the case. Our troops in general conducted themselves well, and they were liked by the South Vietnamese, although the South Vietnamese are a very xenophobic people. There are exceptions without question. But the majority of the population were very much in favor of our sending troops to support the South Vietnamese forces. So, I think Mr Ball's judgement in that regard was faulty. That is not what lost the war.

Charlton: By 1967, a year after George Ball told the President it was a losing war and he ought to get out, there was a major defection within the government, and perhaps the most important: your civilian boss McNamara, who was so identified with all the earlier policies, and who had given you so much support. He too decided that you couldn't win in 1967. Now obviously I imagine that you had a severe trial of will with him about this, as the ground commander. I wonder what you can tell us about that, and what you thought of his conversion?

Westmoreland: Well, with respect to Mr Ball's advice, 'Get out', it was easy to say but how could we do it? In view of Mr Kennedy's emotional address, in view of our participating in the overthrow of Diem, in view of the fact that we made a commitment as far back as

1946, if we had turned tail and moved out at that time the Republicans would have made this a major political issue against the Democrats. And they would have played back Mr Kennedy's charge, his idealism. Here we are saying we're going to fight for freedom and protect freedom, and now we're doing just the opposite. So I don't think George Ball's advice at that time was practically realistic.

Charlton: Just let's take McNamara in 1967—and this obviously was a most important decision within the Government at the highest level, perhaps the top civilian protagonist of the war, and the civilian boss at the Pentagon. What can you tell us about the arguments that you had with him at this vital time, and what do you say about his conversion to the belief that you could not win in 1967, and his recommendation to the President—as we know from *The Pentagon Papers*—that you should give up and stop trying to guarantee a non-Communist South Vietnam?

Westmoreland: I didn't have as many contacts with Secretary McNamara as you suspect. I was not in day-to-day contact with him. I probably saw McNamara maybe twice a year. I didn't have any major confrontations with him. But when I saw him I gave him my views as honestly and as forthrightly as I could. I do recall a meeting in this time frame that you referred to, 1967. We had a conference in Guam and I gave a briefing on the situation. I said if we cannot find some way to stop the flow of men and supplies, down through the panhandle of Laos that we referred to as the Ho Chi Minh Trail, this war could go on indefinitely.

Also in 1967 I happened to be back in the United States because my mother had passed away, and I came back for her funeral. Then I was asked to come to Washington, and a National Security Council meeting was assembled and there I was on the other side of the table. The President had in front of him what I wanted in the way of forces. I had the optimum force, and then I had what I called the minimum essential which would continue to make progress but would prolong the war. Mr McNamara asked me: 'If you get your optimum force, how long do you think it'll take to wind this down?' And I said: 'Well, if I get the optimum force, I think we can wind it down in three years after I get the forces.' Now it would have taken probably a year to get the forces, because they had to be mobilized. He said: 'Well suppose you get your minimum essential?' I said: 'Mr Secretary, in my judgment—but there are many imponderables on this—it will take at least five years.'

Charlton: Now, in the popular versions we have had now of what was actually going on at this time, the suggestion is that one of the reasons for McNamara's disenchantment was your constant requests for more troops all the time, is that so?

Westmoreland: Well, I was a field commander with a mission, and my mission was to bring the war to an end. You can't bring the war to an end unless you have the resources to do it. It was impossible to execute the strategy that had been adopted by my government without additional forces. I would ask for a request that would be cut back. I'd ask for the same request again, and to include what I thought was needed, and that would be cut back. And the thing just dragged on and on and on. In other words I got piecemeal reinforcements rather than receiving what we could have received: necessary forces that could have done a lot of things if the political restraints were removed. I kept hoping that those political constraints were going to be changed based on pressures that were being applied by my cables, and presumably by the Joint Chiefs of Staff. (And of course I knew there was an election coming up, and I thought maybe a new President would take another look at that.) We couldn't go into Cambodia. *They* were building up sizeable logistic bases and troop concentrations in Cambodia, and in Laos, and north of the demilitarised zone.

Charlton: From the very beginning you have made it clear to us that you regarded the war as being of much longer duration, and you were telling your superiors that. And you were not hiding from them the possible size of the commitment needed to carry out the objective of bringing the war to an end. Did you, at the very beginning, anticipate the need to go into Laos and Cambodia?

Westmoreland: I certainly was making plans. I had a plan to go into Laos, I had several plans to go into Laos. I had all kinds of plans. Any prudent military commander is constantly making plans, contingency plans. And I built bases and I built roads in anticipation of the authority which I hoped would be forthcoming. But I dealt with my military chain of command. I dealt with the Joint Chiefs of Staff. General Earle Wheeler, and I think very wisely, wanted to hold to himself the political maneuvering with the political authority. I never objected to that at all. He was the Chairman of the Joint Chiefs of Staff, and he was the man that dealt with these sensitive political problems. Frankly if I had gone in and said: 'I want x number of troops to go into Laos, and so forth,' well it would have rocked Washington and it would have set us back. And that was the feeling of General Wheeler: he had to play this thing very delicately.

Charlton: I want to quote to you again from *The Pentagon Papers* something that McNamara says in 1967, coincidentally with his change in position that the war could not be won and must settle for something less than a non-Communist South Vietnam. Of the strategy being pursued, the strategy of attrition, he says this: 'It is possible that our estimates of attrition losses substantially overstate the actual Communist losses.' For example, he says 'they apparently lose only one-sixth as many weapons as people, suggesting the possibility that many of the killed are bystanders, or unarmed porters'. What is your comment on that?

Westmoreland: Well, we had to make the best estimates we could as to the losses inflicted. I certainly do not suggest that our estimates were accurate, but there was nothing studied more than this, analyzed more than this. All I can say is they were the most honest estimates that we could make.

Charlton: But on the specific point he made on the number of weapons recovered among the dead, and that very high ratio of dead to weapons suggesting that a great many innocent people—I suppose is how public opinion would regard it—innocent people were being killed by the strategy?

Westmoreland: I don't accept that. There's never been a war in the history of my country that gave more careful attention to avoiding civilian casualties. I would say almost every conference I had with my commanders I emphasized this. Now I don't mean to say that all of the bodies left on the battlefield were necessarily military. They could have been porters. But they were serving a military purpose. They were in effect supply handlers.

Charlton: In fairness, McNamara also said that he was unsure whether so many of the killed were bystanders or 'unarmed porters', as he put it, but the inference was there.

Westmoreland: But in all fairness, I don't believe our estimates were too far off.

Charlton: But when did it become obvious to you that the strategy of attrition had failed, in this sense that the North Vietnamese had consistently demonstrated that they could accept indefinitely a cost in lives while imposing upon you a cost in lives which was not indefinitely acceptable to the United States?

Westmoreland: We were—by virtue of the political constraints imposed in the strategy of the government, which was to put pressure on the enemy until he decided to negotiate or accept a divided Vietnam, and at the same time expand the area under government control and improve the stability of the government and the economy of South Vietnam—we were in effect with those constraints fighting a war of attrition. I became particularly disenchanted with the political strategy in 1967, and that was at the time when I mentioned that if we couldn't stop the flow of men and material down the Ho Chi Minh Trail the war could go on indefinitely. And it was during that time frame that I came up with the strategy of withdrawing our troops and turning over to the Vietnamese. Now then, when the Tet offensive occurred I had a change of mind. I didn't have a change of mind in turning over to the Vietnamese: I thought the time schedule that I'd projected was even more valid if we would follow up the enemy's defeat. But I knew eventually we were going to defeat the enemy militarily, and we did severely—although the press did a miserable job reporting it and gave the American people a contrary view. The enemy's other objective was the political, and to create a public uprising. He struck out totally on that: there was no public uprising.

▌In 1967, General Westmoreland was disenchanted himself with the effectiveness of the strategy of attrition. He had come to the conclusion that the time had come to turn it over to the Vietnamese. Was that in effect a decision to extricate the American armed forces from Vietnam?

Westmoreland: Well eventually, but it didn't have a time schedule. I stated I thought we could start the process on a *token* basis in two years, and by that two years I meant the late winter, mid-1969; and that we would talk, we would effect token withdrawal. Now, I did not visualize how long that process would take. My thought was it might take ten years, and our rate of withdrawal would depend to a great degree on the conduct of the enemy, and what we were able to, say, negotiate with the enemy. And a very important element of that strategy was the increase in bombing in order to weaken the enemy in the North, weaken him by accentuating the pressure: and in strengthening our friends by modernizing their equipment and by leaving our troops there as long as necessary but have in mind the gradual thinning out of our forces.

Charlton: But it hadn't weakened him. By the time this period was over, his infiltration rates from the North to the South despite the bombing were higher were they not? And more than that the Communist structure, the organization in South Vietnam was intact.

Westmoreland: In 1967 I think you're right, although we'd made great progress. But now, following the Tet offensive, his infrastructure and his guerilla force, and his main forces to include the North Vietnamese forces, were severely crippled.

Charlton: You said the Tet offensive changed your mind. Can you just make that point for us: what do you mean that it changed your mind?

Westmoreland: I think 'changing my mind' does not connote my real feeling. I thought the Tet offensive gave us an opportunity that I had not visualized, an opportunity to weaken the enemy much more rapidly than I anticipated, as a part of the strategy of weakening the enemy and strengthening our friends, until we become superfluous. This was a windfall in that regard, but sadly we didn't take advantage of that windfall.

Charlton: No, in fact it was the stroke which took America out of the war. Would you not agree?

Westmoreland: I agree, psychologically. The enemy won a tremendous psychological victory in the United States. But he suffered a political defeat in South Vietnam.

Charlton: A military defeat?

Westmoreland: No, *both* a military defeat and he also suffered a political defeat in South Vietnam because the South Vietnamese did not rally to his side, there was no public uprising. The fact that the enemy did hit some of the cities—a number of them—served to solidify and (I would say) give added confidence to the South Vietnamese who basically fought very well. In other words it served to unite the country to an extent that I had not seen before that.

Charlton: But General, with respect, almost immediately after it you put in a request for 200,000-odd more troops. Is that consistent with what you've just said?

Westmoreland: Well yes, it very definitely is. It was taking advantage of an opportunity. There's an old axiom that when the enemy's hurting you increase the pressure, don't decrease it. In anticipation of the enemy both militarily and politically, and consistent with our strategy of trying to bring the enemy to the conference table, that gave us a great opportunity to increase the pressure, which would give the Hanoi regime the essential incentive to come to the conference table and negotiate seriously. But the 200,000 troop plan was not a request for deployment but an input to a contingency plan associated with a more aggressive strategy under consideration in Washington.

Charlton: *The Pentagon Papers* give the impression that that request for more troops was based upon the worst possible case, the assumed collapse of the South Vietnamese forces and the injection of more divisions from North Vietnam.

Westmoreland: The contingency plan for more troops, which was contingent upon a new strategy, was one of the factors involved. The other factor was that if the thing did turn and we did have to encounter the worst possible case, we would have had a contingency plan to respond to that. So you're right, it served two purposes.

Because of television General Westmoreland fought the most widely visible war in history. Unlike other wars, whose audience was confined to the few camp followers and hardened military wives—who watched for example the fighting from the heights of Balaklava—Westmoreland had a mass audience every night in the intimacy of their own homes. It was a war without censorship. Television opened another front, the battle for public opinion in the United States. I asked him about this at length, and we will read what he said in our next chapter in which we deal with that topic more fully.

But this instant and open reporting of the war in Vietnam also brought to light disturbing instances of illegal behavior, of torture for information, of summary execution, which in addition to the violence of the fighting contributed to an impression that the Americans in Vietnam were supporting a shabby dictatorship. Were the Americans corrupted? did they corrupt? There were things which did not become public knowledge for some time, like the massacre by American troops of the population of the village of My Lai. Was General Westmoreland aware at the time of the impact such things were having on public opinion in the United States, and the rest of the world?

Westmoreland: Certainly there were excesses of that type. But they were the exceptions rather than the rule. And of course by giving visibility to the exception, the sensational spectrum of the available news, impressions were created without any question. This was not conducive to rallying support in our country or internationally for our efforts, which were very idealistic and very moralistic in the first instance.

Charlton: What about the corrosive effects that a war of this nature was having on the discipline of the troops themselves? For example large-scale actions, with the enormous modern firepower available, taking place among civilian populations, not by choice of course but that was the nature of the war?

Westmoreland: There weren't too many of those. We moved into an area, we tried to move the civilian population out. We tried to protect them. We would drop leaflets and so forth. We had rules of engagement that were very precise in that regard. I'm not suggesting that they weren't violated from time to time, but in general they were adhered to.

Charlton: Well, I don't mean it to be specious. I'm asking you whether you wouldn't agree that the war, because it was being fought against troops who were at times indistinguishable from the civilian population and fought as civilians among civilians, whether that itself did not have a corrosive effect on the discipline of your own troops? In your book you have much to say about one particular incident, the massacre of civilians by American soldiers at My Lai. It's perhaps important to hear you on that particular incident which was an example of the breakdown of discipline under the peculiar conditions of the war.

Westmoreland: There is no question that there was a breakdown at the time of the incident there at My Lai. But of course this is very small compared with the massacre of civilians at Hué by the North Vietnamese. Unfortunately you don't hear too much about that, but South Vietnamese civilians were killed by the thousands there. The My Lai incident was a most regrettable one. Orders were clear. Every soldier had a card on how to treat an enemy in his hands. This was a case where the leadership fell down. Bad judgment was used by several officers, and the chain of command broke down in that the incident was not reported; and admittedly at least at the company level, covered up. This is a sad chapter, but it was an aberration. There was not an incident comparable to that during the course of the whole war.

Charlton: In your book you refer to it as a diabolical nightmare, with a cold-blooded break for lunch, that went on all day.

Westmoreland: Well yes, I mean the evidence that came out in the trial of course has pointed that out. It was a dreadful thing, yes.

Charlton: And deeply upsetting to you?

Westmoreland: Deeply upsetting. I was unbelieving, until I got evidence that convinced me that something irregular had happened, and the more we got into it the more horrible it became.

Charlton: General, I wonder if I can ask you, looking back in great wisdom over that extraordinary time in Vietnam, whether you think

that the war was lost in Washington—as the French believed a decade or so earlier it had been lost in Paris—or does it seem possible to you, and more reasonable to suppose, that the war was lost because from the beginning it was a war whose methods were largely unfamiliar and whose nature was never sufficiently understood?
Westmoreland: No I don't accept that at all. I don't accept it at all. I think that we could have succeeded in accomplishing the objective that my country adopted as national policy, if wiser political decisions had been made.

❙ General Westmoreland can justifiably claim that he was subject to a greater degree of political control and intervention than any other American commander in war. He claims that from the beginning he thought it would be a long-drawn-out affair, and that success would depend to a great degree on the staying power of the American people to support it. Thus he conducted a campaign designed to get it over with, quickly. He believes America lost its nerve following the Tet offensive of the Communists in 1968. This he concedes was a psychological victory for them, but also a military disaster. But only a week before it happened President Johnson had been telling America that seventy per cent of Vietnamese were living in relatively secure areas. So military disaster or not, the Communist ability to attack all the major provincial towns and cities, and even briefly get into the American Embassy in Saigon itself, overthrew all the assumptions of American policy.

While the Communists sacrificed many thousands of their cadres in that last masterstroke, to have pressed the advantage against them would have meant widening the war into perhaps Laos and Cambodia, which was by now politically unacceptable in the United States. In America the political balance supporting the war had been changed. General Westmoreland was never 'defeated' in the field in Vietnam, but he lost the war. That paradox has bitten into him deeply. Like Gulliver in Lilliput, he mirrors America's frustration.

7
Protest at home

The right to dissent is sacrosanct in the United States and is buttressed by many hallowed clauses in the original and amended Constitutions which exhort the liberty of the individual against authority. Public opinion after World War II had given its support to the perceptions of America as a global power with a policy of containment. The fact that Vietnam was an undeclared war, for which the nation had not been mobilized, had many of the ingredients of inbuilt unpopularity as had been the case with Korea. In addition, public opinion was confronted with the unique visibility of the war and warfare on television. It was, too, the first war America had conducted without official censorship.

Like the war itself, protest against it was highly visible too. But it was not until 1968 when things were going wrong, that popular protest began to hamstring the President. Even then public opinion, as measured by the polls, was not demanding withdrawal. But the request in 1968 by the Army for 200,000 more troops to go to Vietnam led Johnson and the new Secretary of Defense to have second thoughts, by when the political pressures of dissenting public opinion—which undoubtedly contributed to the growing opposition in Congress—was placing restrictions on the President's freedom to act. The battle for public opinion in America developed, in General Maxwell Taylor's view, from 1963 onwards, by which time the United States had helped to overthrow President Diem.

Taylor: From that time on it was quite apparent that the American public opinion, the American understanding or misunderstanding of the situation, was indeed critical. After I came back from Vietnam in 1965 I repeatedly urged various means of trying to get the country to understand what I thought was a fairly clear situation.
Charlton: What prevented that, do you think?
Taylor: Oh, very difficult to say. First was the fact that our Government is not organized for that kind of thing at any time except in time of war. Secondly, the press—not all but the vast majority—was opposed to the Vietnam policy and very vocal. The television also.

Allowing television on the battlefield after our troops got there created an impossible situation at home. Even in World War II I think we would probably have left Britain, or France, or Germany to come home if the bloody pictures which were available on those battlefields had been flashed into the American living-room as was the case in Vietnam.

Charlton: Did you make any recommendations to the President about that?

Taylor: He knew the situation perfectly well, but he and his advisers were afraid of the internal situation if he tried to establish what in effect would have been some kind of censorship, wartime censorship. You see, we hadn't declared war, a fact used as an argument against censorship.

Later than the period General Taylor referred to, during the time the American expeditionary force was in Vietnam, there were hundreds of correspondents based in Saigon from the world's major television networks and newspapers down to those of the smaller American towns. Comprehensive facilities were established by the Americans for the correspondents to travel round the countryside and into action with the forces—American units had their own press relations officers. It fell to General Westmoreland, the ground commander, to fight the most widely visible of history's wars. What were the implications of so doing?

Westmoreland: It had a profound emotional effect on the American people, without any question. I heard an expression by one of our TV personalities who analyzed it this way, and I think it's a very astute observation. He said: 'The American people got tired of the Vietnam TV series, and they saw it as if it was not necessarily real but fiction, and they saw so much of it that they became totally disenchanted with it as if it was a commercial series of programs which a public can tire of. It went on so long and they just got bombarded with this day after day'. Now what did they get bombarded with? They got bombarded, with a few exceptions (word-documentaries that tried to give a balanced picture) but basically they were bombarded with news reporting which emphasized, of course, the sensational. There is another interesting phenomenon. This was the first war in history without any censorship, and the first war shown on television. The American news media had no experience with this, and they tended to report the war like crime on the police beat, or no-holds-barred political campaigns. What is news? News is most often the sensational, the bizarre, the offbeat. So the media tended to emphasize the negative side. I think it's only natural that the authorities, the military and political, tried to balance the equation, and put the accent on the positive. Hence an adversary relationship was created between those trying to carry out national policy and representatives of the news media.

Charlton: Would you say that the reporting of the war led to the isolation of America's armed forces from American public opinion in a way that just hadn't happened before?

Westmoreland: Well, yes, to a degree; and associated with that was the fact that a cross section of the American people were not involved in the war: the unwise and discriminatory policy of allowing a man to go to the university campus of this country and excuse him from military service.

Charlton: But among the things which will be remembered about the television coverage of the war were things that were at the time famous and I'd like your opinion on them. For example, the film of American troops with a Zippo lighter setting fire to the thatch of a poor man's house.

Westmoreland: I was informed that the CBS reporter was told by Lieutenant-General Lewis W. Walt, the Marine Commander, that the well-fortified hamlets were being used by the enemy as a safe-haven from which attacks were being launched against American and Vietnamese personnel and installations, and that he had heard him give permission to his marines to burn houses which 'hid or camouflaged pill-boxes'. There was no explanation given to the TV audience as to the liability that the thatched huts posed to the safety of our troops. It was reported at the time that the Zippo lighter was passed to a marine by the reporter or a cameraman. But the sad thing was that the impression was given to the viewing audience that the action of the American Marines was totally calloused and thoughtless. Misconceptions of that character were not unusual.

▎In the absence of censorship, some images of the Vietnam war had an instant lasting and unflattering impact on America's perception of itself as a nation at war, and one such early jolt was the image of a superpower setting fire to the thatch of a poor man's hut in Asia, filmed in the field by Morley Safer, one of the senior and many correspondents of a major television network, CBS. William Small, Vice-President in charge of its news division, was asked first about this particular incident—the village CBS filmed burning—and then about the general approach which CBS exercised in its news judgments in Vietnam [see fig. 3].

Small: It was not uninhabited, except in the sense that many villages became uninhabited at part of the day and then the people returned at night and so on. Secondly, the accusation is typical of the attempts by the military and other officials to discredit the press. Morley Safer didn't hand a Zippo lighter to a Marine, the Marine had it; just as in another incident we filmed, the cutting of ears off enemy dead, the military tried to spread the story in Washington, where I was at the time, that our cameraman had handed a knife to a young soldier and said: 'Do that so I can take your picture'. Those things have never been substantiated, but they're typical of the attempts by officialdom to try to discourage the people from believing anything that they found harmful.
Charlton: Just back to the cigarette lighter for a moment. If your correspondent, Morley Safer, didn't hand the cigarette lighter to the Marine, did any other newsman, or did the Marine do that himself?
Small: I, of course, was not there but Safer was, the camera crews were and it was done spontaneously, not by one Marine but by several. If you look at the footage, as we have since, many times, this was not an isolated incident. There were several Marines, they were going to burn down that village.
Charlton: A much more important principle is involved isn't it? The size of the screen itself is filled only with one image at a time, and in that case a very particular and a rather hostile and deeply troubling one to the natural decency of the great majority of Americans. But it goes to the heart of the problem; and the phrase which has been used is that it generalizes from the particular and that is the nature of television. In the case of Vietnam that had the peculiar effect of disposing public opinion against the United States.
Small: But in large part all of journalism generalizes from the particular. But it is not all one-sided. It's reportage on both sides of the issue, and could as likely have supported the war effort as the reporting did in World War II. The difference was that this was not a war against Adolf Hitler who was killing vast numbers of people and who was invading France and threatening England and who would in time be on our own shores in this country—this was a war against a small country in Asia which most of us had never heard of perhaps, and no-one ever quite understood why we were there. Was it to keep

the Chinese from coming? Well, no-one felt that the Chinese really were going to land on the shores of San Francisco, except a few extremists. That was the problem with Vietnam: no-one in high place ever sufficiently explained that America truly had a role there.

Charlton: Can you quote examples where you were in direct conflict with the Administration at high levels?

Small: Oh yes. That would often happen. Presidential press secretaries were unhappy. George Christian, Lyndon Johnson's press secretary, once told me that when Walter Cronkite returned from a visit to Vietnam—I think about the time of the Tet offensive—and he went on with a half-hour essay on why America was losing the war, Christian said that 'buttoned the coffin shut'. You could see it all through a Government, you could hear the echoes that Walter Cronkite had declared that America had lost. Dean Rusk once said to me, as he said to other people on similar occasions, this happened to be at a cocktail party, where he thrust a finger into my chest and said: 'All American journalists want to win Pulitzer Prizes for their reporting, but some day they're going to ask what side are you on; and I don't know how you fellas will answer, but I will say I was on the side of the US.' You could protest and say: 'Mr Secretary, it isn't the job of journalists to be on this side or that side but only to report', but he didn't see it that way.

Charlton: But what efforts do you think you made, or what was it did you believe possible to make, to redress that imbalance—because it was a war in terms of reporting it between an open society and a closed society?

Small: Well I don't know how very open various South Vietnamese regimes were at different times; or for that matter the American regime. As we know from the revelations in *The Pentagon Papers* there was a great deal, some of it of massive importance, that was kept from the American people. Indeed I would contend that had *The Pentagon Papers* been made public at the time those events happened, that the public demand to end the war would have come much earlier.

Charlton: But on the ground in Vietnam were you very conscious of deliberate attempts to conceal from you what was actually happening? My own impression is that one could go anywhere and do anything almost with the American forces in Vietnam.

Small: Not true. Not really true. To begin with your transportation was in effect what we in this country call movement by thumb, you had to hitchhike with a military unit. Well, it's true in most wars, it still prevents you from doing a great deal of going out physically on your own; and I think we saw the results of that. I think the best example of our inability to know everything that's going on is the fact that the My Lai massacre story came long after the event, and obviously if it's going to embarrass them they try to keep it from you. I'll cite one example in our own reporting, and the year escapes me but I remember it as being somewhere around 1966/1967. There was a grotesque habit that some soldiers had of cutting the ears off an enemy corpse and sort of putting them in your pocket as a souvenir. It was not widespread but it did happen and we heard it often enough that we asked one of our crews to go out and see if they couldn't discover whether this was true or not. We filmed such an incident taking place and our reporter put it on the air and there was a tremendous flap back in Washington—I was then Washington Bureau Chief—all kinds of official denials from the Pentagon, all kinds of charges, some open and some sub-rosa, that CBS had rigged the story, that we had staged it, that it hadn't really happened, except that there it was on the film and it had happened.

Charlton: Now, what was CBS's attitude to that as a matter of policy? Did you believe that that was gratuitous or due particularly to the peculiarly corrosive effects of this kind of conflict in which the Americans were engaged? Did you believe that you ran the risk of generalizing from the particular in that case or not?

Small: As I remember the report there was no attempt to generalize and say this was the practice of every GI over there. The soldiers on the whole did not act that way. But some did, and we felt that an important thing to report. It showed the callousness of men who live the kind of lives that soldiers do in that kind of a war, and so we did report it. The reaction was strong back home because officialdom would always like to portray one's own army as heroes and the enemy as villains; but life is not black and white.

When the Vietnamese Communists attacked suddenly throughout the countryside of South Vietnam in 1968, it was an unexpected reverse and refutation of the officially expressed optimism about the course of the war. The visibility of that war was, of course, one-sided and certain of the images which came from the field in Vietnam at that time sharply reinforced a public mood of disappointment or cynicism and so weakened the already evaporating will to go on with it. One of these was the summary execution in a Saigon street of a Vietcong prisoner by the Chief of Police which was shown in bloody particularity during fighting in the capital [see fig. 4]. At a time when American resolve was being put to the severest of tests, that unlawful summary justice must have suddenly reinforced all the arguments that the United States was acting in Vietnam in support of a shoddy military dictatorship. I was watching those pictures that night in Washington with one of the news editors of NBC News, Elliott Frankel.

Frankel: My own reaction was one of extreme horror, even shock, having seen the unedited footage of the guy being shot, you could see the thump almost as his head jerked and then falling down and seeing the grey matter spilling out on the floor, and my immediate reaction was: 'My God, are they going to put this on television?' My second reaction was: 'I'm glad I'm not doing the nightly show tonight and I don't have to face this terrible responsibility.' And they did edit it somewhat and it was still tremendously shocking. Some of the other networks I'm told played it in slow motion, played it one scene as we do in instant replay in some of our sports programs, and it did touch off a tremendous discussion among the people afterward. We all afterwards repaired down the local saloon for some refreshment and there was quite a spirited discussion going on—should we have used it, should we not have used it? I guess that the rationale for people who used it was we wanted to show the kind of a regime they had in Saigon, these are the kind of people that are our allies. Let's put this on and show them up. And the people who were against it saying you're brutalizing the American public who have already been overly brutalized by having scenes of the war put into their living-room every night.

Charlton: I remember very well your immediate reactions to that, and I wonder if you can remember what you in fact did. I remember you standing up as soon as you saw that picture and yelling out: 'My God, that's the way to win the hearts and minds.' You could see what effect that was going to have on American public opinion when it was shown; and as you say, particularly that it would have confirmed the growing suspicion that they were acting in support of a power which was not worthy of support.

Frankel: I think this feeling had been growing on the American people for some time. For a long time before that television—and I'm saying all networks—had been acting more or less as cheer leaders and emphasizing coverage of combat and showing our brave boys in action against the enemy. There was very little attempt to explore the deeper problems involved in the war—of land reform: the political problems, you know, how secure the Saigon government was or what was the nature of the enemy that we were fighting. There was very little of that and it was around that time I think that some of the top commentators began questioning the war publicly.

Charlton: This was very late in the day. It was 1968 before you started wanting to know more about the origins of the involvement and what kind of a war it was, and what else was happening in Vietnam. Up till then, all the American public had seen largely was combat photography, the military side of the war, without that other perhaps more important side of the American effort, the attempt to build an economy, to give them new varieties of rice, new machinery, all that kind of thing.

Frankel: Well, that's true, because this is the way to get the ratings. Also we wanted to show our boys fighting over there, and we'd got to show that we were supportive. There was also the feeling that this was more exciting than a lot of showing a bunch of film, talking heads as we call it, of people just debating pros and cons. We did one program, it was a weekend program, a magazine-type show, we devoted a whole half-hour program to the problem of land reform in South Vietnam and we got all kinds of very interesting press. It turns out some of the newspapers hadn't even covered this. We'd been trying to do something about it, and we stumbled across this and we got all kinds of very advantageous, for us, newspaper publicity. The fact was that the ruling people still owned most of the land and the poor peasant was getting very little of it.

▍The disaffection of America's idealistic youth over Vietnam became profound and led to bitter divisions, perhaps deeper than any America had experienced since the Civil War. The unrest on the university campuses, which were sometimes battlegrounds, provided a sustained and articulate opposition. One of the more influential younger voices on the American left was Frances FitzGerald. She first went to Vietnam in 1966 as a journalist writing for liberal magazines and newspapers, and sought to apply the talents of a young American's scholarship to what she saw in Vietnam in her book, which was popularly acclaimed, called *Fire in the Lake*.[1]

FitzGerald: I had no real sense of mission in going there. It seemed to

---

[1] Random House, New York, 1972.

me that we had everything to learn about it, and once I arrived there I realized that even more strongly. There were words being used by American officials at the time—words like 'revolutionary development' or 'democracy in Asia', 'rooting out the guerillas' or 'the infrastructure'—and after I'd been there a few weeks these words looked to me completely autonomous of the situation, like sort of clouds or blimps floating overhead. My work there, and why I decided to stay for a year there, was to try and figure out what the relationship of these words was to the situation in Vietnam. I think that all of us of my generation certainly were very naive at the time. I know I myself didn't think very politically, that is I was always interested in electoral politics but never understood even from Harvard University courses the real bones of it, what politics really means.

Charlton: Did you see America in Vietnam in a way that you hadn't before, which confirmed whatever prejudices you had about it?

FitzGerald: No, I would say I was totally surprised by Vietnam, and what I found there about the United States is something that I hadn't suspected about it. Not that I imagined that American society was perfect at all but that rather it was possible to proceed by reformist attempts at changing society, helping the poor, helping the blacks and so on. What Vietnam taught me was people have to do things themselves, and this is true in this society as well. So when Americans often—I mean, I'm talking about, I don't know, colonels or aid representatives—would say with all goodness of heart that they were trying to help the Vietnamese, trying to build wells, trying to start chicken production or so on, they didn't see this very fundamental principle, that the people they were dealing with were being pulled farther and farther away from their own society. In the end what happened was that we recruited almost everybody into the army or the bureaucracy. There was something like a million men in the South Vietnamese army and in a population of eighteen million that means about all of the able-bodied men; and so what we'd done was simply as it were hired them. It went no further than that.

Charlton: But that was the effect of American aid. Let's talk about the cause rather more, and what was causing this was a war which was being dominated by those who believed in class struggle. They were making all the initiatives and provoking all those responses. Did you come to accept that class struggle was what the mass of the people in South Vietnam wanted?

FitzGerald: In the first place it was an anti-colonial war and I think that's terribly important to begin with.

Charlton: That's talking about the 1940s and 1950s until the French left. I mean, did you still conceive it as colonial war when you got there?

FitzGerald: No. I think it was still a colonial war because...

Charlton: Why did you not think of it as a war for the colonial succession?

FitzGerald: Simply because there was no other side in this war. We —as Dan Ellsberg once said—we were not only on the wrong side, we created the wrong side, and we created it with aid. You can see this process happening from the very beginning of the Diem regime on.

Charlton: But if you created it you also created something which was willing to accept enormously high casualties over a very long period. The South Vietnamese were dying in very large numbers.

FitzGerald: Not as large as Americans would have liked until quite late in the war. The proficiency of the orphan was not something that anybody was terribly proud of.

Charlton: But how do you explain the fact that the Army, however inefficient, however different in motivation and in spirit as you saw it from their opposite numbers—the Communist soldiers—continued to accept battle and casualties at the level they did for so many years?

FitzGerald: Even with a tremendous lot of money they were not in fact willing to accept those casualties. They would have stopped fighting, indeed regiments were running away in 1964. Now when the US came in with large amounts of troops in 1966, they took over the real burden of heavy fighting. What continued on through 1971 was that the US rather systematically destroyed the local economy. It made it impossible to live. It made it very difficult for the guerillas to live, but much more than that it made it almost impossible for the people of the countryside to go on as they were. If you were a young man in 1966 through 1971, your chances of survival could almost be calculated. If you went into the National Liberation Front your chances of survival in 1966 were, let us say, fifty per cent; your chances of survival in the Saigon Army, let's say fifty per cent too at that time. By 1969, the percentages were totally different. Your chances of survival in the NLF were about ten per cent, if that. Your chances of survival in the Saigon Army were about ninety per cent.

Charlton: Did you ever feel that a liberal democracy and a liberal democrat like yourself, with a genuine human concern, had any alternative to offer to that process of wars of liberation, in which violence is the means and class struggle the basis and key to change?

FitzGerald: I really insist on this colonial business, because it was not the Vietnamese that began the violence, it was ourselves by going in there. We were the ones that created a government that didn't exist beforehand.

Charlton: Can I press you a little more about that? Why a colonial war when America never had any intention of occupying, in any sense, Vietnam? It wanted to give the Vietnamese independence.

FitzGerald: Colonial refers to questions of sovereignty, and obviously we did not ever want to have American sovereignty over Vietnam. But we did want to bend it to our will, we did want it to behave as we wanted: we wanted it to be a defense against the Communist North, against China and so on, and we were willing to do almost anything to see that it was bent to our will. There were all kinds of lovely idealistic theories floating around, and there were all kinds of people who really thought we were trying to help the Vietnamese, and maybe President Johnson even was one of those; but the fact is we were never really interested in that at all and furthermore I don't think we were ever really interested in Vietnam. It seems to me the extraordinary thing about the Vietnam War and what made it so much to be condemned, both from the strategic and from the moral point of view, is the fact that there was nothing we could possibly use there, nothing we could possibly do with it. I mean it's one thing to mount a defense against Soviet tanks in the middle of Europe and it's quite another thing to have anti-Communist regimes in South-East Asia.

Charlton: Both are designed to meet the same threat are they not, the imposition by force of something which you believe it is important to resist?

FitzGerald: Well, almost everything is done by force. After all what we are resisting in Europe is the actual invasion of Europe by Soviet power. In Vietnam what we were doing was trying to stop a local government from coming to power. It's extremely difficult and different intervening in somebody else's civil war or government, it's an entirely different thing from trying to stop the advances of yet another major power.

▌While the war was ten thousand miles away from the White House, and yet inside the home of every American, the inability of the Government to suggest when or how it might end to a country perplexed by conflicts and the stated aims and purposes of that war, naturally became a more powerful influence as things were seen to be going badly wrong. The committed opponents of the war outside the government began to recruit their own constituency. J. K. Galbraith had, as he says, 'never had an open mind about the war' and remembers how he sensed and saw the balance of the wider public opinion start to tilt against it.

Galbraith: For a long period I spoke against it but without any large audience. It was in low key, it wasn't in the center of American attention for a long while. I was, and I remain to this day, an admirer of Lyndon Johnson. We were the same age, we first showed up in Washington at the same time. I'd always liked him, he was one of the most interesting men I've ever known. I campaigned for him a great deal in 1964 because he seemed to be a safer figure than Goldwater. And then as time passed—the bombing started, troop commitment which I felt so unhappy about came, and gradually my relations with the President came to an end. I began, as did others, looking for a vehicle. I had once or twice been offered the Chairmanship of ADA —Americans for Democratic Action—and I took it in 1967 because this seemed to offer a platform.

Charlton: By this time then you were determined to organize opposition against the war?

Galbraith: Sometime in 1966 or early 1967 Arthur Schlesinger and Richard Goodwin, William vanden Heuvel and I all had lunch together and I remember Arthur saying: 'If this thing gets worse in the last seconds before the final destruction, we'd better be able to say that we opposed it.' We all committed ourselves at that time to really working against the war, which meant breaking with the Administration. I identified myself for a time with something called 'Negotiations Now'. Then we had a great struggle within ADA, and brought ADA down solidly against the war. Then I began what was a long and fascinating, I may say, association with the man who deserves more credit than anybody else for bringing our involvement to an end, and that's Eugene McCarthy. If you want to ask who it was that was ultimately responsible for turning the tide against Vietnam, it was Gene.

Charlton: Why so?

Galbraith: Because first of all our politics is the politics of leaders. We first tried to organize around the notion of negotiations and peace, and until we had somebody who would really run for office, and run for the Presidency, we got nowhere. And in the autumn of

1967, after Bob Kennedy had decided that if he did it, it would look as though he were engaged in a kind of parochial family war with Johnson, George McGovern was up for re-election and he didn't want to do it, so Gene came forward.

Protest in America was a relatively brief candle which became incandescent in the two years from 1966 until 1968 when Lyndon Johnson decided to withdraw himself from the Presidency and begin negotiations. It flared up again when his successor, President Nixon, widened the geographical scope of the war in 1970 by the brief American thrust into the Communist sanctuaries in Cambodia. The explosive response on the campuses of the United States—when four students were shot as the National Guard opened fire during the violent demonstration at Kent State University—set immediate political limits to the President's freedom as Commander-in-Chief further to commit his troops on the ground. But for the most part, protest seemed to relent with the disengagement of America's forces. Subsequently, even when President Nixon ordered in the bombers to help smash the all-out North Vietnamese invasion with armor of the South in 1972, and mined the harbors in Haiphong, bottling up the Russian ships there, the public demonstrations and outcry never reached the intensity that they had possessed in 1968.

While President Johnson was loosing thunderbolts to force a quick and decisive result, and agonizing in the White House over his intractable inheritance of that war, public confidence in his policies was declining, and unrest and demonstrations beat a tattoo throughout America. They were nervous and violent times. In 1968 Robert Kennedy and Martin Luther King were both assassinated. And it was at this time that Eugene McCarthy, Senator from Minnesota, a diffident and often cynical figure, became a hero to all those committed to getting America out of the war. He had the allegiance of the large constituency of liberal democrats, which had previously been symbolized by Adlai Stevenson. When did Mr McCarthy decide American policy in Vietnam was wrong?

McCarthy: I had doubts about the policy almost as soon as one could determine that it had been fixed. But I would reserve judgment on those who were supposedly expert and who were telling us what we should do and why we should do it. I began to suspect in that period of time when they kept losing Presidents of the Republic,

Diem and General Khanh and so on, at almost every instance it would turn out that the person they had told you was stable and reliable was not so. I forget what year it was but I think it must have been 1965 probably, before we were deeply involved: at that time President Johnson for a short time was having twenty-five or thirty Senators down at the White House every week or two and he would bring in the Cabinet members and talk about current problems. On this occasion Rusk spoke to us, among others. We talked about General Khanh who was then the President, and how he'd reconciled all the differences, Christians or Catholics, Buddhists and whatever else. He said: 'We've stabilized.' I think it was Wednesday night, and on Friday they threw Khanh out. So I assumed that Rusk didn't know very much about the political situation. He was reporting to us a stable government and within two days it was gone.

Charlton: What was the essence of your argument about American involvement in Vietnam?

McCarthy: The first speech I made about the war—serious speech—I said I wasn't going to argue the legality of it or the morality of it; but it looked to me as though there was no proportion between what we were going to do, by way of military action, and the possible good that might come out of it.

Charlton: When did you cast your first vote in the Senate against the various appropriations?

McCarthy: I guess I cast some votes against appropriations but I never thought that was the approach to it. I thought what you should do is to argue the case. The vote against the appropriations is sort of a last desperate act.

Charlton: More positively, you supported the Gulf of Tonkin Resolution.

McCarthy: Well everybody supported that in 1964. If you read the presentation of that by Fulbright, he said that they say this doesn't give any power, it's just a gesture. There was no question of passing power to Johnson. It was like saying—send it down, it will make him feel better. But we had a vote—and that was 1964: we were scarcely involved—and the proposition was: 'Is it alright for American boats to fire back if they're fired upon?' It's pretty hard to vote against that. Now Johnson was pretty careful about it. The press would say that it didn't really give him any authority. But Rusk was the one who was inclined to use it, and he'd say: 'Look, you gave us the authority, legalized it.' So in 1967 Wayne Morse remembered to take it up for reconsideration and we were voted down. Five of us voted to take it up to the Senate. In effect we didn't even get to that. The vote was simply to take it up for consideration. We only got five votes to even take it up.

Charlton: Can you tell us particularly about the time when public opinion began to become obviously a part of the strategy of fighting the war? In a sense American public opinion forced a change of course very early, at the time of Diem's overthrow in South Vietnam. American policy was responding to public discomfiture and disquiet, particularly the press reporting about the nature of the South Vietnamese government America was supporting. Certainly by the time American troops went there in 1965 it had become very much a factor in the whole strategy of the war.

McCarthy: Johnson and McNamara thought it would be a short war, and it was one of the reasons why they provided all sorts of exemptions from the draft, exempting college students and exempting people who would go to graduate school. It was calculated on their part, they didn't want to get the draft working among the people who would protest, the writers and the professional people and so on. They assumed that they could end the war so quickly that they'd never have to answer for it. Later on they had a lot of trouble with the draft and the enactment of it because the four years ran out and they didn't know what to do with college graduates.

Nixon then gave this thing about—you can be nineteen at whatever year you want to be, and all sorts of terrible evasions that developed from it. The early part of the war was fought pretty much by the military and by regular army people plus draftees who were not the kind who would protest. It was largely fought, you know, by the poor and by the blacks. But as it went on, the numbers increased and the draft pressure developed. I think there was a personal response in those classes of Americans who were more likely to speak out and be able to speak out, and that was beginning to develop.

I thought that the most significant early protest was one that was sponsored by clergy and others united against the war. That was I think in November of 1967, and Senator Morse spoke, and Ernest Gruening did, and I spoke: I think we were the only three members of the Senate who did. But this was a clerical group which covered pretty much the whole spectrum of religion in this country. They came to town, and they represented the whole country. Before that there'd been nothing really organized, just sort of scattered protest and scattered criticism. Then we began to build on that with the various letters we sent to the President, protests and so on and speeches against the policy. And the press began to pick it up a little bit more at that point, but there were only about three papers or four in the country of any consequence that opposed the war.

Charlton: What was your mailbag like, would you say?

McCarthy: I don't think we had much in the mail. It was more a question of a public judgment expressed by a smaller number of people. It wasn't a protest that developed by some kind of mass letter-writing sort of thing—not in my case anyway.

Charlton: But how would you characterize in retrospect the peace movement? Would you say that it was substantially formed by people who were confused as to the aims and purposes and shocked by seeing the war on television, people who felt that the aims of the war had never been sufficiently explained to them? Did it represent a deeper moral feeling than that, that somehow a fundamental injustice was taking place?

McCarthy: Well I think it was a mixed case. The clergy and others emphasized the moral aspect of the war, and I think there was something of that in the country. But there was also a selfish response eventually on the part of those who didn't want to fight, or their parents who didn't want them to. I thought the mothers of fifteen-year-old boys were the most anti-war people of all. They thought the sacrificial age was there, that the war wasn't going to end, and they were really agitated at the prospect of their young boys at seventeen or eighteen being drafted and going off to fight. And then there was the pragmatic judgment; and actually the business community, whatever their purposes were, they were mixed I think, but they sensed it wasn't even a war. They could make an argument against it on economic grounds too. I don't say that was their principal motivation in opposing it, but we did have businessman groups organized publicly opposed to the war, which I think was unique in the history of this country; any military action has generally had almost uncritical support from leading financial and businessmen.

The moral issue as I saw it finally got down to the question of whether there was any proportion between the destruction and what possible good would come out of it. Some of the others made a more specific moral judgment and just said it's bad in itself and so on. I suppose you can make judgments of that kind if you want to. I just prefer not to.

Charlton: But that was more a criticism against the way the war was being waged than the cause itself.

McCarthy: Well not necessarily. I would have been against it if they had fought it with nuclear weapons. The proportion would then have been even worse. You started with the judgment that people had made for us about people in South Vietnam wanting to have a free society. But the price of getting it was the destruction practically of a total community. You make a pragmatic judgment on it, you don't pursue it to all-out destruction. But in any case I thought that they had underestimated the kind of war they were caught up in, had great doubts as to whether it would succeed.

Charlton: Can we talk about 1968, the year of the Chicago Convention at which there was widespread disorder?

McCarthy: Firstly we kept maybe a hundred thousand young people from coming to Chicago. We were afraid what would happen. There only were about ten thousand there. We probably should have had more come so we had just as many as there were police and guards. They anticipated a hundred thousand and therefore they had more military power than they knew what to do with, you know, and a sort of a hyped-up disposition to use it. I don't know whether anything much could have been done as long as Johnson and the people who controlled the Convention were set on making no concession. Rather curious, the whole Johnson role, from the time of his withdrawal in March when he said he was going to withdraw so that he wouldn't be accused of political motivation in what he might do.

The only base upon which that would have made much sense was that he was going to end the war somehow. But instead of that he persisted in conducting or trying to force whoever followed him to conduct the same kind of war. And I think in his own way he'd figured this out, that if he'd stayed in he could have been nominated but he would have had to admit that the war policy was wrong, and by pulling out he could really control who would be his successor, I think. Either it could have been Nixon or Humphrey. So whoever succeeded, he was going to see it would be a person who would have to, in office, carry on the Johnson policies.

Charlton: Now what did you understand those as being at the time? His defenders say that he had taken the decision to de-escalate the war after Tet and to probably withdraw America and undertake Vietnamization. Is that what you thought?

McCarthy: I think that he and Rusk had in fact thought they had won, and they thought they might de-escalate because of the victory. But I don't think they were talking of de-escalation in the face of defeat or an admission of the realities.

Charlton: Were things dangerous in the United States because of the protest movement which reached its peak at the time of the Chicago Convention?

McCarthy: Oh they weren't dangerous on any massive scale. Later on Cambodia was in some ways the national danger. Violence in many places was greater in the Cambodian situation than it was in Vietnam.

Charlton: But the Government always had a mandate in your view and legitimacy?

McCarthy: Insofar as the Congress was concerned, there were only I suppose really fifteen Senators who had made some position of criticism of the war by the time of that Convention. There were only actually about five or six that supported me in the Convention—Senator Morse and Senator Gruening and Senator Hughes and Senator Hart—and then there were a few others who were quite outspoken against the war like McGovern. Mansfield was against the war but he didn't do anything about it at Chicago. Fulbright was against it; he didn't make any overt commitment. So that there was no political instability, or I'd say any real public danger. I think the war would have ended just about the way it did if we had not even made a protest in 1968. If there'd been no criticism I'm afraid the war would have run out, afraid that our protests didn't end it any earlier than it would have. It just sort of stopped, you know. I've heard criticism of Kissinger taking the Nobel Peace Prize for watching the war end that he'd advocated.

8
The Pentagon Papers

Vietnam, having begat within America a conflict between citizen and Government, produced some notable encounters. Among the more revealing of them was the personal exploit of Daniel Ellsberg and his unauthorized removal from their filing cabinets of forty-seven volumes covering thirty years of the most intimate secret exchanges within the American Government on Vietnam and giving them to *The New York Times* to publish. They were known as *The Pentagon Papers*.[1] Two years after American combat troops had gone to Vietnam on the strong recommendation of the Secretary of Defense, Mr Robert McNamara was a man besieged by crippling doubts and hurt by the violence of the protest that decision had brought within America, much of it aimed at him personally by those who were calling it 'McNamara's War'. As Secretary of Defense, McNamara had mastered and ordered the elaborate new technologies of the defense industries; now his nerve and his former convictions appeared to be failing.

On 17 June 1967, he asked his staff in the Pentagon to make a special study which would retrace America's steps into the soggy labyrinth of Vietnam. In that commission given by McNamara one senses perhaps his own arrival at a point where he had lost his sense of purpose and direction.

It is revealing too, perhaps, in another dimension. Unlike the North Vietnamese who had had the same political leadership for all those thirty years and had been everywhere before in the arguments of their long revolution, the knowledge of the Americans was often confined to the span of a single administration and therefore had to be relearned at various intervals with the arrival and departure of new governments. *The Pentagon Papers* were a comprehensive collection of documents—the abstracts and brief chronicles of thirty years or so of action and decision at the top level of American Government. The staff archivists and historians of the Pentagon who fished them out recorded their view that the answers to some of the more important questions were still elusive. To that extent the *Papers* are unrewarding;

[1] Quadrangle Books, New York, 1971.

but they did reveal or confirm much of the secret side of the war and the undisclosed doubt and pessimism of the early sixties and in particular the subsequent soul-searching of McNamara. The man who was given the job by McNamara of editing this survey of the recent historical past was Leslie Gelb, who was thirty when the study was undertaken and a member of the Pentagon's Department of International Security Affairs.

Gelb: *The Pentagon Papers* began with a list of one hundred questions about the war that the then Secretary of Defense Robert McNamara and a few of his closest aides wanted answered. Most of these questions were about current events, questions like how did we know how many Vietnamese Communists we were really killing; how did we know when a hamlet was truly pacified. Some of the questions were historical like: was Ho Chi Minh really an Asian Tito; were there occasions in our past involvement in the war where we could have extricated ourselves without any loss in credibility? The original intent of the operation that was set up was to answer these one hundred questions. In order to do so we had to requisition files to answer the historical questions. The guidance I was given when taking on this enterprise was that our effort be encyclopaedic and comprehensive and—what was the other word, 'retrievable'—I think it was something like that. We were to let the chips fall where they may.

Charlton: I'm not sure I understand 'retrievable'; what does that mean?

Gelb: I think that Mr McNamara said he wanted an index of useful, handy information. After we requisitioned these historical files we found that they shed interesting light on the current data. So interesting in fact that a number of us thought we really ought to take much more care with the historical questions to illuminate the answers to the current events questions, to give some perspective. There had been no institutional memory to the war, particularly back in Washington. I therefore drew up a list of some twenty-eight or thirty studies that I suggested be undertaken. The suggestion was sent to Mr McNamara, he approved it, and the effort became what you have seen. But only then, some four to six weeks after it had begun.

Charlton: But these were fundamental questions being asked, it would seem, very late in the day. After all, America had been involved in Vietnam to a greater or lesser extent since 1945 or 1946, all the way back to the old days of OSS, the forerunner of the CIA, so why was it necessary to ask such fundamental questions at this time if the answers hadn't already been given?

Gelb: I can only speculate about that. One answer might be that by this time, 1967, Mr McNamara had become deeply troubled by that war in a way he hadn't been before and he was after answers to questions he had never asked himself before, however late it was to ask them. Another possibility was that Mr McNamara was going to do a favor for President Johnson. He was going to prepare the answers to all the dirty and difficult questions that could be asked about the war in the upcoming Presidential campaign. He had performed a similar service for President Johnson in 1964 when he ran against Barry Goldwater. The third explanation that I've heard is that he was really doing this for Bobby Kennedy and not Lyndon Johnson, that he was preparing ammunition for a Kennedy insurgency against Johnson for the Democratic Presidential nomination. But those are all speculations on my part, I have no inside information.

Charlton: But do you believe that that study was undertaken in the belief or knowledge that when it was all put together the cumulative effect of it would be to force a change in policy?

Gelb: I have no idea whether that was in Mr McNamara's mind. As I said, the enterprise began with answering questions; not with doing the kinds of studies that we ultimately did.

Charlton: But when you, charged with putting it all together, saw the cumulative effect of it would you agree that its probable and likely effect was that it would force a change in policy?

Gelb: No, because I didn't think anybody would read it; it was voluminous, even the summaries of each study were long and government officials don't read things that are that long.

Charlton: How did you approach the problem of selecting the documents in the first place?

Gelb: The whole enterprise was very haphazard. I was the director of the project. I didn't spend any more than half my own time on it because I had other daily responsibilities—and that was true for a good many of the people who worked on the studies. It was very difficult to get people to do the studies. It was even more difficult to get trained historians to do them; and it was often impossible to keep people for more than two or three months. They couldn't finish the studies they had begun. Someone else would have to come along and undertake to finish them. So the studies were very uneven in quality.

Charlton: What attempts were made to get trained historians? One of the criticisms I've heard of it is that the approach to it wasn't scholarly at all. They were being written by quite low-level people who had no training in historical method for example.

Gelb: Yes, I think that's true in a good many cases. There were efforts made to get historians to come in and do it but they weren't terribly inclined to do work on it. I tried to get Henry Kissinger for example, and he came in on several occasions and read but he wasn't prepared to write anything himself.

Charlton: Can we just go back for a moment to the hundred questions. What was the relevance and importance of asking questions in that form?

Gelb: Well, I think it was a McNamara technique, one that he had used when he first came into the Department of Defense. He asked a number of questions at that time in order to ascertain what our capabilities were with respect to strategic nuclear weapons and doctrine. It was a technique that he had used back in the Ford Motor Company too, and behind it lies the assumption that if you ask the right questions you're going to get the right facts and you're going to be able to give the right answers.

Charlton: Did you all sit round and come up with questions, or did he ask the questions?

Gelb: I was given a couple of pieces of typewritten paper with some hundred questions on them. I'd never seen them before. I thought that McNamara had written these questions, along with one of his principal aides, John McNaughton, and a military aide by the name of Robert Gard, those three people.

Charlton: What were your own reactions when you had access to these documents yourself, when you actually started pulling out things going all the way back to pre-Geneva Accords?

Gelb: Well I was quite overwhelmed. At one point during the enterprise we must have had thirty or forty file cabinets filled with documents. It was beyond my capacity to begin to absorb a lot of this material. We had access to almost all the paper material in the United States Government at that time. We had access to State Department files, CIA files, a number of White House files although not complete; we had all the National Security Council files and a complete record from the Pentagon. We didn't do interviews and that is indeed a shortcoming, to the extent that you believe people's memories are accurate about what happened. That's a big hole in the study. But as far as documentation is concerned, we had documents from all over, including virtually open access in the State Department.

Charlton: So there's no reason to suppose that there are other documents in other archives which would qualify importantly the impression left by *The Pentagon Papers*?

Gelb: Well, you take a look at President Johnson's memoirs, *The Vantage Point*, and you show me how many documents he presents that weren't in *The Pentagon Papers*. I found only two, two memos that were sent to him. Otherwise I think the documentary record we have is rather complete. But, as you know, there are important things done in discussions, that we never did have access to. In that sense our archival record was incomplete but not in the sense of extant documents. We had them. Nor was the study marred by a uniform prejudice among its authors. While the authors were by and large untrained as historians they had all sorts of different views about the war. I would say at least half of the thirty-six-odd people we had writing the studies were supporters of the war out and out, complete. I originally was a supporter of the war myself until about 1966. Some others had questions and a very few could be classified as doves.

Charlton: What about yourself, what were your own views?

Gelb: For that time I was classified as a dove. Even then my views changed over the years. I guess initially I was surprised that the leadership of the intelligence community was so clear-eyed about the difficulties of the war, about how long it would take to have a resolution of it, that did surprise me. At first I thought it demonstrated a good deal of cynicism on their part, for here they understood privately what the difficulties were and they weren't saying it publicly. It was a view that I held until much later. After I left the Pentagon and started to look at the public record I found by and large most public statements made by administration leaders over the years did indicate that it would be a long haul. But the statements that got the most attention, the most publicity, were those that seemed to indicate that peace was around the corner.

▌In 1971 the still classified and secret *Pentagon Papers* suddenly appeared in public print in *The New York Times*. The man responsible for passing them to the newspaper was Daniel Ellsberg. Ellsberg was to achieve further prominence when following the publication of *The Pentagon Papers* the office safe of his psychiatrist was burgled, as we know from the Watergate inquiry, on the orders of President

Nixon. Ellsberg had been one of what were deprecatingly called 'whiz kids' in the Pentagon. They were young academics recruited by the Kennedy Administration to work with the military on the apocalyptic scenarios of strategic nuclear war, involving intricate intellectual war games with missiles and bombers. Ellsberg's enthusiastic application is remembered as a sharp contrast to his also fervent and influential conversion over American policy in Vietnam. Ellsberg spent two years in Vietnam from 1964 as the ground fighting was becoming more intense and the United States faced the choice of losing the South or putting in its own troops to prevent a Communist takeover. He was recruited by John McNaughton, an Assistant Secretary of Defense and McNamara's desk officer on Vietnam, to become McNaughton's own assistant. McNaughton, who appears to have been a considerable influence on the thinking of McNamara, was killed in mid-1967 in an air crash in the United States. In due course Ellsberg, who spent most of his working life on secrets and in secret, came to the conclusion that secrecy in the case of Vietnam was for him no longer justifiable.

Ellsberg: John McNaughton, who was then Assistant Secretary of Defense for International Security Affairs, asked me to be his special assistant in the summer of 1964. He told me that he was McNamara's desk officer (as they said) on Vietnam, and that he spent seventy per cent of his time or so on Vietnam and he would want me to spend a hundred per cent of my time on Vietnam. Prior to that I had worked since 1958 in the Rand Corporation working with the Pentagon as a consultant, mostly on matters of strategic nuclear war and then on the question of crisis decision-making in the Government. So, I knew nothing about Vietnam to start with; I was anxious to see a decision-making process from the inside. I had an academic background in economics, specializing in the theory of decision-making, subjective probability and the analysis of decision processes. So my background was a little more suited to the process than most. Really these people were just in the spirit of staff assistants of various kinds, planning people as in every government; a peculiarity of America is the existence of a few research firms which are granted access to a large amount of classified information and that do work closely with the Government.

McNamara ran the Vietnam war inside the Defense Department very much from his hip pocket (as they say) from his own office. He dealt directly with the Joint Chiefs on this and he involved very little civilian staff planning. The fact is, McNamara was using McNaughton as a rather lowly assistant to manage this because he himself was acting as a so-called action officer on this. Thus I got involved in a process that very few civilians were really involved in. I came to the problem in 1964 at a time when the Government internal thinking on Vietnam was extremely pessimistic, very, very gloomy. That was especially true of my own boss, McNaughton, who actually wanted to be out as a result of this, although he loyally staffed the process of escalating the war in 1964 and later.

Charlton: But this period of course was accompanied by publicly expressed optimism.

Ellsberg: Public optimism. So from the beginning I was introduced to a great discrepancy between private gloom and pessimism, despair almost, throughout the year 1964 and early 1965; and a public impression during the election that the problem was under control and that there was no need for escalation. Everything that I did was secret in the sense of classified. Actually at one point the cable traffic from Vietnam was so overwhelming day by day that I asked that I received nothing but Top Secret or 'no dis.' (which meant no distribution) cables and that cut down my traffic to about five feet of cables, two piles two and a half feet high on my desk. So everything we did was secret from the public, all the lies that were being done, the illegal actions that were being prepared, the aggressive actions against North Vietnam, all of those were by their nature kept secret from the public—and a lot of other things as well.

Charlton: But what specific brief were you given by McNaughton? Was he asking you to prepare what in effect appeared to you to be preparing the way for an American withdrawal from Vietnam?

Ellsberg: Well, this reflected his own belief, I believe, that the situation was so bad in Vietnam (and he didn't differ in his appreciation of how bad it was actually) but he was able to imagine that it was so bad that it would be in the US interest to cut our losses and to leave. Thus it would be his job to give advice to McNamara on how to arrange that if it should be desired. But if you ask me in what spirit he gave me that I can tell you exactly, because it's hard to forget. He said: 'Don't use a secretary when you write this, do all your own typing; no one must know of this job, you must not tell your closest friends'—and he named some of them in the Pentagon, people who would normally have been natural for me to consult with. He said: 'And before you even do this I want you to be very clear that you could be signing the death warrant to your career in even working on such a task.' He said: 'Many people have had their careers ruined for much less than this'.

Charlton: Why should he emphasize the need for secrecy so much to you?

Ellsberg: Every American of our generation, even given the difference in our age, had vivid memories of the McCarthy period and the consequences for the Democrats of having allegedly lost China in the late forties.

Charlton: Was another possible reason for his secrecy, could I ask you, whether he himself was authorized to make such a study with such objectives—after all, preparing for the withdrawal of America from Vietnam?

Ellsberg: As far as I'm aware this was a rather natural form of his advance planning on a situation like that. What made it sensitive was simply, as I said, the self-evident possibility that such a policy change would lead to recriminations later.

Charlton: But what did he say to you, as he asked you to undertake it, and how did he define what he wanted you to do?

Ellsberg: What are better and worse ways to lose the war in Vietnam? What are the pros and cons in other words of a particular way in which we might choose to get out or be forced out of our involvement in Vietnam? Cutting our losses in Vietnam in 1964 would not at all have been comparable to quitting the war in 1965 or 1966 after we'd committed combat units and after American casualties had been accepted. In other words, this was the last time in which a loyal bureaucrat I think could conceive of it being appropriate for the US just to cut its losses and get out.

Charlton: What, if any, was the link between the study you undertook for McNaughton in 1964 and what subsequently became known as *The Pentagon Papers* much later?

Ellsberg: There was no direct link. The spirit of officialdom in Washington in 1967 and 1968 when *The Pentagon Papers* were put together was quite different from that in 1964, because in the interim of course we'd committed 500,000 troops. So in the summer of 1967 I'm not aware of a single official, junior or senior, who was seriously considering as a possibility that possibility that did occur to John McNaughton in the fall of 1964, some three years earlier, which was simply getting out. After the escalation of the bombing and then the troops in 1965 I, like essentially everyone else in the Government, accepted the feeling that we were fully committed in Vietnam. Now the question was how to succeed or to avoid failure, although most people who had been to Vietnam concluded after some tour there that we were not going to succeed in what we were doing; and after the Tet offensive in February 1968, essentially everyone—with the exception of Johnson, Rusk and Rostow as some people used to say —had concluded that our effort was hopeless in Vietnam. The effort of the Government still was carrying out the orders of Johnson and Rusk which had to do with continuing the war in Vietnam. To look critical of what we had done in Vietnam was not a dangerous position in 1967 and 1968. It put one in the mainstream of American opinion.

Charlton: Can you just clear up whether you worked for the Rand Corporation or the Pentagon at this time?

Ellsberg: I was being paid by the Rand Corporation; but in effect I was being loaned to the Pentagon for a Pentagon study.

Charlton: And in what circumstances did you leave the Pentagon, having started work on *The Pentagon Papers*?

Ellsberg: I just finished my study of the 1961 decision-making, went back to Rand, later came back and worked on the actual current decision-making in March of 1968 that surrounded the Tet offensive and Clifford's coming in and looking at new options. That involved me actually in higher level decision-making documents than I had seen since I'd been back in the Pentagon in 1964. Then I went back again to the Rand Corporation and volumes of the study became available: a number of them came out to Rand in California in the course of the study. Ultimately the entire study was deposited at the Rand Corporation by Paul Warnke, Leslie Gelb and Mort Halperin.

Charlton: Wasn't that unusual? How did the most intimate secrets of a country's diplomacy, which *The Pentagon Papers* certainly were, get to a private corporation like Rand?

Ellsberg: It's not at all of course unusual that Defense Department documents should get to Rand, and that's what these were. What was unusual was that they existed as a study. It is essentially universal for officials to take with them all the documents that have passed through their hands. One can assume for example that Henry Kissinger has in his possession outside the government many many thousands of pages, probably hundreds of thousands of pages, of top secret documents that he dealt with in the government.

Charlton: Having completed your study, how would you describe your own frame of mind about Vietnam and how committed were you to doing something about the ending of the United States involvement there?

Ellsberg: Well, my attitude changed quite a bit from 1967 to 1969.

In part that came from the fact that I learned in 1969 that a new President now, President Nixon, intended to continue the war. I had worked for the new administration—first in the Hotel Pierre in their temporary headquarters before they actually went to Washington—in December of 1968 and then worked for Henry Kissinger on Vietnam options in January and February of 1969. By the end of 1969 I knew from the people who had worked on those things with me in the Government who remained in, that he had chosen the option essentially of staying in Vietnam, contrary to what the people believed. Second, I had read *The Pentagon Papers* in the interim. That had a much greater effect on my thinking than even the two years in Vietnam.

Charlton: All of them? All *The Pentagon Papers*?

Ellsberg: What had particularly changed my impression was the earliest of *The Pentagon Papers*, which I had put off reading until the end because I thought them likely to be less relevant. To the contrary I discovered that they gave a perspective that nothing else did, they showed me that our intentions in Vietnam could not be described as legitimate ones.

Charlton: Which period are you talking about?

Ellsberg: 1945/1946.

Charlton: The very early period.

Ellsberg: Yes. There was no way of saying, as even say *The New York Times* likes still to say and President Carter still likes to say, that we went into Vietnam with the best of intentions; shoring up a colonial domination, the French colonial domination of another country, is not in the United States defined as good intentions. That's what we had done.

Charlton: So you came to the position that you were ultimately to take, after *The Pentagon Papers* had reached the Rand Corporation where you finished reading them.

Ellsberg: I didn't finish reading them until September 1969, and I began copying them to give to Senator Fulbright of the Senate Foreign Relations Committee that same month.

Charlton: You decided to photocopy *The Pentagon Papers*?

Ellsberg: Yes.

Charlton: Why?

Ellsberg: Nixon's policy was to continue the war in contrast to what the public had been led to believe in the 1968 election and in the course of 1969. Second, after reading *The Pentagon Papers*, especially the early parts, I discovered what was quite a new thought for me, that this policy could not be changed by working within the Executive Branch alone. My entire life, professional life, had been spent on helping the President ultimately have better information on which to base decisions. Suddenly it was apparent to me from this twenty-year-old history, more than twenty years, that a succession of Presidents had gotten quite adequate information on Vietnam, as realistic or as pessimistic as I could provide, and had chosen to continue the war.

Charlton: How did you actually do the photocopying?

Ellsberg: I took the papers outside the Rand Corporation overnight. I was the only researcher at Rand authorized to see them at all, so they were in my possession in my safe. The only other person at that time authorized to see them was the then President of Rand, Harry Rowan. So I took them from my safe out overnight to a firm owned by a friend that had a Xerox machine, and I would Xerox them all night and return them in the morning.

Charlton: You did the whole lot?

Ellsberg: Seven thousand pages.

Charlton: And alone?

Ellsberg: A few evenings I had help from my friend Anthony Russo, and on a few evenings from my son and daughter.

Charlton: So there was no selection made of the documents you copied, you copied the lot?

Ellsberg: No, on the contrary, I thought it was essential to have every line and every page there lest they be undermined by the charge that I had made some selection to stack the cards and to present an unrealistic impression, so I thought that even the boring parts and the parts that no longer seemed germane had to be there when I gave them to Congress, to make it clear that I had personally made no selection on it.

Charlton: And at this time you were still an employee of the Rand Corporation, no reason to suppose that you were going to leave it?

Ellsberg: You mean no reason by others to suppose that—No.

Charlton: And you had no reason to suppose that you would?

Ellsberg: Well, from the moment that I decided to copy *The Pentagon Papers* I expected them to be out shortly one way or another. I hoped that Congress would put them out in hearings. My mistaken impression at that time was that I must be violating some law by doing what I was doing. I was sure that would be taken very seriously and I thought I would be put in jail without bail.

Charlton: What law, for stealing the documents?

Ellsberg: I didn't know what law might apply. We'd often been told that it was against the law to copy such documents and of course in most countries, including the United Kingdom, it is against the law.

Charlton: Did you know all this at the time you were photocopying, did you go into all that?

Ellsberg: Everyone knew that there was an Official Secrets Act in England and that we didn't have, strictly speaking, an Official Secrets Act. But it was widely assumed that we had some functional equivalent of an Official Secrets Act. We were often told that in writing within the Government. That was a lie. In fact it turns out that the First Amendment asserts that the Congress shall pass no law abridging freedom of speech—and freedom in the press has always been taken by Congress and by the Courts to preclude any act like your Official Secrets Act. So the actual situation in our country is that the official government documents can be stamped Secret and Top Secret and so forth as an administrative matter, and one can be fired of course from the Executive Branch, as I expected to be fired, for disobeying the regulation of safeguarding those documents, but there is no statutory basis for that system. And in fact the Constitution precludes such a basis.

Charlton: Were you aware of this before you did what you did?

Ellsberg: No, I wasn't sure of that until I was indicted so my assumption was that I would be thrown in jail for the rest of my life.

Charlton: Yes, I mean there can have been little or no doubt in your mind that you were committing some kind of criminal act.

Ellsberg: I had no doubt, though I was mistaken. Of course I had no doubt, and was not mistaken, that I was doing something that my former superiors or my colleagues had not authorized me to do and would be horrified to learn that I had done.

Charlton: What, at the time, was your essential justification to yourself for doing what you did?

Ellsberg: Well, as I listen to that question now I wonder if it has occurred to you to ask any of the other officials that you have interviewed how they justify to themselves not doing what I did? Have you asked them what made them feel they had a right to keep their mouths silent about the lies that had been told that they knew of, about the crimes that had been committed, about the illegalities, about the deception of the American public. Each of them I would suppose, and I say that without even knowing which ones you've interviewed, has known such things, had the opportunity to tell the public or to give documentary evidence as I did, and again I say without knowing their names, none of them did it. I wonder how they justified that to themselves, did you ask them?

Charlton: No I haven't but I'd still like to ask you. How did you justify it to yourself?

Ellsberg: Well, I think that's implicit in the question I've asked. I came to realize that I had been very wrong in imagining that I had the right to conceal from the public all this information that had been in my possession as an official or a consultant all those years. Having discovered that I'd been wrong all those years I decided to start doing what I should have done in the first place.

Charlton: Having photocopied the documents what were your immediate intentions, what did you have in mind to do with them, did you have a specific objective?

Ellsberg: Yes, my intention was to give them to Senator Fulbright, and my hope was that he would use them in hearings of some sort.

Charlton: Did you approach him personally?

Ellsberg: Yes. He was very enthusiastic at the prospect of getting them. I handed several volumes to him personally, including in particular the volume dealing with the Tonkin Gulf. He had of course himself been abused by Lyndon Johnson and manipulated into being the floor manager of the Tonkin Gulf Resolution and having told him of the whole scope of the documents, I said: 'I've brought a few here with me right away, would you be interested in the story of the Tonkin Gulf?' and he said: 'Indeed I would' and he took it from me.

Charlton: Subsequently there were no Congressional hearings. Did Fulbright tell you why there were not?

Ellsberg: One result that did follow was that the Foreign Relations Committee under Fulbright did finally and belatedly vote to repeal the Tonkin Gulf Resolution; and later that came to a vote in Congress and it was repealed by Congress, although by that time the Administration said that it made no difference. As for holding the hearings that he had promised me, Nixon was so successful at deceiving the public on the subject of his having changed the policy from Johnson's that Fulbright felt that a history such as *The Pentagon Papers* would seem no longer relevant.

Charlton: Did his views about the nature of that history differ from your own? Did he draw different conclusions from *The Pentagon Papers* than your own?

Ellsberg: No, I think they even had little surprise for Fulbright, and there was no difference in interpretation. It was a question of how

the public would react and whether they would be seen to be relevant. As Fulbright said, after all they're only history.
Charlton: So how did the photocopies get from you to *The New York Times*, as they subsequently did, to become public knowledge?
Ellsberg: I first gave them to Fulbright in November of 1969 and had given them all to him by the spring of 1970. Several times it looked as though hearings were about to be held and they weren't. By the spring of 1971 two more invasions had taken place—invasion of Cambodia in 1970, the invasion of Laos in 1971. It seemed likely that escalation was going to go still further, as it did in the fall of 1971 with the renewal of the bombing of North Vietnam and ultimately the mining of Haiphong in 1972. So I felt that I couldn't wait any longer in informing the public of this history, for what it was worth, so that they could better exercise democratic influence on our policy there. There was a question as to what newspaper might be willing to print these. I went first to the *Times* because they are the most authoritative, and the most likely to print large amounts of documents.
Charlton: Did you give any advice to *The New York Times* at any time on publishing *The Pentagon Papers*?
Ellsberg: No, they did not turn to me in any way for any comment. In fact I didn't even know when or entirely if they intended to publish until it came out.

▌When *The Pentagon Papers* were made available by Ellsberg to *The New York Times* important constitutional issues were involved in publishing them. The Government intervened to try and stop them, the case went to the Supreme Court which decided by a majority of six votes to three that *The New York Times* could publish and that the First Amendment to the Constitution guaranteeing the right to a free press surmounted other considerations. James Greenfield of *The New York Times*, the paper's foreign editor, was placed in charge of the project to make public the revelations of the American involvement in Vietnam at a time when America was bringing home its troops but was still waging war. What issues were in his mind as he set about this task?

Greenfield: One of the first things we talked about was the privacy of government, not because we didn't want to publish but we wanted to know this hand grenade that we had in our hands, how it was going to explode. So we sat down and we asked ourselves questions that in effect our opponents would ask us: is this going to destroy the privacy of the inner governmental circles; in other words if we publish does this mean that no-one in an inner governmental circle can talk frankly to one another? Well, that argument was really destroyed by a great deal of research that we did. By then about forty or forty-five books had already been written by people who had participated in the Vietnam war discussions within the Government; and we very methodically, over a period of several weeks, indexed what was contained in those books. We decided that if there was ever any privacy it had already been destroyed or at least made public by this rash of books that were written by the insiders.

Charlton: But surely only by implication. I mean that it is one thing for books to draw upon sources from personal knowledge yet not to disclose them. Your decision had to involve the actual disclosure of the most secret interchanges at the highest levels of government in the country.

Greenfield: Right, what you're talking about is a matter of degree. Ours went a bit further I admit but the fact is that the basic interchange in government had already been revealed by the participants; we were adding quite a bit of meat to the bone, quite a bit of juicy meat.

Charlton: How did you satisfy yourselves that the documents which you had were not selective themselves to the point of distortion in that they had been selected by somebody who had taken an open and hostile position to the whole American commitment?

Greenfield: Well, that's a good question. As a matter of fact it went even further than that. We had to determine whether we thought they were real, the first thing we had to do, and we did this through cross-checks of people who were involved and whose signatures were on it; we did it very quietly and I don't think they ever were quite sure what we were doing—I know they weren't—to determine that the documents were real. Now whether or not they were slanted is something; the very weight of them sort of weighted against the slanting. What we wanted people to know was that this was what the Pentagon had put together and if you look at the final version, if you look at that thick book which we finally published, you will see that every paragraph in that book can have a numerical notation that comes from the documents.

Charlton: Now you say that the issue primarily for you was the privacy of government, but surely the context in which you had to consider privacy of government was the fact that your country was at war and you had nearly half a million troops fighting in Vietnam. Now how did you face up to that?

Greenfield: I think you have to look at it against the background in which we published. If the Government was weak at that time we the press—we *The New York Times* but we the press in general—had not done the weakening. The weakening had already been done in our estimation by the fact that a war was being pursued in which the powers in Washington already knew that literally half the country was strongly opposed to it, if not more. It wasn't a question of a sudden revelation of facets that would weaken an effort by a government. There weren't any great headlines in *The Pentagon Papers*.

We worried about other things of course, we worried about such things as codes, we were breaking codes. Was anybody going to lose their lives? Was anybody going to be killed by this? We went over those documents in a minute form, and I come back to our conclusion that we were printing perhaps instant history, I don't know. But certainly we were simply telling a story in more detail, in more perception, in more inside terms; we'd told the story already. Everybody had told the story about Vietnam, you know.

Charlton: Nevertheless public opinion may have got the impression that the documents *and* the comments were part of the Pentagon study. The comments you added were thought by those who actually took these decisions and acknowledged the authenticity of the documents to be highly contentious and distorted.

Greenfield: First of all we did *not* include the comments in the explanation of what was in the *Papers*. In other words we very purposely kept those stories about what were in the *Papers* absolutely separate and we separated our comment on them and so forth, pictorial comment and others. Let me tell you that when we first began writing the papers, when Mr Neil Sheehan and Mr Hedrick Smith wrote their first versions, we scrapped them because they had both been in Vietnam, they could not resist their own comments. We scrapped the first version, and believe me as an editor there was blood all over the floor because when you have somebody rewrite a seventeen-thousand-word piece from beginning to end you are in trouble already and we were all cooped up in several hotel rooms, never leaving them practically, so it was a very difficult thing. But the fact is we said, no, we want every paragraph, as I said, to come out of the *Papers* so that a footnote can be made and so forth. Those pieces have never been challenged because they all refer back to the original documents. Now we did something that no other newspapers did, when we dealt with the *Papers*. We printed the text, the full text of the documents which we were quoting and we did that very specifically because we wanted the reader to be able to go to the original document and make up his own mind. We also found that there is nothing that catches the flavor of a man, a policy, a thought, position, as to print the original documents and that's what we were criticized for. My answer to that was, if we are going to do the thing at all let the reader know right from the start from the horse's mouth what really was on that man's mind. Well nobody likes their memos printed in full but our feeling was that it was the only way to really get the ultimate flavor, not to run it through our typewriter but let the reader read it as it ran through their typewriter. Now we have been criticized for many things about *The Pentagon Papers*, and we will live with them.

My great disappointment is that *The Pentagon Papers* had relatively little impact except among people who learned things and so forth, but I'm not sure that there was any real lesson learned from them.

Charlton: You believe that they did have little effect on popular opinion?

Greenfield: No, I think they had effect on popular opinion, but I don't think they had an effect on the decision-makers. In other words I see no diminishment of secrecy within government, I see no attempt in the past years to build policies based on public opinion, nor do I think if I were a Congressman or Senator, do I really see any great desire on the part of government to share information with Congress. Now that all may change in the future but the fact is that those were the basic problems that *The Pentagon Papers* brought out.

Charlton: How did you assess public opinion at the time when you had made the decision to publish?

Greenfield: We even went as far as to tell the publisher that this paper could be wrecked. We warned him. We told him we didn't know what public opinion would be. We didn't know if suddenly we would wake up two days later and the public would say this is a terrible thing you have done. You know when we first talked to the lawyers they were absolutely flabbergasted because we said we had seven thousand secret documents, and we had to explain to them that we deal with secret documents every day. So that the principle was not whether we dealt with secret documents or not, because we get them all the time. But we get them one and two and three. They were just staggered by the numbers. We tried to say to them don't think in those terms.

Charlton: What was it sustained you really though, what was the fundamental thing on which you rested?

Greenfield: First of all we asked ourselves very frankly was this a good story? Then we tried to say why shouldn't this be printed, after all we have been printing stories for years now. After all we had a country as near an open psychological revolt almost as you could get, and we said isn't this information that the people of this country ought to have? What reasons would we give ourselves not to print this story, after all the things we've printed about Vietnam.

The Pentagon Papers themselves filled more than forty volumes, and the form in which they reached the public was the selection made from them by *The New York Times* with chapter headings and introductions to the selected documents made by the staff correspondents of the newspaper. William Bundy offers the comments of a government insider.

Bundy: You have to speak of three different things. You have to speak of the collection of documents themselves and of course they are authentic, there's no question of that. They represent a very substantial percentage of key decision-making papers, but they don't contain a great deal of the State Department files, they don't contain a great deal on some of the negotiations, they don't contain a great deal on our dealings with our allies and on the degree to which, at least in late 1964, early 1965, our major allies—including Britain—supported us or interposed no objection and said that what we were doing seemed reasonable to them. It doesn't contain a whole lot of things. It's the omissions I'm pointing to.
Charlton: Which would change the character?
Bundy: It changes the overall picture. It's an incomplete picture. Now that's the basic documents. Then you have the individual chapters that were written by this team that McNamara assembled, and they vary. Some of them are very good, and some of them are mediocre; but they're honest, serious efforts.
Charlton: Were they high level judgments?
Bundy: No. These were civilians, some with historical experience, some without; these were serving officers at the colonel level. They were a very intelligent group and they were as good a team as you could expect on this kind of project.
Charlton: But you don't recognize them yourself as being an accurate reflection in that respect of what happened?
Bundy: They were not a team assembled by Hugh Trevor-Roper and supervised every step of the way by him. They were not trained

historians. They had the original documents. You have the material written up by this team. Then you come to the *New York Times* stories based on this material and I must say I consider those, to put it mildly, uneven and in some respects quite misleading, particularly misleading on the 1964 period and whether there was a Johnsonian decision that he was going to get into this war, that he was concealing this during the election year, that the Gulf of Tonkin was a put-up job. All of that I think is historically wrong and put together by innuendo and by the misleading use of snippets of evidence, that it's bad history.

▌With the publication of *The Pentagon Papers* we have reached the years of the Presidency of Richard Nixon. Vietnam was now in turn his inheritance as it had been Lyndon Johnson's.

9
Trying not to lose

By the time President Nixon was elected at the end of 1968, there had been more than twenty years of warfare in Vietnam. Earlier in that election year, the request of the American military commanders for an additional 200,000 troops for Vietnam had been refused. President Johnson's denial of that request was a recognition that the strategy adopted since 1965, of seeking a military victory, was no longer achievable within a time and at a cost which was politically acceptable to enough Americans at home. President Johnson's decision to stand down and not to run for a second term of office, while at the same time largely ending the bombing of North Vietnam, had proved a sufficient inducement to the Communists to agree to open talks in Paris. For the first time since World War II it seemed that America was in retreat. It had been forced to seek a negotiated settlement to end the war. The new President's freedom to act was circumscribed by the need to placate American opinion and calm the unrest about the war at home. A steadily diminishing role for American troops in the fighting had been implicit throughout the Presidential campaign. President Nixon was compelled to start repatriating the expeditionary force. When he came to office, there were half a million American troops in Vietnam. Within two years, that figure would be brought down to 70,000, and the 300 American combat deaths each week, down to an average of 10. But the political commitment to the survival of a non-Communist South Vietnam remained, as President Nixon himself more recently reaffirmed—he was being interviewed by David Frost.

It looked to me at first that the reason for our being in Vietnam had perhaps not been adequately understood by the American people. I thought that Kennedy and Johnson were right in going into Vietnam. I was very critical of the way the war had been conducted—particularly President Johnson because of course he had the major responsibility—that they could have conducted it in a more effective way. I had some ideas as to what could be done; but I wasn't about to go down that easy political path of bugging-out, blaming it on my predecessors. It would have been enormously popular even in America, but that would have been at an enormous cost, eventually even to America, but particularly to the whole free world.

So while President Nixon had set in motion the disengagement of the American army in the field, it is clear that he was unwilling to accept a humiliating exit from Vietnam, because of the damage that that would do to the quality of America's guarantees elsewhere in the world. Informed advice to the American Government, was by now even more deeply divided about whether South Vietnam had the makings of an independent nation. Any analysis of its strengths and weaknesses depended upon how that question was answered. The Communist Tet offensive of 1968 had strengthened the hand of those who argued that it did not. And what therefore was left for Nixon to attempt? He made a new appointment to the Department of Defense, as Head of International Security Affairs, Professor Warren Nutter. When he went to the Pentagon, this was what the Nixon Administration had in mind.

Nutter: The question of winning militarily was really ruled out. There was no way at that point in time to bring to bear the kind of military force that would have been necessary to conclude the war. Although it was always possible at any time to do so, psychologically, politically it was just totally ruled out inside our country and throughout the world. We couldn't have done it. So there was no thought given to that. Now what were the other options? The other options were essentially three: that is, we could try to negotiate a settlement, which we were already engaged in doing, in Paris and Hanoi. We could simply abandon Vietnam, get out as quickly as possible—what some people referred to as 'a bug-out'. Or we could make an effort to train the Vietnamese to take over the responsibility themselves for defending the country and gradually withdraw our own forces, and reduce our involvement to one of providing them with the materiel and the equipment and the know-how to carry on their own defense. At the time the decision was made to go with a combination of negotiations and what later came to be known as 'Vietnamization', which was essentially the last option I mentioned.

Charlton: Now, would you agree that negotiation was controlled totally by Hanoi, at this time; that any concessions were entirely in their gift?

Nutter: Oh yes. There was no movement made at all at the negotiating table. It was ridiculous to even refer to the process as negotiating because they insisted from the very beginning that there must be a linkage between a military settlement and a political settlement, that the two could not be in any way considered separately, and as far as the North Vietnamese were concerned the only settlement possible was one in which we both lost the war militarily, gave up militarily, and simultaneously threw out the existing government in South Vietnam, so that the Communists could impose their own government. Since that was absolutely contrary to our commitment, we were in a position where no movement was possible at all.

Charlton: So this other option, as you say, was the process of what was called 'Vietnamization', turning over once more to the Vietnamese, going all the way back to the idea of the original involvement in the 1960s, that the Vietnamese ran their own war, aided by the materiel that you gave them. But would you agree that by this time it was quite unrealistic to suppose that a viable state could be made in South Vietnam? Was that accepted?

Nutter: Oh, I don't think that that was taken for granted at all. It certainly wasn't by me, and by many of the people in the Pentagon at that time. I don't know how much optimism there was in the State Department, that South Vietnam could still survive as a viable entity. But certainly where I was in the Pentagon we had not ruled out a stable state in South Vietnam at all. As a matter of fact by 1973 we hadn't ruled it out. When we *first* got involved, the thinking was in terms of providing the South Vietnamese with help to defend themselves and maintain a separate state. But then for a period, at least since 1965 for a period of four years, that had been completely abandoned and in fact the opposite course had been taken and we imposed upon them our own way of handling the military affairs, and had removed from them virtually all responsibility for any military action. They had virtually no responsibility left. And we suddenly, after Tet we decided to train them at least to protect against the Vietcong, against the internal threat, but never against the external threat. So our thinking was perhaps, one would want to say, simple-minded, but it was in these terms: 'Well let's try, let's see if we can't train these people and equip them to do the job. Why can't they fight as well as the fellows they're fighting against?' We were really, I think, more optimistic than you suggest.

▌That optimism was encouraged by the views of those who considered that the military strategy as so far conducted had got the priorities wrong. In addition it was by now more fully appreciated that the Communists had suffered crippling casualties in their Tet offensive, which while it was a political masterstroke which forced America's own disengagement, had left them temporarily at least unable to exploit their advantage. And in that particular respect the arguments were much like those which followed the defeat of the French at Dien Bien Phu in 1954. One voice to which President Nixon listened at this time was Sir Robert Thompson, who believed that there was an alternative strategy which would allow troop withdrawals to go ahead.

Thompson: What we had been saying was that the Americans were fighting main force battles, against largely North Vietnamese units and some Vietcong regular units. That in fact was practically all that they were doing. They were depending on this war of attrition, that they would be imposing such costs on these military units in casualties that they would give up. That wasn't the case. Now where I get criticized was: 'The Indians are coming through the windows'. Well, quite obviously you've got to stop that happening. But what the Americans should have been doing at this time was coming back to the main issue, which was what were they going to end up with? They still had to end up with a South Vietnam that was capable of doing this itself, and of surviving in these circumstances. In other words, rebuilding South Vietnam; building the South Vietnamese forces; building the organizations inside South Vietnam to manage a war of this nature; rebuilding the South Vietnamese economy; regaining control in the populated areas. These were, in my view, the priorities. Here you've got to make a very clear distinction between priority and effort. I accept that if the Indians were coming through the windows you'd got to use a major effort to stop that. But that was not the priority. This was a containment operation, which you'd got to do while you did the priority tasks of rebuilding the South. That is where the Americans failed absolutely between 1965 and 1968.

My first advice—at this period—was given to Dr Kissinger, while he was still adviser to Governor Rockefeller of New York, and before Nixon had been elected. I had a long talk with Henry, in which I said that the American strategy should be changed to one of containment of the North Vietnamese, and going back to these priority jobs of what came to be called pacification and Vietnamization. If the Americans did that, they would be able to withdraw 100,000 troops in the first year, there would be such an improvement in the internal situation. You've got to remember that one of the reasons for this was that the Tet offensive had in fact destroyed most of the Vietcong regular and regional units inside South Vietnam. In other words they had nothing, or very little, left to defend their rural base areas with. This enabled the South Vietnamese to regain control in the countryside very rapidly, which is what happened between 1969 and 1970. I've never been so staggered in my life at the speed with which control was regained in the countryside.

I American public opinion had long been proved to be a powerful factor in the strategy of war for the Communists. Hanoi relied on the war's unpopularity with the American people to force a total withdrawal. For their part the Americans now wanted to give a less impatient strategy a try—one which would substantially reduce American casualties, and make clear to Hanoi that by their own efforts they could not bring about a withdrawal of American forces. Sir Robert Thompson believes that Nixon wanted to win the war, if he could. A fresh trial therefore of will and endurance was coming. The Paris negotiations initiated under President Johnson made no serious headway. Here is Mr Nixon's 1977 summary of what he considered was negotiable during his first term of office.

> *We decided we needed a new approach. And the new approach that we developed was that we would have a mutual withdrawal of all American forces and all foreign forces—including, of course, North Vietnamese forces—within twelve months of an agreement, and a supervised election and a supervised ceasefire. That was our first step. As the months wore on there was no progress in Paris on that. They turned thumbs down whether it was a question of first stopping the bombing, which they said might bring progress in the negotiations; and then they said we had to have something with regard to withdrawal. Now, we'd offered mutual withdrawal. They said: 'No, that isn't enough.' And so we got down to the bottom line with them very early, a line they hung to right into the last, until 8 October 1972.*
>
> *As far as my ideas as to how we could bring the war to an end, we should continue to negotiate and try to find some new formula that would bring the two parties together. We should combine that, if negotiations reached a dead end or a roadblock, with increased military pressure, because we thought that with increased military pressure that that might help. As far as that complete military pressure was concerned it was to be combined with training the South Vietnamese forces so that they could take over more of the burden of the war—because, as Vice President Ky pointed out, several months later I believe it was, 'the Americans have captured our war'. And that was the case when we came in.*

The later judgments of those involved in the new policy of Vietnamization were more skeptical in retrospect than they remember being at the time about the underlying will and determination to support it. Did people like Warren Nutter, at the time, believe that in leaving Vietnam they would indeed leave something behind which would prove self-sustaining in any reasonable time?

Nutter: Yes reasonable, I think. In the Pentagon we never thought in terms of less than four years as we sat down and looked at the problem just of getting our own people out.

Charlton: But ten years? Fifteen years, what?

Nutter: Ten or fifteen years, we would have thought, yes, as a reasonable timetable. That is to say, if we had withdrawn our forces in four years, we expected that they were prepared to defend themselves, if we gave them the materiel. Then another four or five years of survival, and growing experience, and improving political stability and maturity or whatever one wants to call it. That of course is a very short period of time in history; but we felt, yes, they could make it.

We always assumed, I think, from the very beginning—at least as long as I can remember back—that the North Vietnamese would pause only long enough to lick their wounds and prepare themselves once again for a push such as they had executed in the Tet offensive, and that this would just recur from time to time. And our estimates were that it would take them two or three years to put themselves together and re-equip and regroup and then that they would come back. So that at all times I think we were fully prepared for this kind of activity, this kind of warfare. And it came as no surprise to us whatsoever when they attacked full scale in 1972.

Charlton: But to make Vietnamization credible did you suppose that that could go on and on, and that the United States would fund the process?

Nutter: That's a much more difficult question, and I don't think anybody was so optimistic as to believe that this was going to be a simple thing to accomplish, that the American public or the Congress and so on would just carry on forever. And, of course, looking back, one knows that this is exactly what the North was counting on all along, that sooner or later we would run out of patience.

The conviction of the Communists in Hanoi, that the Americans would run out of patience, was also of concern to the South Viet namese, in whose name Vietnamization was being undertaken. President Thieu had little option but to accept the new policy, and in many ways welcomed it as returning some of the sovereignty over their own decision which the Americans had exercised alone. But the South Vietnamese were nervous about the pace of withdrawals of American troops and appealed directly to American public opinion for understanding. As Thieu commented in 1970:

It is very clear that the Americans have not withdrawn from Vietnam. When we talked about withdrawal, when we used the word withdrawal, that means abandonment and I don't believe the Americans will abandon South Vietnam. I think now the situation permits us to go progressively along. So we have no reason to retain them forever here, and we have to replace them: that's quite normal. But the replacement of US troops by Vietnamese troops should be gradual and very progressive. It takes years and years, but we are now feeling more and more confident and we try to do our best to alleviate the burden of US people. And I think if the Vietnamization plan is very well done, it's the best solution for us, and for the Americans too.

There were two components to the policy of Vietnamization, that was handing back to the Vietnamese the war which Air Marshal Ky told Nixon: 'The Americans have captured'. The first was the strengthening of the South Vietnamese armed forces, the second a renewed attempt to police and pacify the villages of South Vietnam. With the strategy of attrition pursued from 1965 until 1968 largely discredited, President Nixon's closest advisers were now men who had opposed it. Among them was one who had been intimately involved with Vietnam almost from the beginning of the American commitment, William Colby, who had been Station Chief of the CIA in Saigon in 1959, and later in charge of the Far East Desk in Washington, under Lyndon Johnson. President Nixon sent Colby out to Vietnam in 1969 with ambassadorial rank to take personal charge of the new priority—pacification.

Colby: I think the strategy of attrition to me was not an answer to the war. Because what you're talking about was an attrition of North Vietnam. This then led to the bombing of North Vietnam, and I think CIA's assessment of both the bombing of North Vietnam and the major military actions was that they really were non-conclusive: that the real war was at the village level. If you could strengthen the village you would recruit away the potential enemy. He would be on your side. He would be holding your self-defense gun instead of holding the infiltrated AK47.

Charlton: Were there any votes for the Americans in the villages of Vietnam after the period of attrition was over?

Colby: Well there were still a lot of people who were still fearful of Communists. That is a characteristic which I think is frequently not appreciated sufficiently. There were literally millions of Vietnamese who fled from their homes, toward the government. There were very few who fled toward the Communists, the reason being they wanted to live in this kind of society that they hoped for on the government side—a nationalist society, one with some degree of protection, one with some degree of economic hope. They felt that on the other side there was regimentation, the Communist control. There was also the danger from the American bombardment, clearly. There's no doubt about that. But there was equal danger from being bombarded in the government centers by the rockets and so forth from the Communist side. The refugees in great part did vote with their feet, as to which side they preferred, and which side they thought would give them some hope for the future.

Charlton: But one of the impacts of attrition must have been enormous war-weariness, a disposition to give up.

Colby: I must say the Vietnamese are a very tenacious people. And you found very little of that. You had also in addition to the fear of Communism—literally Communism on the part of many South Vietnamese—a concern about the North Vietnamese. You had the regional difference which is a very important difference in Vietnam, between the South and the North. And this fear of being dominated and run from the North was a real factor in their approach towards the North Vietnamese. I think therefore that you can't say that either votes were lost or won by the program of attrition. I think that was a military fight that was sort of in my mind. It was essential at a certain period, but it was not the strategy that was essential in order to win the battle.

Charlton: Can I ask you to address yourself to the program which has aroused a good deal of criticism in the United States among opponents of the American ambitions in Vietnam, the so-called Phoenix Program. What was the Phoenix Program?

Colby: I'm delighted, because this is one of those things which is grossly misunderstood, and I think dangerously so. Fundamentally a political program, all these different programs to support a political result, of letting people choose which side that they would be on, helping them if they chose the government side. Now, one feature of that is that they had to be free of North Vietnam divisions, which is what the military did, to keep those away. The other thing they had to be free of is a secret apparatus within the population which would shoot them, which would kidnap them, which would otherwise terrorize them into support of the Communist insurrection. Now you could go around and try to protect them against that, and not be successful, unless you knew what the enemy was, who they were. This was a problem of knowing who members of the secret apparatus were. During the rather chaotic years of the mid-sixties, Vietnam was a very dangerous place on both sides. There was a lot of very brutal and unpleasant things that happened, as these two apparatuses—the Communist apparatus and the government apparatus—struggled against each other. There were grenades in market-places, there were assassinations and there were killings and all the rest of it, between the two forces. The Phoenix Program was an attempt to apply to the government side of that struggle some proper intelligence techniques, so that it would be efficient, and some proper standards of behavior so that it would be acceptable to 'American standards'. Item: instead of just accepting an accusation that somebody's a Communist in order to put his name on a list, and result in his being captured or something, insistence that there be three separate reports from different sources, proper dossier built up as to who this person is, description of his job. Is he a leader, is he a chairman of a committee, or is he just a simple follower someplace who has to go out and do his service because the other side is around?

If it's the latter, forget it. We're not interested in him. We're only interested in the so-called A and B categories, not the C categories of the enemy apparatus. Rules about how long people could be held, how they would be treated in the detention procedures, training and proper method of interrogation rather than torture. Torture is obviously abhorrent to a moral standard. It also just happens to be non-efficient, because if you want good information you'd better use good techniques or you'll get bad information. If you use bad techniques you will get what you want to hear instead of what's really the case.

There are techniques for proper interrogation: the use of the mind, the use of other information, clever approaches toward the handling of prisoners which all armies teach, proper POW interrogations, a variety of programs of this nature to define precisely what the enemy was, who they were, to make sure that the targeting—and it is targeting—to try to capture these people; capture is not kill, obviously they're not much good if they're dead. But if they're alive they have information. Capture them, get them to accept the amnesty. This was what the Phoenix Program was.

You've heard the statistics about the Phoenix Program. 17,000 identified people in the apparatus chose the amnesty. 28,000 were captured. 20,000 were killed. This is frequently turned into an accusation that 20,000 were assassinated. That is not true. 20,000 were killed mostly in military actions. The fight takes place outside the village tonight. Several people killed on both sides. You go out in the morning to see who they were. Sure enough you find Mr Jones lying there, he's the head of the local guerilla squad. He was on your list as the head of the local guerilla squad, thanks to your intelligence. You were hoping to capture him if you could. But in the fight that took place he happened to be killed. He didn't take amnesty, he wasn't captured. He was killed. But he wasn't assassinated. I issued directives against participation in assassination by any Americans in any way. I further said: beyond that I insist that if you hear of any involvement in one, you are not to turn away and ignore it, and say that that's something for the Vietnamese, none of my business. You are to object, and you are to tell me. And a few of our advisers did tell me and I took them up with the government, Prime Minister, and I had people punished for their role in that. I think then that the Phoenix Program was the application of proper intelligence techniques to a necessary battle and to conduct it on a proper level instead of an improper one. Did it a hundred per cent succeed in that? No. Did it essentially succeed in that? Yes. Because I think that while some things may have happened that don't fit anybody's standards, they were reduced and almost eliminated thanks to the Phoenix Program.

▌The Americans were under no illusions while they made this renewed effort at pacification that the Communists would launch no major attack again when ready. In an attempt to forestall that and also to give a forewarning of the response to be expected from him, President Nixon had sent American forces into Cambodia in 1970, into the sanctuaries where the Communist guerillas trained and rested and which they used as jumping-off points for major military actions. Some of these, on the Cambodian border, were only fifty miles or so from Saigon. When the President did that, back in America the campuses of the universities exploded. At Kent State in Ohio, the national guard fired on a crowd and killed four students. So the President discovered anew that there would be violent constraints at home to his use of American forces in ground fighting.

As President Richard Nixon faced the campaign for re-election to his second term in 1972, North Vietnam made *its* move and the bombing of the North was resumed. Sir Robert Thompson again:

Thompson: Whatever the critics may have said about pacification and Vietnamization the North Vietnamese and the Vietcong understood that it was working and that they were in fact losing ground inside South Vietnam, that the South Vietnamese strength was being built up in all senses. Therefore they had to do something about it and the only instrument that they had left to do anything with was the regular army of North Vietnam, and they put it in in March 1972. We knew it was coming—we didn't quite know how much or exactly when and where. They put in twelve divisions. Now, naturally when you do an initial attack with twelve divisions you get some initial successes. Everyone thought the South Vietnamese were going to collapse but even in the north where the third division gave way, the North Vietnamese only made eighteen miles in three weeks, which isn't exactly an electric advance. This was partly, of course, because the South Vietnamese held in the north, they held at Kontum and they held at An Loa. Now the fact that they held on the ground made it possible for American air power then to inflict enormous casualties on the attacking forces, because here we were dealing with mass troops, and we were dealing with troops using T.54 tanks and all sorts of things that are targets for an airforce. So the casualties inflicted on the North were twice what I had expected.

Moreover, in the bombing of the North, you had now got not bicycles carrying down petrol in water bottles, you had to have trucks if you were going to keep T.54 tanks going, if you were going to keep 130 mm guns firing you had to have trucks and trucks and trucks, thousands of tons of stuff a day, absolutely made for an airforce to hit. The invasion was smashed by American air power. In July 1972 the South Vietnamese started their counteroffensive and with three divisions recaptured Quang Tri against six North Vietnamese divisions. The South Vietnamese at that time, thanks to good luck, coincidence or good planning, had their units back up to strength, whereas the North Vietnamese were down to 50 or 60 men in a battalion, their recruits coming in were 16- and 17-year-olds.

The whole thing was just about to change in South Vietnam. So what did the North do? They said: 'We'll negotiate'.

▎The months before this all-out invasion of the South by North Vietnam we know today were marked by a period of statecraft and secret diplomacy conducted by Henry Kissinger in which he and President Nixon sought to change the whole context in which Vietnam had been viewed. It transpired that Kissinger had been meeting secretly for three years with a member of the Politburo of North Vietnam in the Paris home of Jean Sainteny, who contributed to the first two chapters of this book. Also in July 1971 the White House had announced that Kissinger had been to Peking secretly to see Chou En-lai and Mao Tse-tung, and that President Nixon himself would visit Chairman Mao in 1972.

It seems that this was the time when Vietnam was beginning to be seen by President Nixon and Dr Kissinger as an episode rather than an all-consuming concern. In which case, was Vietnamization at heart a fig leaf concealing another and more fundamental change?

Nutter: With hindsight it's become more and more clear to me that probably the leader of the Executive Branch, President Nixon, was more interested in finding some, as you call it, fig leaf to cover a fundamental change in our posture in the world than anything else; and I am not at all sure that wasn't the main interest of Henry Kissinger at that time.

Charlton: But as far as you were concerned in occupying your high position in the Pentagon at the time, you believed that you were genuinely implementing a policy which was meant to last and was meant to be credible?

Nutter: That's right. I may have been too naive, but I took it all quite seriously and I think that the Secretary of Defense [Melvin Laird] took it quite seriously and sensed that we were going to make a real genuine effort to provide an alternative solution to this problem.

We felt that the United States had made one of the most solemn commitments and the most clear-cut commitments of its existence to protect the principle of self-determination for South Vietnam, and that if we failed in one way we should find another way to succeed; and that we shouldn't just abandon this in a kind of cynical way and go on our way. In other words I thought we were trying to do something along that line, but I'm not at all sure that that was joined by everyone. Moreover, leading up to the second election of President Nixon it became more and more clear that the timetable that was set for various benchmarks in foreign policy was geared almost exclusively to the elections so that it was imperative that Vietnam be settled by 1972. There was just no doubt that that had to happen, because otherwise it would be an election issue that would not be favorable to the President. Similarly the whole unwinding, or the beginnings of the policy of détente and so on, the haute politique—all of that fitted into what now, as one looks back, seems to be a timetable designed primarily to ensure a re-election with a mandate.

Charlton: So within the highest reaches of the Government, you're saying that there was a secret diplomacy which you knew nothing about which was in fact trying to achieve the opposite ends of your own efforts?

Nutter: Oh yes. There were always two tracks for everything. At that time Henry Kissinger was fond of speaking about different tracks simultaneously—but the second track in almost every case was a secret one, which involved him and the President and a very few other people. So there was also a kind of an official process going on of negotiation; and then there was the real process of negotiation, which was behind the scenes and known only to him.

Both Kissinger and Nixon have yet to give their own accounts of the secret diplomacy of their time. As Professor Nutter reminds us they are the only witnesses for their own intentions. As for the Vietnam negotiations one account in particular, though, has won the approval of Kissinger himself as being 'substantially correct'. It was compiled after long inquiry by Tad Szulc, one of the senior political writers in Washington, and published by the authoritative journal *Foreign Policy*.[1] What then was Kissinger's position as the North Vietnamese and he began serious negotiations to settle the war in July 1972?

Tad Szulc: I would say that it was a concept that the war had to be ended within a certain period, a certain time frame which evidently he conceived as being the first Nixon term in office.

Charlton: Do you believe that Kissinger was given freedom by the President to make that essential concession? In other words, to give up, if not the guarantee, the support of the idea of a non-Communist South Vietnam?

Szulc: I think there were several levels of perception here. In the first instance I would say yes, Kissinger believed that this was a desirable

[1] 'How Kissinger Did It.' *Foreign Policy* No. 15, Summer 1974. Washington.

objective. I think there's no question that Nixon did give him his own ideological background and his view of the world. So in that sense the two of them were on the same wave-length. Now what happened subsequently was the way this whole concept began developing in other directions. What I did not know, which I think is enormously fascinating, is whether Kissinger himself ever had doubts in his mind whether it was feasible. Or better still, at which moment did it become clear to Kissinger that this could not be attained and therefore such concessions as allowing North Vietnamese to maintain their forces in the South after cease-fire would be required? I suspect that Kissinger realized this shortly after he began his secret meetings in Paris with the North Vietnamese, maybe sometime in early 1971.

Charlton: That was the essential concession wasn't it, that a cease-fire in place (as it came to be known after the agreements were signed) was in fact giving up the guarantee of non-Communist South Vietnam.

Szulc: I would think that by any standards of reason, by any standards of appreciation of what a guerilla war is, by any standards of looking at the military deployments in South Vietnam on the part both of North Vietnamese regulars and Vietcong regiments, evidently cease-fire in place meant two things: one, that you have given up, or are giving up the notion of 'mutual withdrawal', and two, that you're inviting inevitably a new war with other American Presidents.

Charlton: Your article claims (and Kissinger himself has agreed that 85 per cent of it was absolutely correct) that Kissinger's disclosure to Brezhnev that the Americans were not going to insist upon withdrawal of forces from the South appears to have astonished the Russians. Now he weakened his whole position by disclosing that, because he believed that it was not just desirable to have a settlement in Vietnam. A settlement in Vietnam became of overwhelming importance, as far as Kissinger was concerned, to fit his whole strategy of détente with the Soviet Union.

Szulc: Therefore you sacrifice certain objectives for other objectives. I think a decision had to be made that if we were going to go into high gear into détente with a summit then you had to bring the Vietnam thing to an end in some coherent way. I think at that point Kissinger had to concede (or Nixon, this we do not know): if I do want to move with détente then maybe this late in the game of three years or three and a half years of war under Nixon Administration with no end in sight, with more and more troops being withdrawn, that you simply have to make that concession even if you don't make it publicly. Do you weaken your position? Of course you do, but without options. This is where the famous Kissinger remark which (without direct attribution) I quote in the article becomes very relevant—the remark being that essentially Vietnam was a cruel sideshow to the larger objectives of American foreign policy. Once you've said that, you've said everything.

Charlton: He made this remark at exactly this time?

Szulc: In this time frame in the context of these negotiations, these moves, and I think everything that's happened since bears out that this was really what he was talking about and what he had in mind, it would seem to me, looking back at the record now.

All the time the Americans were going ahead with their withdrawal of combat troops from Vietnam it left them less to bargain with and more vulnerable to a volatile issue: the fate of their own prisoners of war. They were mostly pilots shot down over the North and now housed—as they themselves called it sardonically—in 'the Hanoi Hilton'. The release of the prisoners could only be achieved by a negotiated settlement, and was therefore a fundamental counter for both sides. Warren Nutter at the Pentagon had personal charge of the prisoner-of-war question.

Nutter: When we came into office we discovered that, as I think was generally known in any event, the fundamental decision had been made in the Johnson period not to say anything about the prisoners, that this was to be treated with official silence. There were various rationales on the basis of which this decision was made and the basic one put forward was the feeling that saying too much about the prisoners and so on would invite more difficulties for them, because they'd be maltreated in any event. When we came into office very few people were aware, in the American public or anywhere else, of how many prisoners the North Vietnamese held and what kind of conditions they were being held in, and how they were being treated and so on. So, we had to face the question of what our policy should be, and we made a decision very early on that we would go public on the problem of the prisoners. We would do our best to educate the public and the world at large on this problem as quickly as possible, and that for three reasons: first because we were convinced this was the best way to ensure better treatment for them, we knew they were being maltreated, tortured, in the most crude ways.

Charlton: I'm interested that you should say that. What was the nature of your information about that?

Nutter: I wish I could tell you all, but I mean we did know. We knew very definitely that this was happening and I don't think it would be in the best interest of future problems of this sort to say how we knew, but we did. We knew they were being mistreated and we knew that many of them were in solitary confinement and so on. After a lot of soul-searching we felt that the best leverage we could bring to bear to get better treatment was to expose the problem to public view and turn the searchlight onto the North Vietnamese so that they would behave better. Secondly, we wanted to get them released as quickly as possible, and that meant that we were going to have to get this issue into the negotiations and if we were going to have any success there we felt we had to have a preparation of public opinion behind us on that matter. And third—this is closely related to the second objective I think—is that we wanted to avoid the prisoners being used, being held as hostages for various political and economic ransom that the North might demand of us in the process of negotiating and reaching a settlement. We felt the best way to avoid their using the prisoners that way was to make it a public issue so that we could bring to bear the humane attitude of the world on this matter. So we did go public as quickly as we could.

Charlton: With what response?

Nutter: It was very difficult to get the matter before the public. It took us much longer than we ever imagined to get any serious public discussion of the issue. The media didn't respond very well. It was, I would say, an uphill fight to get this out as a matter of common public knowledge, but we managed after a couple of years.

Charlton: Presumably because there were equal and opposite suspicions that the Nixon Presidency was using the prisoners for political purposes?

Nutter: Yes, I think that's fair to say. I think there was a feeling on the side of those who'd come to oppose the war absolutely that this was an effort to get some public opinion behind the war by using the prisoner issue. I'm sorry that that was the feeling because I don't believe that was ever the intention.

Meanwhile the draft of an agreement during the second half of 1972 between Kissinger and the Communist government of North Vietnam made clear that the Americans had given up their insistence of many years that there should be a mutual withdrawal of forces—their own and North Vietnam's. The draft left the Communist forces in the South and also gave to them there an equivocal jurisdiction. When this was made known to President Thieu of South Vietnam he refused to accept it in the form in which it was put. Thieu, execrated by the North and opponents of the war elsewhere as an American puppet, was to show at least a substantial measure of his independence by proving obdurate. There was also a feeling at high levels in the American Administration that Kissinger might have conceded too much too soon. Did they encourage Thieu to hold out for improved terms?

Szulc: I could not document it. We do know things like, for example, General Haig [his deputy] looking with certain alarm at that which Kissinger was doing. On the other hand, Ambassador Bunker, who had his influence in Vietnam, I think was closer to the Kissinger—shall we say—flexible line than people like General Haig. So I think in that sense Kissinger's problem was not so much the White House as President Thieu—who of course was involved in a battle of survival which at first was political.

Charlton: And who saw it for what it was.

Szulc: And who knew exactly from the word go and who saw that document, the first draft, he knew exactly what it meant, because he knew what the deployment of troops were and he knew what the chances of violation of the 'one-for-one' replacements and so on were. You'd have to be very foolish, which he was not, not to have realized it. But one may wish to say again, to use a Kissinger comment which I will paraphrase, to the effect that OK, this is certain, we have to end the war, but before we do it two things have to be done. Number one, we have to make South Vietnam as strong as possible, therefore, the two programs known as Enhance 1 and Enhance 2 which were the massive deliveries of aircraft, helicopters, whatnot, to the South Vietnamese. And the second objective being to make North Vietnam as weak as possible at the time of peace—and that I think to a very large extent, at least in my mind, explains the fury and the magnitude of the so-called Christmas bombings in 1972.

But before that in October and with Thieu still holding out, the North Vietnamese had broken the secrecy in which the negotiations had until now been conducted. They cried betrayal and they published the essentials of their understanding with Henry Kissinger.

Szulc: They went public—Hanoi radio came out on a day in October 1972, virtually giving away the essential aspects of the agreement. The famous so-called virtuoso performance by Kissinger took place at the White House, in which he said, yes indeed, this is essentially correct that peace is at hand—and this is October—and then suddenly it developed that peace was not at hand because we still did not have Thieu ready for delivery. Then we went back to Paris. There was a situation in which we re-opened certain points and then, sometime in December, Kissinger took the view—presumably obviously with Nixon's assent and knowledge—that the North Vietnamese have been 'taught a lesson', and again this also related to what we were discussing earlier which was the need to make Hanoi as weak as possible at the time of the ending of the war.

▌President Thieu's objections concerned the old and fundamental issues. Thieu wanted improved supervision of any cease-fire and rewording of the agreement to make clear that the proposed National Council of Reconciliation and Concord, in which the Communists would participate, was not to be considered a government of the South. Sir Robert Thompson believes that Nixon was once again the dominant figure at this critical time.

Thompson: The rock was Nixon. When there was a breakthrough at the negotiating table and the North went back on a lot of things that it had previously been insisting on, like a coalition government and so on, were prepared to leave President Thieu in power and so on, this was the breakthrough point. Kissinger at that point would have signed that initial agreement before the actual election in order to ensure the election. Now this was at the end of October, with the election on 4 November. Nixon refused. He said it wasn't good enough because the enforcement clauses were not there, or not sufficient enforcement clauses. In fact the enforcement clauses never really got into the agreement.

▌It is clear from Warren Nutter that President Thieu was not the only one who thought Dr Kissinger had overridden some legitimate objections to reach agreement.

Nutter: Exactly what went on between Kissinger and President Nixon at that time I think is known only to them. We'll perhaps get either consistent reports or contradictory reports when they write their memoirs, I don't know.
Charlton: But would you agree that there was a dramatic contrast

between Kissinger's expedition to Hanoi—he announced that 'peace is at hand', he came home, the peace was found to be unacceptable, he was sent back and then Hanoi was bombed—there appears to be a curious moment there where Kissinger and the President were not aligned in their interpretation of that peace?

Nutter: I think that statement on Kissinger's part was one that he later regretted. I think it was hasty. Already at that point in time, if I remember the timing reasonably well, it was clear that all the matters had not been settled at all, and in particular that Thieu was not happy with the wording of the agreement and was going to present a problem.

Charlton: But more specifically than that, that Kissinger was willing to settle for less than Nixon was: is that a possible interpretation?

Nutter: That is possible, yes, if you mean that he was willing to settle for fewer assurances of North Vietnamese adherence to the agreement ultimately. I think that is conceivable.

Charlton: He presented Nixon with that as a negotiating triumph which after a period of consideration was rejected.

Nutter: That may have been the case, but on the other hand by that time enough was known in other parts of the Government so that the President was receiving comments and advice from other quarters as well, that this agreement had not been buttoned down and that there were problems with the South Vietnamese. Some of us felt that the South Vietnamese were raising quite legitimate questions, and so I'm not sure that the President was completely in the dark about the alternatives.

So it was that the negotiations once more stalled, the Americans launched a major wave of air strikes against Hanoi in the two weeks before Christmas 1972.

Hanoi was the most heavily defended target in the history of war. It was surrounded by thousands of anti-aircraft guns and missiles, and more than twelve hundred Russian missiles were fired off at the raiding aircraft in ten days. The American losses initially were heavy, including sixteen of the giant B.52 strategic bombers. But in the end they overwhelmed the defenses. Their new laser-guided bombs were more accurate than anything used before. Industrial capacity in North Vietnam was virtually brought to a halt. Within days the American bombers roamed with impunity over the North. The casualties announced by the North Vietnamese were 1200 civilian dead in the fortnight.

Nutter: I think it was important in getting the prisoners released, but fundamentally because it led the North Vietnamese to believe that it was in their interest to sign the agreement that had been virtually signed before they said 'we won't negotiate any more'. Whether the North Vietnamese were hoping for something happening in the election, I don't know, but in any event they broke it off. I think the important thing about the bombardment, the bombing around Hanoi, was that it made them think again about this, and they decided maybe they'd better sign the agreement. Of course, the agreement committed them to so very little that could have been verified or counteracted that I think the decision was a pretty wise one. Otherwise they could have suffered some much heavier damage. Bombardment taught them I think several lessons—and maybe taught the Russians some lessons—because it was a little embarassing to have B.52s flying in daylight over a city which was defended by Soviet missiles and being successful in very precise bombing tactics. I don't think that was the fact that got the prisoners released. I think the prisoners got released because the North Vietnamese finally agreed to sign the agreement.

Charlton: How far do you think President Nixon might have been prepared to push that threat? I'm thinking of the invasion of Cambodia, and if you take another example both that and the bombing of Hanoi were seen at the time as a strategy deliberately contrived to produce uncertainty in the minds of the Communists as to what he would do. You couldn't be certain that he would do this, but you couldn't be certain that he would not. Now for that itself to have been credible, do you say that there might have been a moment where that bombing could have gone much further?

Nutter: Oh yes. The bombers were actually very careful not to bomb the heavily populated sections of Hanoi. Some bombs spilled over and there were some mistaken runs and there were some civilians killed, but not a great number. You look at the numbers the North Vietnamese released, it wasn't all that many civilian casualties, and we were always very careful about that. But it was crystal clear from the fact that the bombers were there and that they managed to drop them. They dropped them exactly where they had planned to drop them and if they wanted to move into the center of town there would have been no trouble at all.

This was actually of course the problem that existed at the very beginning, 1969. If we had been prepared to go in for saturation bombing or anything on the order of what was done in World War

II for example, in my own opinion the war could have been ended very quickly at any time. This was considered morally reprehensible and inexcusable and so on. So whether he could have actually done that or not I don't know, but I think that the North Vietnamese were sufficiently uncertain, and sufficiently afraid that he might, they didn't want to take the chance. Of course it wouldn't have been necessary only to do that, there were various governmental headquarters and so on, all of which were pretty well-known, that could have been bombed. I don't understand why the North Vietnamese didn't sign the agreement to begin with, because they weren't really running that much risk. I think all the way along they were more cautious than necessary as history has shown—because of their experience back in the early 1950s, when they felt that they'd made a terrible blunder not to insist on a political settlement; and here South Vietnam had survived. But by this point in time for them to have imagined that the United States would go on indefinitely supporting the South seems to me was a bit too cautious.

One other point perhaps was of significance to the judgments being made by the Americans at the critical time of the final negotiations which ended their own involvement in the war. By 1972, Nixon's personal nemesis had begun to loom for him.
Szulc: Well, now we know it—I didn't obviously know it at the time, we didn't know in 1972—how deeply Nixon was enmeshed from the very beginning in Watergate. I think we tended to underestimate at the time how deeply concerned he was with it. He also had a campaign to run, because there was an election, as you recall. To what extent did his attention flag, it's very hard to say. As you go over Nixon's public activities during that year, the people he received, and his appointments in the White House, public speeches, the conferences, he seemed to me very much engaged in the formulation of planning of foreign policy. Yet, Kissinger himself perceived that there he was going through the motions more than being actively involved. We don't know, I don't know, whether Kissinger realized himself at the time, how deeply he, Nixon, was involved in Watergate and how his attention was being diverted; it's a very fascinating point.
Charlton: I was going to ask you exactly that, whether Kissinger realized that the authority of the President was slipping and that that gave Kissinger a freedom of maneuver.
Szulc: I certainly would not exclude it because there was a very interesting combination of human beings. A very insecure President

psychologically, and in his own way a very insecure Secretary of State—Secretary of State subsequently, National Security Adviser at the time—who played his own insecurities against Nixon's.

▎The bombing of North Vietnam in 1972 had produced a world outcry but also a signed agreement. While the Hanoi government had accepted terms by October which they had previously rejected, such as the right of the South to self-determination in supervised elections and the participation of the Saigon government in a new National Council of Reconciliation and Concern, they also forced a cease-fire in place—which left them with 120,000 guerilla soldiers in South Vietnam. There are bitter critics of the December bombing of Hanoi who say that the improvements to the draft were insubstantial, measured by the reality. Among them is Paul Warnke. Could any better agreement have been achieved?

Warnke: I think we could have ended up with a much better negotiated settlement back in 1968/69 than we finally got in 1973.
Charlton: How would this have materially differed?
Warnke: I think there would have been the possibility of some sort of a political compromise in the South, but the longer the war went on, the weaker the political situation in the South became. So finally in 1973 there wasn't anything they had to bargain with.
Charlton: But are you saying seriously that you think you could have got withdrawal of the North Vietnamese forces from the South? That's what the issue was.
Warnke: Not without some sort of a political compromise, and our trouble was we weren't prepared to compromise politically. That was the real difficulty.
Charlton: But that's why I'm querying when you say that you could have got a better settlement. You may have got the same settlement, not a better one?
Warnke: No, no, I think we would have got a considerably better one; we'd been prepared to decide that you could not preserve the political status quo in a negotiated settlement. The problem was all through our negotiations that we weren't prepared to settle for anything that would mean Communist participation in the government of South Vietnam.

Of course the North Vietnamese and the Vietcong weren't prepared to settle for something that meant the continuation of the Nguyen Van Thieu government in control in the Independence Palace, so the consequences of the negotiations in that were serious. So eventually what it came down to was a negotiated unilateral withdrawal of American troops.

Charlton: It's the difference, isn't it, in time scale. In 1968 you might have got a disguised sellout, if you're talking about introduction of third-force politics into the Saigon government, the National Liberation Front.

Warnke: Except I would not characterize that as a disguised sellout. I would have regarded it as being an opportunity to determine just what the political balance of forces was in South Vietnam.

Charlton: A disguised sellout in the sense that it was the abandonment of the original aim of a non-Communist South Vietnam.

Warnke: That is absolutely correct. I don't call that a sellout. I call that a realization that you had been wrong.

Paul Warnke resigned to return to the law. But President Nixon's own appointment to the same office was Warren Nutter. The day after the Paris agreements were signed in 1973, he too resigned from the Government. His own disillusion was a forecast of what was to eventually come.

Nutter: Yes, I thought that was a good time to leave, the 28th of January.

Charlton: Can you tell us why you thought it was a good time to leave and what your own views of those agreements were and their consequences, and how divided American Government was at that time over the desirability of that kind of settlement?

Nutter: I don't want to suggest at this point in time, and being able to look backwards and see all the events that happened, that I was prescient and I knew exactly all the difficulties that were going to come about and that I wanted to get out beforehand. Fundamentally my decision had been to leave in any event. I didn't feel that the agreement was really going to be enforced, and that it left the South Vietnamese in a terribly vulnerable position with most of the Northern troops still in place and able to be reconstituted and built up and all the rest. And I didn't have that confidence that we would continue to support the South in the way that would be necessary. I quite frankly didn't think the agreement was the best one we could have gotten, and so I then felt that it was better just to go on my way and let someone else worry about the problems.

Charlton: What sort of an agreement could have been got do you think?

Nutter: The President I think *had* created an atmosphere of uncertainty. He had been re-elected by a very wide margin. I think with a bit more persistence we could have gotten better guarantees of withdrawal of the Northern forces, or could have gotten better protection for violations. 'Better' means at least something. We could have created some kind of a mechanism for responding to violations which would have at least had some legitimacy and so on, which we didn't. In fact the North wasn't in all that strong a position at that time to insist on all the points it had been insisting on—so I think we could have given the South a much better chance.

Now as everything evolved afterwards I'm not sure that would have made a difference anyhow, because when the chips were down we pulled the plug, we decided—if I can mix up that awful metaphor—we decided we just weren't going to give them the gasoline, we weren't going to give them the bullets and so on, and that made the position just impossible, and so they were defeated.

10

South Vietnam—shadow or substance?

To Marxist theoreticians the Communist victory in Vietnam was the victory of class struggle and a vindication of its precepts. The final triumph over the nationalists in the South and the Saigon government was held to be the historically inevitable triumph over a westernized bourgeoisie, which perhaps too conveniently ignores the fact that the Communist leadership itself came largely from the same class and were themselves the sons and daughters of that bourgeoisie, the 'Frenchified elite' in Vietnam.

When the Americans took the decision in 1963 to overthrow President Diem—the Catholic nationalist leader that they had supported for nine years—they transferred their support to the generals of the armed forces. Out of this new meritocracy of the army which they wanted to create they believed would also come a more vigorous political leadership to achieve the goal of an independent non-Communist state of South Vietnam. Nguyen Cao Ky was one of the younger officers, born in the North and one of the million Vietnamese who came South in the exodus of 1954 when Vietnam was separated into two zones at the time of the Geneva Agreement. Ky was a pilot of an undoubted personal courage, who became chief of the air force. He emerged from the spate of coups which followed the assassination of President Diem, to become Prime Minister in 1965. He seemed at the time to symbolize that more aggressive will to withstand the Communists which the Americans were anxious to cultivate and promote. Later when Ky's personal rivalry with General Thieu—another member of the governing High Army Council—threatened more political instability, he stood down from an attempt to become President of South Vietnam under the new constitution. General Thieu became President and Ky his Vice President almost to the end, until Saigon fell to the Communists. Stepping down to accept the lesser post of Vice President was, according to Lyndon Johnson writing much later,[1] an act for which Ky had received insufficient credit.

---

[1] *The Vantage Point*. Holt, Rinehart and Winston, New York, 1971.

Air Marshal Ky was a flamboyant romantic. His reputation was tarnished by frequent allegations that he was in some way involved in opium smuggling out of Laos. (In this chapter he comments on these allegations.) He was a man of some sensitivity who read and wrote poetry. Those who were in Saigon in the early 1960s, in the days before the American commitment became so large that it diverted attention from the voices and efforts of the Vietnamese themselves, will remember how each Sunday afternoon at a quarter to three an aircraft used to fly over the city. The pilot was Ky. It was the time of the political shambles and the immature coup-making which followed the overthrow of Diem, and from the air Ky would shake an aerial fist at the plotters and the Army barracks below, and so give warning of the consequences which he could cause to fall upon them if they pursued their distracting personal ambitions any further. Ky was present throughout, personally engaged, and himself a later symbol of the lost cause in South Vietnam. He got out at the very end. In 1977 he was living in a relatively modest house in one of the straggling suburbs of Los Angeles. He kept a liquor store and was the acknowledged leader of a large community of 40,000 or so Vietnamese who were washed ashore with him on this western beach of the United States after the last collapse, one of those in whose name America's longest war was undertaken and lost.

I first asked Nguyen Cao Ky about his family background.

Ky: My family is some sort of mandarin family. My grandfather, great-grandfather were mandarins. My father was a teacher, but he belonged to the old generation of Vietnamese. He was very influenced by Chinese culture and tradition. He was very against the French domination. That is why he quit as a teacher and in his last few years he did nothing except hunting in the jungle in North Vietnam and where just before the take-over by Ho Chi Minh in 1945 he was helping the resistance in any ways he could.

Charlton: The resistance against whom?

Ky: Against the Japanese occupation at that time. Because of his many trips to the jungle he got sick and died when I was twelve years old.

Charlton: What about your own sympathies when you came to have them politically, were you yourself at first sympathetic to the objectives of the Vietminh?

Ky: At that time you know that all the Vietnamese nationalists were fighting hand by hand against the French and against the Japanese.

So we were united at that time, and we didn't know anything about Communism.

Charlton: And nothing about Ho Chi Minh himself?

Ky: No, no.

Charlton: It was a name completely unknown to you in Vietnam?

Ky: At that time, yes, But after the defeat of the Japanese in World War II Ho Chi Minh became a national hero. But after that when the Communist Party with Ho Chi Minh at the head started the destruction of other nationalist parties such as Vietnam Quoc Zan Dang and other parties, and after they organized the country under the Communist way, the things they did to us made all the Vietnamese see more clearly what Communism is. The way that they pushed people against other people, the father against the son and daughters against mothers, at the so-called public trial. When you see your own son denounce the father, that is something in a thousand years we Vietnamese could not accept, that kind of philosophy.

Charlton: Can you tell me a little bit about your own ideas at this time. For example you wrote a lot of poetry, didn't you, as a young man.

Ky: Oh, as a young man I always dreamt about flying or farming. Those were the only two things.

Charlton: But did you write poetry as a young man?

Ky: Yes, because you see most of the pilots, and I mean the good pilots, the true flyers, are some sort of poets.

Charlton: When you equate flying or wanting to fly with poetry what do you mean? Did you have a romantic idealism like the sort of thing that the French fighter-pilot, Saint-Exupéry, expresses in his poems?

Ky: In a poor country a hundred years under French domination, flying high in the sky is for all of us something that is untouchable, very difficult. But for the poor Vietnamese young boy at that time it was a dream, so I seized the first chance to be a pilot.

Charlton: How did you get that chance, where?

Ky: I was second lieutenant in the army with many thousands of my friends from the college and high school. We were *drafted*, contrary to some unfriendly press outside. They always reported I was an officer in the French army, in other words I fought alongside with the French colonists against the Vietnamese people. It was not true. I never served with the French armed forces. I was drafted by the Vietnamese government and I spent ten months in the Military

Academy in North Vietnam and I graduated as a second lieutenant of the Vietnamese army. I served in an outpost near Haiphong for about three months. Then when I was there in that small outpost I received a note from the Minister of Defense. They asked for volunteers for the air force. So after passing examination I was accepted as cadet, and because at that time we didn't have any flying school in Vietnam they sent us, the first group of pilot cadets, about 35 or 40 of us, to North Africa, to Marrakesh in Morocco. I graduated in basic training. I went to France for two years for advanced training both in transport and bombing and strafing. Then I come back 1954 just after Dien Bien Phu and after the division of the country.

Charlton: By this time the Kuomintang and the Nationalists had been defeated in China, the Communists were on the frontier with Vietnam itself, and the colonial power had been defeated at Dien Bien Phu. So what did you as a young Vietnamese nationalist believe it was possible to do after those two enormous events?

Ky: Well, I think we knew that acceptance by the Communists at Geneva Conference about the division of the country was just temporary and they would come to the South some day. So at that time we were busy to build a new strength in South Vietnam.

Charlton: And were you convinced that it should be possible to do that?

Ky: Because I have the firm belief that the majority of the Vietnamese are against Communist doctrine, the Communist way of life and way of thinking.

Charlton: Did Korea have any influence on you as a model for what might be achieved, a demarcation line drawn across the country, partitioned into two, into a non-Communist and a Communist section.

Ky: No. You remember when I was commanding the air force, and when I was Premier I always talking about unification, and I always told my fellow countrymen that Vietnam in the past was divided at one time for a hundred years, but at the end Vietnam was unified again. So this time when Vietnam was divided in 1954, I always believed that history would be repeated, and some day Vietnam would be unified again. And it happened, but this time the Communists achieved that historical goal, unfortunately not us, not the non-Communists.

Charlton: Did you believe that it was going to be vital for the armed forces to play the essential political role, to be the instrument, not just of salvation of Vietnam, as you saw it, but also the instrument of social change as well?

Ky: It's my opinion, not because I am a military man, but I firmly believe that the military should play a dominant role because when you look at the countries in Latin America, in Middle East, in Africa, in Ethiopia, in Asia, in Thailand, in Taiwan, in Korea, all those poor and undeveloped and newly independent countries were governed by the military. Vietnam is not like Britain or America, where the military are apart. As I said earlier, I was drafted. The government closed all the schools, so all the young generation of Vietnamese at that time were drafted. So the military people in Vietnam were not apart, so I think it's stupid to make a distinction between the military and the people because we *are* the people.

Charlton: On the other hand this brought you into conflict immediately with the Americans who were trying to encourage the formation of civilian governments which would win respect and authority, not just in Vietnam but in the outside world, in the United States in particular. Were you from the very beginning skeptical about that?

Ky: I think that's something wrong with American knowledge about Vietnam. I said we are a people's army, we came from the people, we are not a different class. Second, as a representative of the vast majority, we were fully aware of our historical responsibilities, particularly myself. I always thought that my responsibility was to build a strong Vietnam, to stop Communist aggression, and second to bring to the people happiness and justice, social justice.

Charlton: What was your attitude to the coup against Ngo Dinh Diem? Did you play any active part in that yourself?

Ky: No. At that time I was a junior officer. I was a lieutenant-colonel and I was commanding officer of a small flying unit, the first air transport group. So I was not really actively involved in politics. But concerning Mr Diem, well, like Ho Chi Minh, in the first five years he was really a popular man. Myself and my family, we are not Catholic, but I really encouraged all my family to go and vote for him. Before he came to power, he was very popular, he had a very good reputation as a nationalist, and I think we really respected him. Actually, you know, I really admired him, and most certainly he was very popular and I can say that it was the first really honest Presidential election in Vietnam. But then five years after that, in 1963, after five years in power, absolute control, I think Mr Diem thought that he was God. At least he believed that he had some message from God to stay there and govern the way he thinks was God's policy.

Charlton: How important is the Diem episode for you as a Vietnamese and a leader of Vietnamese nationalists in retrospect and at the time? How important did that episode of his overthrow and assassination seem to you?

Ky: It is very important, very important because it was a big turn of history, whether the overthrow of Mr Diem was wrong or right. But right after that you see a big big enthusiastic atmosphere among the population. Big Minh [General Duong Van Minh] at that time was treated as a big hero. It is no doubt. But again what was wrong was that you eliminate Diem and replace him by a bunch of generals who were more dumb than Mr Diem himself. I still believe that at least Mr Diem had some ideal to serve, but the group of general officers who replaced him had no ideals at all. I think they were old, corrupted and not capable to carry out the so-called revolution that they used for bringing Mr Diem down.

Charlton: What impact did the fact that the Americans had conspired in the coup against Diem, at least promoted his overthrow, have on the future relations between the Americans and you in the military, their allies?

Ky: I think since the Americans helped that group of generals to come to power, I had the feeling—because you know I was an outsider and too young and I can see more clearly—I think most of them, the Vietnamese generals, had the feeling that they owed something to America. And because they always look at Mr Diem with big fear and respect and now they see that, well, the Americans can do it with Mr Diem, so with them there is no way that they could go against the rule of the Americans because they will be eliminated right away. Even Thieu, Thieu after he became President, he was the typical general officer belonging to that generation. Every time he discussed a problem with me, particularly for the negotiations in Paris, when I come back to tell him such things he only asked me what the Americans think about it. Thieu always worried about America. He believed that the Americans could do everything. That's why most of the time he tried to please America.

Charlton: Now after the assassination of Diem came a dreadful period in the war for the South Vietnamese, and successive governments within the space of a very few months and then your own coup...

Ky: I ask to stop you. I never staged a coup. I never had my own coup.

Charlton: Well I didn't mean you personally, I meant the military take-over from civilian government.

Ky: No, on the contrary I was against a coup. Any time I was involved I was on the side of people who were against the coup. I have always been against the internal fight among the military to have power. When I took over the civilian government there was no coup and I never asked the civilians at that time, Mr Suu as Chief of State and Mr Quat as Prime Minister, I never asked them to step down and hand the power to me. On the contrary I remember that night because Mr Suu, the Chief of State, and Mr Quat, the Prime Minister, they belonged to different political parties, so there was a conflict. As a Prime Minister, Mr Quat proposed the law in something, some project, and Mr Suu refused to sign. So that night Quat as Prime Minister called on us, the Military Council, at his office [8th June 1965] and he said: 'I cannot govern, I resign and I hand the power to the military'. That is all.

Charlton: Can you tell us about the earlier occasion when Ambassador Taylor attacked you all, you younger military leaders?

Ky: That is right after the military had taken some measures against the so-called High National Council at that time. It was a figurehead body with Big Minh and the other old politicians. They were sitting at the Palace and talking about politics and trying to—well, they talk, never act—and the Military Council decide to get rid of them. General Maxwell Taylor was Ambassador. He had just come back from a trip to Washington where he told American President, 'Well we have stability, we have the garrison, we have the government, we have the military, everything is fine'. Then just as he came back to Vietnam that thing happened. Well, before that, when he just came back from Washington, he invite us at his home for a dinner—myself, General Khanh and a few other members of the Military Council—and he told us that that is what he spoke to Washington and he doesn't want to see any trouble, any coup happen. And right, two days after that, in fact, Khanh took the decision to get rid of all the High National Council.

So that morning we meet together at the headquarters of the general staff, and Maxwell Taylor call Khanh. I don't know what they talked about on the phone, but after that Khanh told us that Taylor wanted to meet with a few of us down at the American Embassy. So Khanh point to me and said, 'You go Ky' and I said 'OK'. So I went down with Mr Thieu. When we entered Maxwell Taylor's office he looked pale, very very angry. He didn't say hello to us, he just said, OK sit down and he really gave us a lecture as an old general officer teaching the young officers. He asked why we did that. I think I was the only one to answer him. I said: 'Mr Ambassador, we did it because we think it is good for the country, for Vietnam.' He said something about his dinner. Maybe I misunderstood it, but what I understood at that time was he told us that: 'Well, I invite you for dinner, I tell you what we want and you did something different. I think I waste my dinner.' I told him, I said: 'Listen, you don't waste your dinner because I can tell you Mr Ambassador that I never had a such good piece of steak. As a poor man in a poor country I never had the chance to eat such good steak that you gave to us. So you really don't waste your dinner. No, I really appreciate your dinner.' So that is what I told him and after that I left the Ambassador.

Charlton: This dressing down Ambassador Taylor gave you all, isn't it perhaps an interesting reflection on what the relationship between the Americans and the Vietnamese military leaders really was? How did you react to the way he spoke to you that night?

Ky: When we came back to the headquarters of the general staff and when I report the conversation to the session of other members of the Council they all were very angry; and you know what, they want to call right away a press conference and tell the press about Ambassador Taylor's attitude. I think the Americans heard about it, so they send someone to us really asking us not to act that way. I remember this man. He said: 'We will not worry about Mr Taylor as Ambassador, but he was some sort of hero among the military and we spent years and years to make a hero, a military hero. So please don't destroy it.' I think the guy is very smart because when he made such an appeal to us we agreed right away.

Charlton: But there was a specific reason, wasn't there, for Taylor's displeasure with you? It came at a moment when the Americans were about to undertake the bombing of North Vietnam for the first time to achieve two things: to make possible a more stable government in Saigon, and they believed that bombing the North was a necessary recipe for that to encourage a greater degree of resistance in the South, a more cohesive resistance; and of course they wanted to signal their readiness to take reprisals against North Vietnam for its continuing attacks. So were you completely unaware that this campaign was about to be undertaken of bombing the North? Were you not consulted or informed about it, or did you take your action knowing that that was coming but not believing it would have the effects that it did?

Ky: At that time I was commanding officer of the air force only, so on all the political decisions between American and Vietnamese I was not consulted. I wasn't aware of that and I doubted that even the Vietnamese government at that time was consulted by the Americans. I don't think so, because with my experience later on I think all the important military or political decisions were made in Washington, and they let us know maybe twenty-four hours warning.

Charlton: Did you try and protest about that yourself?

Ky: About the bombing?

Charlton: No, about the lack of consultation on policy. Did you believe that you had a contribution on policy planning to make?

Ky: I protest many times by expressing my opinion, by telling them what I think. After I become Premier I have many meetings with American officials—including President Johnson on many occasions—and on each occasion I told him what I think was the right way to deal with the war and to deal with the Communists and to deal with South Vietnamese people. Most of the time the Americans just smile, and very politely, but the problem is they never listened to me. They never did the things that I asked.

Charlton: You have longer association with Americans than most Vietnamese at a very high level, and of course your knowledge of English made it possible for you to converse with them in the same language. Can I take the last point that you made first about the difficulty of relations with the Vietnamese and the Americans. What were the difficulties do you think, were they cultural for the most part?

Ky: Yes. I remember the first time I met with the Ambassador Cabot Lodge when he come back the second tour, and Mr Lansdale at that time accompanied the Ambassador to meet with me at my office, and I remember I mentioned to Ambassador Cabot Lodge when he asked me: 'What is your government program of policy?' and I told him just two words. I said: 'Social revolution'. After the session he said to me, he said: 'Well you know, I don't think it is good to mention the word "social" and the word "revolution" to the Americans. They are reluctant about "revolution"; and about "social" because it sounds like Communism.' I said: 'Now look, there is a big difference between Communism and Socialism. And why revolution? Isn't that what we need here in South Vietnam, revolution.' So you see that is, in my opinion, the basic difference between Americans and we, the Vietnamese. I see the need of a complete change in South Vietnam in everything, but the Americans didn't see it or they saw it a different way.

Later on you know, when I had to deal more often with Americans, I realize the difference was really big. For example when we talk about the way to stop the expansion of the Communist ideal. As one American official told me: 'Well if we give to the Vietnamese in the South a bigger house, more material, more facilities, in other words give them a really high standard of living, and more luxurious living, they will not listen to the Communist propaganda'. I tell them: 'No, it is not true.' The Vietnamese have a very little need for material; but for spiritual things, yes, this is more important. A Vietnamese can be a happy man even if he is a poor man, but you see that is a different thing. The second is I told them what Vietnam needs is a man like Ho Chi Minh for the North Vietnamese, a true leader for the Vietnamese, not an American man. But that they never understand.

One Ambassador, when the people ask him about Mr Thieu and myself he said: 'With Mr Thieu I feel more comfortable'. That is typical American. They come, they make friends and they try to support people with whom feel comfortable. What does that mean? It means the 'yes man'. With me it is the contrary. I knew at that time that none of them felt comfortable with me, even Mr Nixon. I remember when in 1971 I had a breakfast at the White House with Mr Nixon—and Kissinger and four or five American officials were there—and I told Mr Nixon at that time about the effectiveness of American aid. I said to him that most of the money you give to us went to the pocket of a minority, corrupted American and Vietnamese. I think he was not happy the way I told him. When I said it, our Ambassador sitting next to me, he really give me a big kick under the table. But that is the way I deal with them. They don't feel comfortable with me.

Charlton: You were saying that you were convinced that a successful stable government in the South did not depend upon the material advantage for the people provided by the Americans. But what was the sort of spiritual quality that you thought it should be possible to bring? It needed strong leadership to begin with, but what else? I mean, how would your own revolution have differed from the Communist variety?

Ky: As I went through the ranks and spent all my time with the soldiers—I am not the sort of a general who got promotion you know spending his time sitting behind a desk—so I can say I know exactly what the feeling of the majority is. As you know, at that time because of war so there are a lot of profiteers, particularly among the officers in the government. So what happened to the Vietnamese society at that time was a minority on the top profit everything from war while the vast majority, particularly the military, had nothing. So when you see a captain going to the front and leaving behind a big family and knowing that his wife, his children didn't have enough to eat you can't expect him having a high spirit for fighting; so my idea at that time was to give the best to those who deserve it. I mean the military, the fighting soldiers.

Charlton: How could that have been achieved and why wasn't it?

Ky: Well, if you can take out the money first, take the money from the pocket of the profiteer and give it to the poor, to the soldiers. Second, that if you receive from America and use it to improve the poor, the standard of living of the poor. In other words what I call a 'social justice'.

Charlton: How did you view the arrival of the American armed forces in such large numbers? The disadvantages of that were plainly obvious to both the Americans themselves and presumably to you, the danger that the Americans would be seen as the return of the colonial power; but how was that whole episode viewed by you?

Ky: When they decided to bring troops it happened before I become Premier. I had nothing to do with that. Later on many occasions I told President Johnson. I said to him: 'Now if you mean to bring maximum, big number of American troops then we should go right to the North, use all that military power in a very short period of time to get rid of the military war. But if your policy is to sustain alone, and sustain a war then that kind of a war should be fought by the Vietnamese and in that case we just need a very limited number of American soldiers.'

Charlton: And when you put that argument to him what was his response?

Ky: I even told him that when you look at the North Vietnamese we know that without big help from China and from Russia they cannot sustain a long invasion in the South, but we never see and we never heard about the Russian or Chinese in the North. Here in the South all we hear every day every hour is the Americans say this, the Americans do this. Where were the Vietnamese, where the nationalist Vietnamese in the South? So I told him why don't you just do the same thing. Stay in the back and let us do the fighting, let us perform the show. As I said earlier to you, everything I told them, they just smiled to me, very friendly, very politely but the next day they did what they decide.

Charlton: What is your short answer, if there can be one, to perhaps the essential difficulty that I think the South Vietnamese faced successively in world opinion, which was the belief that the Americans were acting in support of an essentially corrupt power?

Ky: It was true, and it was true when the Communists' propaganda condemn us as not nationalists but 'a puppet and lackey of America'. The way that the Vietnamization was implemented was the wrong way. When they handed the fighting responsibility to the Vietnamese, they handed to the people that they felt comfortable with. One general officer, Vietnamese, he was well known among the Vietnamese as the most corrupted and incapable officer. Every American who came to me said: 'Oh, he is a real tiger'. That is the reason why at the end within 30 days the whole army of a million men collapsed, not because the poor soldiers are less courageous than the North Vietnamese but because all the commanding officers at that time were cowardly and corrupted.

Charlton: Of course you yourself have been tainted by the charge of corruption. How do you answer that yourself?

Ky: That's the only thing that I can say I am very proud of myself, and that's the only thing maybe now I regret, not to be corrupted.

Charlton: The suspicions or open charges that you did have some interest in the opium crops in Laos. What do you say to those?

Ky: I knew that there was a lot of traffic in drugs and everything. I think every people were involved in it in Vietnam during the war, the soldiers, the air force, the marines, the navy, the government. I knew that in some cases the Vietnamese air force were involved in it. When they fly to Laos and Cambodia for a military operation, and when the plane come back the crew brought some drugs, opium. It happened and I knew about those cases. But it doesn't mean me, Prime Minister Ky, that I was involved in it.

Charlton: How were you unable to stop it?

Ky: Impossible. Not only because it was in war, but also because I was the only one among all the officers, military and civilian, in trying to clean the house. I could do it but it would take me five years or seven years, but not here and now.

Charlton: As a Northerner, you had many difficulties as a political figure with the population of the South who don't like people from Tonkin. How big a factor was that in preventing a cohesive approach in the South and putting an end to its sectarian squabbles and strifes, the fact that so many of the political figures in the South had come from the North?

Ky: You see, that kind of a feeling, I think it existed only in the mind of a group of the Southerners, but not among the population because I knew for sure that I am more popular among the Southerners population than among the Northerners because I *feel* closer. You see most of the Southerners living in the Mekong River, in the Delta, most of them are peasants and they like a cock fight, they like a drink—and I like the same thing. I am very popular among them. So you should make a distinction when you talk about the politicians in the South and the people in the South. Second: I think the press and in particular foreign press, the American press you know, they really blow it up out of dimension.

Charlton: Can you deal with the question of bombing and the extent to which in your own view it alienated?

Ky: I think all the Vietnamese in the South were supporting the idea of having the military forces go straight to the North and clear it out within a period of about two or three weeks, particularly among the military in South Vietnam. You remember that the first time we were allowing to go North I—as commanding officer of the air force at that time—I led the mission and when the Vietnamese pilot heard about we were going North the next day and only a limited number of aeroplanes will go, I had to draw the names of volunteers. The spirit of going North at the time was really high and for all the Vietnamese both military and civil. It was what they were expecting for years and years. But again it was a limited action.

Charlton: What about the bombing in the South itself in support of military campaigns against the Communists there? Do you believe that that did have, as many do, catastrophic effect on the peasants and in their will to support the South Vietnamese government, or has that been exaggerated?

Ky: I think that none of us want to see it happen in South Vietnam, a massive bombing, a massive evacuation of people out of their village, out of their home and leave the land uncultivated. It affect the production of the country—particularly the defoliation program. None of us, particularly the peasants, don't want to see it happen but at that time we had no alternative. We are not against it but we feel that the bombing in the South to support the ground operations intensified day after day. We realize that the military situation was not good in South Vietnam.

Charlton: But do you want to leave the impression that the bombing was being carried out on heavy centers of population or not? [No!] In my own experience that was not the case, the bombing was taking place in relatively sparsely populated areas.

Ky: No, because we gave very strict orders. When the ground troops asked us first to bomb the area where they think the enemy was, but then when our fighters flew over and see mixed with the Communists are a big number of civilians, they always report back and ask our final decision whether we go ahead and bomb, both the civilian *and* the Communists. Most of the time we said no, wait until they were separate.

Charlton: When did you know the war was lost?

Ky: A few minutes before the end. I am a soldier. I always believe that even at the last second you can save the situation or die there right in the battlefield. So you see as a soldier you stay and fight until the last second, so until the last second you still have hope.

Charlton: What was your attitude to the Americans at this final phase where Vietnamization had collapsed? You were not being re-supplied to the extent that you were supposed to be under the 1973 Paris Agreement, the Congress had cut off aid to you. Can you describe how you felt personally in those last few months in Saigon with time running out?

Ky: I still feel—and I tried to tell Mr Thieu and other Vietnamese leading figures—that I still believe that with the massive aid from America as we had had years before, with what we still had on hand, I think we could save the works. Now it doesn't mean that I still believe as years before that we could go ahead to the North and overthrow the Communists. But I think with a little chance within the government and the military we could stop their advance. And from there with more stability, more strength from this within the South Vietnamese we could stop them military speaking, and from there we could talk with them about a new political settlement. In other words even accept a coalition government with the Liberation Front or have an open election with them participating in the election.

Charlton: Well that is a fascinating thought which I have not heard expressed before. It was always resisted very strongly by you earlier. What on earth was the inducement to enter a coalition with the Communists at such a late stage as that?

Ky: We were realistic men. When you see that you couldn't achieve the whole accomplishment and then you have to try to achieve part of that. You can't save the home, well at least save the furniture.

Charlton: Earlier, in what frame of mind did you go to Paris yourself for the negotiations? What was your own strategy there on behalf of South Vietnam and how did it fit do you imagine with what the Americans proposed or what you assumed they had in mind?

Ky: We went to Paris for the negotiations knowing that we had not only to fight with the Communists our enemy but also to fight with our friends, the American delegation. I think that is why Mr Thieu sent me to Paris, because then I will be the man who says No to the Americans and to the Communists; and then Mr Thieu will say Yes, particularly dealing with the chief of the American delegation at that time, Mr Averell Harriman. He is old and very tough. He always looked down and consider you as one of his grandsons. Many members of the Vietnamese delegation have trouble communicating with him, and I heard about that before I came to Paris. So the day I came to Paris the first time, and Mr Harriman and Mr Vance (now the Secretary of State) both of them came to see me at my home, you know. The first thing I told them, let me know clearly right now whether you are going to sit down at the conference table as Allies, as a friend of Vietnam or as a friend of Communist side, because everything I heard until now about the preliminary talks and preparation for the negotiation, you are on the side of the Communists trying all the time to impose on us and to make us you know give more concession to the Communists.

Charlton: Did you feel inferior when you were talking to them about the strategy of the war, the policies to be pursued?

Ky: I am not tall. I am not big but I fly high. I never have any inferiority complex. I was young, yes, but I think I know the Vietnamese better than any old American politicians. The war in Vietnam was a Vietnamese war.

Charlton: How important does the Vietnam conflict appear to you to be in retrospect, set in the context of the world as you see it today?

Ky: Even today many people, particularly American people, want to forget about it. In the long range Vietnam War still has a big effect on American people. It was a big wound. They tried to forget it but impossible, and I think Vietnam War will serve as good lesson for the non-Communist countries in the world.

Charlton: What is that lesson?

Ky: When a thing happened subsequently in Angola, immediately people are talking about Vietnam. What happened in Vietnam, what *will* happen to Angola, you see. Zaire today is the same thing. You will see, maybe in a small scale, a different Vietnam War happen in other parts of the world. So I hope that the Americans and all the non-Communists can really learn a lesson from the Vietnam War—to deal with another Vietnam in another part of the world.

11
The fall of Saigon

After the signing of the Paris Agreement in January 1973, it soon became apparent that the Americans had all but washed their hands of Vietnam. The last of their half a million troops were on their way down to the ships and the aircraft which were waiting to take them back across the Pacific. By now Ho Chi Minh's civil war, which he had launched with five thousand followers from sanctuaries inside China in 1945, was rising thirty years old. It had taken the Communists nine years to take and hold the North, another nineteen using it as a springboard, to be within reach of ultimately taking the South. Ho Chi Minh himself had died in 1969. He had embarked on the protracted struggle to take over all Vietnam with the moral approval of the Americans, who had at first been on and by his side in the days following the defeat of Japan. Within a year they had swung round to oppose him. Twenty years after that they had landed an army to fight him themselves. Now they were about to turn their backs on Vietnam altogether. Watergate, the political death of President Nixon, had begun to overtake all other American concerns.

The Paris Agreement of January 1973 was to have a cease-fire 'in place' while the Americans unilaterally withdrew. That meant that one hundred and twenty thousand Communist guerillas would stay in the South. While the Geneva Accords, nineteen years earlier, had left only a short internal demarcation line across the country from east to west at the 17th parallel which divided it into two zones, this time South Vietnam was left defending an open frontier, nine hundred miles long, north to south, and stretching from Laos to Cambodia. The Agreement should have provided for a rough balance of military strength in arms and materiel between the Communist and South Vietnamese forces which would be maintained by their patrons, the Communist powers and the United States. No one seemed to doubt that eventually there would be more fighting and dying to decide the ultimate outcome—at least not President Thieu of South Vietnam. Two months after the ceasefire he saw the probable future as little different from the past.

The people of South Vietnam cannot perform the right of self-determination so long as we have any foreign troops in South Vietnam, and above all the troops of North Vietnam who have invaded the country... If they do not withdraw, I think that they continue to nourish the trend of invasion of South Vietnam and they are planning a new war. Even now almost sixty days after the cease-fire, they continue to infiltrate. They continue to send out to South Vietnam more tanks, more artillery guns, and more troops. That's the first sign after the Accord had been signed that they continue to infiltrate and to prepare another war.

A year before this Paris Agreement the South Vietnamese army, lavishly equipped by the Americans and with the vital support of the American Air Force, had stopped an all-out invasion of South Vietnam by the North. The debris from that unsuccessful invasion was littering the rubber plantations some 60 miles from Saigon. At a place called An Loc were the hulks of more than sixty Russian tanks lying in bomb craters in the streets of the town, their turrets blown off, chalk-marked with victory slogans of the South Vietnamese troops. They were bronzed with rust and the heat of the fires which had cremated their crews. The North Vietnamese crews for those tanks had been trained at the Russian School of Armored Warfare, near Odessa on the Black Sea. Hanoi's generals were being trained in Soviet military academies. It was a modern mechanized army which faced the forces of the South, and to maintain an equilibrium the Americans had undertaken to match on behalf of the South anything which their opponents received. Our principal witness for what were now to become the last months of South Vietnam, and the time of the vanishing American presence, from the Paris Agreements to the Fall of Saigon—is America's last Ambassador there, Graham Martin. He was a career diplomat, who had previously been Ambassador in Italy and in Thailand. What first of all did he think of President Thieu himself, and that shrinking state which the United States was still pledged to go on arming and supplying under the Agreement?

Martin: I did not expect to like President Thieu. I have not normally liked military people who have made a transfer into the political field. Over a period of almost two years I grew to have a different appraisal of President Thieu, certainly one radically different from the conventional image that a concerted propaganda campaign, as I think in both our countries, had given to him. I found him to be an effective leader, and I think if an election could have been held in Vietnam supervised by the Canadians or the Swedes or anyone else in whose objective impartiality we would have no doubt, Thieu would have won at least eighty per cent of the votes. There was a popular support for him. He had become an effective politician as well as a military leader.

The other thing that impressed me was his understanding of the necessity for the economic development of the country, and his concern with that. The land reform program, for those who wanted to make a truly objective appraisal, had worked amazingly well; and the basic support of the South Vietnamese people for the government seemed to us to have been uniformly pervasive. Now this did not apply of course to the intellectual community, or to what I sometimes call 'the Saigon Chapter of the World Wide Community of Alienated Intellectuals', who in every clime will always oppose, will always criticize, who will always demand ultimate perfection, which is rarely achievable. The so-called Third Force I mean did not really exist except in the figment of the imagination of many visiting journalists who would come in for a week or ten days and interview the Saigon intellectual dissidents, and go away with glowing accounts of what a Third Force might do. It is interesting to note that all those figures are now either in re-education camps or have been totally eliminated, and they have taken their place in the dustbin of history, along with similar attempts and groups in other situations.

Charlton: How would you describe the military and political situation as you found it when you got to Saigon?

Martin: The military situation was, as I arrived in July of 1973, a basic stalemate with increasingly the military initiative going to the South Vietnamese forces. As you recall, there had been a massive supply before the Accords in the so-called 'Enhance Program' which was designed to leave the South Vietnamese military forces equipped and prepared to resist external aggression. It was the conclusion of our own military authorities at the time that the South Vietnamese would be successful in doing this, if there were not massive support to the North Vietnamese from outside sources. As we arrived in July 1973, this was becoming clearly evident. It was certainly true a year later, when even the Communist members of the Control Commission, the representatives of Poland and of Hungary, had concluded that the military initiative had clearly passed to the hands of the government of South Vietnam.

While the Paris Agreement was imminent but not yet signed, the Americans had hurled ashore into South Vietnam prodigious amounts of military equipment. The Agreement would permit the replacement of any losses in combat only on the basis of 'one for one' held before they were signed. Inevitably, while they did not match at once the speed of the initial American delivery, the Russians and Chinese began to do so.

Martin: The so-called Ho Chi Minh Trail, for example, had been expanded into almost an autobahn kind of supply route with branches. It was coming over to the border from south-eastern Laos and from Cambodia, and it became a supply route over which vast convoys of trucks were able to bring down supplies.
Charlton: And of course there was no bombing at this time. United States airpower had been withdrawn totally, as a result of the Paris Agreements.
Martin: Completely.
Charlton: Would you describe that as almost the only part of the agreements which had up till then apparently been honored?
Martin: Yes, I think that would be accurate.
Charlton: And what effect were the South Vietnamese themselves, with the air force that you'd left them with, able to have on that ability to stop that kind of reinforcement?
Martin: To have stopped that kind of reinforcement would have required the South Vietnamese air forces to strike into North Vietnam, into Laos, and into Cambodia, all of which was forbidden by the Paris Accords, and the South Vietnamese government did not do that.
Charlton: So the essential and critical thing in trying to ensure the survival of South Vietnam became this issue of supplying it adequately with material. If you couldn't stop it reaching the North Vietnamese forces in the South, you had to make sure that it was matched. It became an even more crucial question?
Martin: It became the essential question of survival. In the beginning I think, shortly after the January 1973 Accords, there was a diminution of military supplies on the part of the government of China and the government of the Soviet Union to the government of North Vietnam. Now this was reversed in the following year, when the erosion of American will to support South Vietnam became rather clearly apparent; and then, I think, both countries, not wishing the other to have become the single most dominant factor in the North

Vietnamese victory, began again the process of massive re-supply of North Vietnam.

Charlton: Can you deal with that interesting point rather more fully: what effect do you believe the interplay between the Soviet Union and China was having with the prospect of, as they would see it, of an American withdrawal leaving a strong North Vietnam with a large and, up till this point, highly successful army in control of events in South-East Asia?

Martin: I think that the January Accords which would have called for the maintenance over an indefinite period of a rough equivalency of balance was acceptable to both the Chinese and to the Soviets, in the basic sense that it was to the advantage of neither the Soviet Union, nor the Chinese, to have a Hanoi totally dominant in all of South-East Asia, which they would have the capability of becoming if they were to be successful. I think the Chinese could never be totally certain that they would not work a predominance of Soviet influence which would provide, as I think Churchill once described it in the under-belly of Europe, but in the under-belly of the Chinese mainland, bases and things which in unfriendly hands would have presented a clear danger. On the other hand the Soviet Union which still hoped, and still does I think, to broaden its influence in South-East Asia, would not have wanted the Chinese to have become the primary big brother of the government in Hanoi, and so there was this element of competition. But it was to the advantage of both for the Paris Accords to have been observed, and if we could have maintained the equivalency of support which we had undertaken to do in the 1973 January Accord, I think that that kind of status quo might have been attainable.

Whatever residual will remained in the United States to see that it *would* be attainable did not have long to wait for proof. In October 1973 war once more broke out between the Arabs and Israel, in the Middle East.

The price of oil rose fourfold. This made the precarious balance contrived temporarily in Vietnam suddenly swing away from Saigon and, commensurately, the opportunities presented to the North rise sharply.

Martin: Two things came, if you recall, in the fall of 1973. First was the Arab/Israel war when American stockpiles were severely drawn down and with the absence of appropriations which would quickly replace those stockpiles in Europe and in the United States. Then the pressures on the American military establishment to reach every conceivable source of supply or places where they could cut back. Then the rationale began that the South Vietnamese were being too profligate, for example in the expenditure of ammunition—although some military people in whose confidence I have reason to rely, have estimated that a South Vietnamese division, for example, was expending ten per cent of the ammunition under active combat conditions that an American division would have expended in a static or non-active hostilities sort of situation.

The second thing was the increasingly effective propaganda campaign being waged in the United States without effective counter from the Executive Branch, which led to Congressional reductions in the monies appropriated for military support to South Vietnam at the very time that the prices for the items were being vastly escalated. Now the combination of these brought about what the military logisticians have estimated to be an eighty per cent reduction in effective military aid, without any knowledge or forewarning to the South Vietnamese that this would take place.

Charlton: How effective were you from your position in Saigon, how effective could you be, in an attempt to point this out and influence this obviously crucial argument taking place in the United States about 'one for one' replacement. As was your obligation in fact under the Paris Agreement?

Martin: One could point this out, and I think the first cable that I recall was in December 1973 when the process had already begun as a result of the pressures on the Pentagon from the diversion of American stocks into the Mideast. Now, one could say a great many things from Saigon and I have not been noted as being loath to do that, but at that time you must remember what was happening in the United States. The beginnings of the Watergate pressures in the fall of 1973 and which continually escalated during 1974 and to the dénouement of August with the departure of President Nixon, did not lead to a great concentration of either thought or effort in the Executive Branch of the United States on Vietnam.

Charlton: And would you say it was that combination of those two things—the failure to carry out the 'one for one' replacement because of the coincidental embarrassment of the need to supply Israel in the Middle East and the economic effects of the tripling of oil prices and the fact that President Nixon was becoming more and more deeply enmeshed and his position was being weakened by Watergate—that led to a fundamental reappraisal on the part of the Russians,

Chinese, and certainly the North Vietnamese, that everything was now totally to their advantage?

Martin: I think they concluded in the early months of the summer of 1974 (and certainly we have evidence that they acted on this in the fall of 1974 shortly after the departure of President Nixon) that the American Government was in such disarray and that the effectiveness of the propaganda campaign being waged in the Congress and throughout the country to bring pressure on the Congress to reduce or eliminate appropriations to South Vietnam would make American support of South Vietnam increasingly ineffective. I think it is also clear at that time that they made the calculated decision that if this were to be the case and we were going to let South Vietnam go by default, that they were likely to get the credit from the North Vietnamese of having assisted them in this. And so the supplies to North Vietnam began a rather astronomical increase.

For their part the South Vietnamese too shared much the same deductions about Watergate when, as after the Americans departed, they watched the detachment and pre-occupation of the United States increase. General Tran Van Don, who was one of the leaders of the coup against Diem in 1963 which the Americans had supported and encouraged, was Defense Minister in Saigon's last government at the time of the approaching final collapse. He recalls the particular significance as they saw it of the decline and fall of Richard Nixon, following his assurances to President Thieu at the time of the Paris Agreement.

Don: Nixon has sent a letter in February to Thieu and said to him—don't worry about what can happen because we are always behind you, if something happens. If some aggression from the North we will react.

Charlton: What effect do you believe Watergate had?

Don: We think that if President Nixon would be in power he could react, and maybe he would react. But Watergate had a very bad effect for our war.

Charlton: It made it clear to you that the President was not free to act any more?

Don: If he [Nixon] was in power as a President he could react if something happened, you know. I think that Hanoi believed when President Ford come into power, non-elect President, President Ford would have to ask the Congress. But President Nixon did *not* have to ask the Congress because we had an agreement. At that time we believed if Nixon was more in power in 1975, he could react. We are quite sure, if Nixon was in power, Hanoi would not launch any attack in 1975.

Charlton: So with the decline and fall of Nixon the last hope, as you see it, of a non-Communist South Vietnam disappears?

Don: That's right.

❚ And did the South Vietnamese have good reason to suppose, as General Don suggested, that the ultimate deterrent of American air strikes would once more be available to them if there were a wholesale military violation of the provisions of the Paris Agreement?

Martin: Yes, I think we had undertaken that we would not idly stand by if there were a massive violation of the Accords on the part of North Vietnam. On the other hand there had been a further evolution in the American political scene, dealing with Cambodia and with further legislation which forbade any use of American power, I believe the legislation language was 'in, over or about South-East Asia', which totally precluded any possibility of doing that.

Charlton: Just to be a little more specific if we can. Did President Thieu have a letter from President Nixon pledging an air strike against Hanoi if the Accords were violated?

Martin: At the time of his resignation I think in the evening of 20 April, as I recall, 1975, he did produce and read to the assembled legislature of South Vietnam and the government of South Vietnam letters which purported to carry those assurances.

Charlton: Can you tell us whether those assurances were in fact given? You say: 'Purported to carry those assurances'—did he have them?

Martin: I say that because I have not myself seen them and I would not therefore categorically say that they existed.

Charlton: Do you have any real reason to doubt apart from the absolute visual evidence before your own eyes, that they did exist?

Martin: No, no, because it would have been quite appropriate for us in the aftermath of the January 1973 Accords, which as you recall the South Vietnamese government accepted with great reluctance, to have given such assurances.

Charlton: In fact, in order to get them to accept those accords at all, they were promised and given something like that—the guarantee of an air strike?

Martin: Yes, I think so.

Charlton: All this time the failure—for the reasons you've given—to carry out the provision for 'one for one' replacement, plus the doubts about America's *will* to fulfil these obligations in political terms in the United States with Nixon's deepening embarrassments over Watergate, what effect were both these things having that you can attest to on South Vietnamese morale itself—in the Government, in the armed forces—and their own will to resist what was obviously coming, another major test of that will by the North Vietnamese?

Martin: I think they were not that convinced in the beginning of 1974 that the American assurances would not be fulfilled. I think it became increasingly evident during the spring, the summer, the fall, that this would not be the case.

▌It was therefore now in the spring of 1975, after discussing it the previous year, that the South Vietnamese decided to carry out a strategic withdrawal from the two northern regions of South Vietnam and bring their forces back to shorter, more easily defensible perimeters which would include Saigon and the heavily populated Mekong Delta. They managed to extricate about half their military forces but left behind their equipment. President Ford sent out the American Army Chief of Staff, General Wyatt, to see whether it would be possible to re-equip these units and to see if they could maintain a defense, if they were. The recommendation General Wyatt made was that they could and that 750 million dollars' worth of additional military equipment should be provided. Congress refused. Because not just in Vietnam, but inside America too a balance had tipped. This time it was the constitutional one, away from the freedom of a President to intervene towards the new constraints of a more populist foreign policy under vigilant conduct by the Congress. President Ford—who had by now succeeded Nixon—might speak but he could not expect to act.

If we cease to help our friends in Indo-China, we will have violated their trust that we would help them with arms, with food and with supplies so long as they remain determined to fight for their own freedom. We will have been false to ourselves, to our word and to our friends. No one should think for a moment that we can walk away from that without a deep sense of shame.

The last Americans left in Vietnam were for the most part concerned with the re-supply of materiel used up in combat. This was the role to which the Paris Agreement confined them, and to which Ambassador Graham Martin insisted that they should be restrained. They were not capable of offering tactical or strategic military advice. Indeed the South Vietnamese no longer either consulted or informed the Americans, even about the strategic withdrawal. Relations between the South Vietnamese and the Americans had become sulphurous.

Martin: I was not in Vietnam, I was back in Washington at that point trying desperately to get the Congress to understand the inevitable end that would take place if we did not begin to honor the commitments which we had made at the time of the January Accords. The decision and the beginning of the withdrawal occurred before I returned to South Vietnam in the last week of March with General Wyatt, the Chief of Staff of the US Army; but we were not consulted and not informed.

Charlton: Is that perhaps a comment on deteriorating relations between President Thieu and the Americans at this stage, in addition to your own rather strict interpretation as you put it of what the Paris Agreements provided for, which was that you had to keep out of this sort of thing?

Martin: I think inevitably there had to be a deterioration when over a period of some at least thirteen to fourteen months prior to that decision they had seen the complete curtailment of the promised American aid, and a waging in Washington of this immense campaign on the Congress to deny all future appropriations to South Vietnam. It was, I think, in January 1975 that Tran Van Lam, who had been the Foreign Minister and who was then currently President of the Senate of the Republic of Vietnam, had visited Washington. He was not even received on the Hill, and it is my understanding that on his return to Saigon he advised President Thieu that not only would the requested supplemental appropriation not be approved, but that in all likelihood that the temper in Washington was that no more additional military aid would be forthcoming at all.

Charlton: Ambassador, with a decision by the South Vietnamese to abandon the northern part of South Vietnam, to pull out of the military regions to the north of Saigon and to redraw a line which they felt they could hold more securely in the south, in the Mekong Delta, that decision to make a strategic withdrawal became a

THE FALL OF SAIGON 237

collapse and was portrayed and reported widely as an undignified rout. I think it's probably correct to suggest the popular view is that was brought about by the increasing pressures by the North Vietnamese, and that under those increasing pressures the moment had come where the whole apparatus in South Vietnam just collapsed. Now what is your own assessment of what really happened?

Martin: Well, the evidence of that, I think, is that the contrary is true. It is unfortunate that so little attention has been paid to a rather extraordinary document, an almost 80,000 word memoir of the North Vietnamese general who was commanding the forces in the South and I think that when that is carefully read the conclusion is inescapable that the strategic withdrawal caught the North Vietnamese completely by surprise. It was not a result of their immediate military pressure, and they had some difficulty really in reorganizing and re-orienting their own thinking to take advantage of it. Now, any military withdrawal when it is not most carefully and meticulously prepared, and sometimes even when it is, has elements always of disaster accompanying it. The panic of the civilian population in the North, which made an enormous effort to get to the South, complicated that withdrawal—and there were elements of disaster which did take place. But as I say, the most telling and compelling evidence comes from the North Vietnamese themselves, that it is simply not true that the withdrawal from Military Regions 1 and 2 was a direct result of overwhelming current military pressure from the North Vietnamese at that time.

The situation which led to the necessity for the withdrawal obviously came from the failure of the United States in having to provide the 'one for one' replacements which we had undertaken to do. The North Vietnamese, after an initial period of shock at their unexpected gains in the North, sent barrelling to the South all of their reserve divisions that had been retained in North Vietnam and the military pressure became very intense. There was a terrific battle on the outskirts of Xuan Loc, which was some I think thirty kilometers to the north of Saigon, where the North Vietnamese division was totally annihilated and South Vietnamese fought with extreme courage and tenacity. Then it became evident that the American Congress was not going to provide the necessary support. My own estimate had been that the Congress would not approve the President's recommendation, so we had prepared the plans which had been kept in being of course, as they are in every embassy in the world, for the orderly evacuation of the American presence.

Charlton: Did you ever have a good reason to suppose that in your great concern to avoid panic, born of the fear that the South Vietnamese may turn on you in view of what they would see as ultimate betrayal of what you had been leading them to suppose would happen, did you ever have a good reason to suppose that that was in fact likely?

Martin: Yes we did. You may remember that photograph,[1] which has gained a certain notoriety world-wide, of the Chief of the Saigon Police Forces shooting a Vietcong during the Tet uprising in Saigon?

Charlton: I remember very well, Colonel Luan.

Martin: Colonel Luan. He among others had said: 'If you Americans think that you're going to, you know, just walk away and leave us you'll never make it to the airport'. Now this was a very real, a very natural reaction. Now we kept that whole situation stable and going. We went through two changes of governments, in other words three governmental authorities, from the time of resignation of President Thieu to the assumption of power by Vice President Huong and then on his departure the assumption, very briefly on the last day, of General Minh. The transitions were not revolutionary but totally legal. Now in that sense we maintained the integrity of the ability to command the South Vietnamese armed forces. They did not disintegrate until the very last day. And so we successfully evacuated every American who wanted to leave—and some 140,000 Vietnamese.

▌Vietnam had one more spectacle to place before its world-wide audience, fed by television on the spectacle of it until they wanted no more. It was the swarms of helicopters carrying the last of America's esrtwhile allies in South Vietnam out to the aircraft carriers in the South China Sea. There they fluttered above the overcrowded decks in the final scramble to get away. Some were pushed over the side to make room for more, and when there was no more room on deck they splashed down into the water for burial at sea. These were the last visible indignities of defeat.

The North Vietnamese have since published in their official newspaper Nhan Dan their history of the fall of Saigon. In it they admit that beginning in 1974 they broke the Paris Agreement by sending, as they said, 'great quantities of tanks, armored cars, missiles and long range artillery and anti-aircraft guns to various battlefields.' They built a new all-weather supply highway, six hundred miles long, down to the South. A new recruitment drive they said gave 'tens of thousands

[1] See fig. 4.

THE FALL OF SAIGON 239

of new troops' to Hanoi's army. They said too, that a key factor in the final outcome of the war was the reduction of American aid to Saigon. As a result the victorious North Vietnamese commanding General, General Dung, said that: 'Thieu was forced to fight a poor man's war. The firepower of the South Vietnamese had declined by sixty per cent because of bomb and ammunition shortages. Its mobility was reduced by half, owing to the lack of aircraft, transport and fuel.'

In Vietnam itself we know, but no longer see, that the vanquished South Vietnamese were marched away to the re-education camps to be 'remolded'. Among the first pronouncements of the new military governor of Saigon was this: 'National reconciliation does not imply indulgence towards the defeated.'

Was the Vietnam War one of the more fundamental of conflicts? Did it mark the beginnings of some historical decline in that the United States and the West can no longer be roused to a political challenge. Was it the victory of Spartans over Sybarites? Or did the Americans invest Vietnam with an importance it need never have acquired? The Americans still alive and who made most of the decisions which took the United States into and out of that war, have all it seems grown older more quickly with the strain of those years. Some are still secure in their beliefs and judgements, others ill at ease, others repentant—but none is unmarked by it. Unity at home in the United States is being restored. At what cost?

General Maxwell Taylor: I think it's too early to be sure how deep the scars are, certainly we bear scars. The thought that we abandoned an ally, seventeen, eighteen million South Vietnamese, who are now in the hands of the Communists in spite of our bungling efforts—they hang on the conscience of many of us, certainly on my own. On the other hand I think these events took place in the United States at the end of the war at an unusual time, the great conflict between President Nixon and the Congress. The action of Congress in cutting off aid to South Vietnam was certainly more a slap at Nixon than a deliberate decision to abandon an ally which it amounted to. In the long run of course I have great confidence in our people, we have great resources and with leadership we can come back and redeem ourselves. However, I must say that if I were a foreign diplomat or adviser to a head of state, I would say: 'We'll have to watch the Americans and see whether we can count on them in the same way we could in the past'.

Charlton: Do you suspect that it marks the retreat of America—I don't mean into a posture of classical isolationism, because you're too involved and enmeshed in the world anyway—but do you imagine that it does mean a period of retreat and detachment from obligations rather than commitment to them?

Taylor: I come from the Middle West. You say of a Russian, scratch a Russian and you'll find a Tartar. If you scratch a Middle Westerner you'll find an isolationist. We'd all like to be isolated, Great Britain would like to be isolationists, France would like to be isolationists, but we can't be—particularly in this world where economic factors constantly increasing our interdependence are tying the good and the bad of every country to those of its neighbor.

I would say however that I would hope our decision-makers will be very slow in accepting new foreign commitments. We certainly had a feeling after World War II that we could go almost any place and do almost anything. Well, we did many things at enormous cost, but henceforth we're going to have trouble feeding and keeping happy our own growing population just as every other nation is. This is not a time for our government to get out on limbs which are not essential. Indeed it may be a time to crawl back from old limbs that have become a little shaky. So I think conservatism and caution is likely to be our guiding principle in foreign policy in the United States for some time.

▌Senator William Fulbright, for many years the Chairman of the Foreign Relations Committee in the Senate, became towards the end of the American involvement a focus for formalized opposition to that war and its continuation.

Fulbright: We *are* in the process of reuniting and of getting over the disillusionment and alienation that developed as a result of that war. We are in a sense an inexperienced country, especially with regard to foreign relations. This real involvement is a relatively new experience for us, and I don't think the American people like it. I don't like it. I don't wish to leave the implication we're isolationists. I have long advocated a much more vigorous power role in the United Nations, and in all of the international/multinational organizations, such as the inter-American Bank and these development programs, and that is the way I think we ought to move. I mean, with the invention of nuclear weapons the traditional methods of so-called balance of power and so on, seem to me to become obsolete and you have to have a new approach. And as a part of that approach there has to be something done about the traditional attitude of one nation to others. I mean, in this chauvinistic attitude that our nation, you know, right or wrong, etc., has to give way to the realities of nuclear power. So I think that a whole new approach should be brought about and that is one of my conclusions from this experience in Vietnam, and how these things develop in a way people did not intend it. I don't think Johnson ever intended to get into the kind of war he did. But things lead up to it and this has a long history, and this emotional fixation about ideologies, such as we have had over Communism, is a disastrous approach.

Charlton: What do you say though to those who do see ideological conflict continuing, as the Communists proclaim it will, and their refusal to renounce their objectives of revolution, of the overthrow of the existing order, wherever that may be?

Fulbright: Well, the professions that they make are not as significant as the actions they take. Now aside of the actions that they have taken in Czechoslovakia and Hungery in recent years, I don't detect this kind of business you're talking about.

We professed to also believe in democracy and freedom, which I do believe in. It's the question of the methods you're going to follow to promote those. There's nothing wrong with them if they think they're right to proselytize, but there's a great deal wrong to allow these to develop where you're going to try and prove it by arms, with nuclear arms. What we're looking for is a way to avoid its developing into another war. I think our prosecution of that war was a terrible mistake. We didn't for example recently intervene in Angola, which I think is correct; and I will say that's one of the benefits of having been in Vietnam. We'd at least avoided involvement in Africa up to now, and I hope we do avoid it.

▎Was Vietnam for Sir Robert Thompson, as Henry Kissinger was reputed to have called it, 'a cruel sideshow'?

Thompson: Yes, I suppose in a way that is right; if you think of all the other problems round the world Vietnam does seem in retrospect to have been a sideshow. I think I would put it slightly another way: if the Americans had come out of Vietnam successfully in 1972 we wouldn't now have many of those other problems. I doubt for

example whether there would have been a 1973 Middle East war. I think that was a direct consequence of the American failure in Vietnam.
Charlton: Why so?
Thompson: We have now got into a situation globally where as far as Russia is concerned she's established two basic ground rules. That the whole of the target area in the world which we have called 'the free world' is now from the Russian point of view a free-for-all, whereas all marxist states are off-limits as far as the United States is concerned. And the second ground rule that has been created as a result of this is that a marxist guerilla movement only has to win once. It can fail just as General Giap failed in Vietnam, at Tet and in 1972, but in the end when it succeeds it only has to win once. We are now in the situation where we're going to see exactly the same thing happening in many African states—and I'm not here referring just to Rhodesia or to South Africa. I think we're going to see changes of government caused by marxist guerilla movements in other states of southern Africa, for example in Zambia, Tanzania, Kenya. Looking further ahead what is the stability going to be in the Middle East with these various sheikh governments, how long are they going to last?

We all saw what happened in Iraq in 1957, how there was a change-round overnight due to the assassination of the King and the Prime Minister. Well if that is going to happen in the Middle East what can the Americans do about it? No one can think they can rely on American forces. We know they can't. America gave it up in Angola. The tragedy of Angola was it was a pushover for the United States to have put Unita into power in Angola as against the MPLA. It would have been easy to do. The United States has got a non-involvement policy, whereas the Russians have got a full involvement policy; and that is what we're going to be up against.
Charlton: Do you think then that Vietnam marked the strategic surrender of the United States?
Thompson: Oh yes, I said that all along, that we're now living in this situation where the United States has strategically surrendered its global position vis-à-vis the Russians.
Charlton: Therefore far from being 'a cruel sideshow', your verdict would be that it must be one of the fundamental conflicts of modern history?
Thompson: I regard it probably as being the most decisive war of this century.

But that is not the verdict of Mike Mansfield, for many years the majority leader in the Senate, harbinger of the attitudes which Sir Robert Thompson fears have gained ground since America went to Vietnam in the early 1960s.

Mansfield: It seems to me the American people want to forget Vietnam and not even remember that it happened. But the cost was 55,000 dead, 303,000 wounded, $150 billion. With some of us it will never be forgotten because it was one of the most tragic, if not *the* most tragic, episodes in American history. It was unnecessary, uncalled for, it wasn't tied to our security or a vital interest. It was just a misadventure in a part of the world which we should have kept our nose out of.

Charlton: But that's expedient isn't it? Must the central issue not be whether the United States can offer an alternative to class struggle and revolution as a means of securing independence?

Mansfield: I didn't look upon it as class struggle. I looked upon it as a struggle on the part of the people of South Vietnam to achieve an independent state in that part of Vietnam.

Charlton: Yes, but you're not allowed that choice. The Communists say that that can only emerge through class struggle.

Mansfield: Well, I know, but you're getting back to the containment policy of China. Why did we go into Vietnam in the first place? Because we got involved in Korea, and we felt that we had to contain China. It was part of a monolithic Soviet-Peking axis which never existed really. So what you're doing is to bring in the ideological aspect of it which as far as I'm concerned played a very minor part of my thinking.

Charlton: You don't believe it is the role of the United States to offer an alternative to that, or to support an alternative to that?

Mansfield: I think each country ought to have the chance to decide what its own form of government should be. That's its business, not ours.

Charlton: But if it can decide it only by force, it's going to need the support of somebody, just as the Communists enjoy the support of the Communist powers.

Mansfield: Well, it's up to the countries concerned.

Charlton: But would you as an act of policy now deny non-Communist movements American support?

Mansfield: I don't believe in intervention unless it's tied to our own security and self-interest. I'm just against intervention per se except on that basis. Now that's why I voted against additional funds for Angola. That's why I was against the intervention of the Dominican Republic. That's why I was opposed to the war in South-East Asia.

Charlton: But if that's a unilateral abandonment by America of intervention, that is going to lead to the extension of Communist influence, isn't it?

Mansfield: All countries don't look upon Communism as the ideal which they seek. I think a stronger force than Communism is nationalism.

Charlton: Just to make the point that for example the Russians and the Chinese support guerilla movements. They intervene.

Mansfield: Should we do it because they do, should we react to what they do? The trouble with this country is we always react, rather than act initially.

Charlton: Yes. So what you disagreed with, was the universal approach that America had in her foreign policy of putting her thumb in the dike wherever it happens?

Mansfield: We didn't. We didn't do it in Hungary, we didn't do it in Czechoslovakia. Why should we do it in South-East Asia?

▎The Secretary of State to Presidents Kennedy and Johnson, Dean Rusk, said: 'We knew we had lost the war when we couldn't tell the people of Cherokee County when it would finish and how much it would cost.' Therefore, was Vietnam in retrospect 'a cruel sideshow' peripheral to the interests of the United States, or was it one of the fundamental conflicts, something which has changed the balance in the world?

Rusk: It may be at least twenty years before we can make a judgment on that point because I don't think we've seen the end of the story, in all sorts of directions. On this I'm in what may appear to be a rather curious position. I would hope that the events of the next twenty years will be so constructive and positive in the direction of organizing a durable peace in the world that the future historians would be tempted to say that President Kennedy and President Johnson and those fellows Rusk and McNamara overdid it, what was done was not necessary after all. At the risk of sounding pretentious, no-one could possibly want the kind of vindication that would come from catastrophe, where a few survivors would look at each other and say: 'Gee, those fellows were right, weren't they'. So I think we've got to try to build toward that durable peace because in the nuclear world there's no real choice; but how Vietnam fits into that, one can't be sure yet. I hope that it will not mean that the fidelity of the American people toward their alliances will be any the less; but that's something that if I were in Europe I would be concerned about.

Charlton: And therefore it is your concern that it did perhaps mark a fundamental conflict in this sense, that it marked perhaps the strategic surrender of the United States at a critical moment?

Rusk: No, I think it probably marked the end of one chapter, and that is the chapter in which the United States and the American people would be called upon to undertake major responsibilities relatively alone. Those days are over, believe me.

America's last Ambassador in Vietnam has served the United States at the zenith of its global influence and power, and he was its representative as the first successful challenge to that power and influence placed new and as yet unknown limits upon it. On 3 April 1975, the Vietnamese Communist troops riding on their Russian tanks broke down the gates of Independence Palace in Saigon and captured the last government of South Vietnam at their last cabinet meeting. The last American representative, Ambassador Martin, had left by the only way then open to him, by helicopter from the roof, as the high tide of Ho Chi Minh's thirty years of revolutionary war lapped around his Embassy. And so out above the Saigon River and the upturned faces, going the way the Japanese had gone, the British had gone, the French had gone, and now the Americans too had gone—back to the ships in the South China Sea.

Martin: I think I had a feeling of just sort of enormous relief that it was over, and that we had gotten all of the Americans out successfully. I'd been walking a tightrope for almost three weeks of trying to keep everything stable. I felt enormously lucky that it had all worked into place as I had conceived it, and that we had gotten all the Americans out who wanted to come. We had also gotten out large numbers of Vietnamese, not as many as we would have liked, but under the circumstances a rather remarkable performance to have gotten out 140,000 of them. I remembered Secretary Kissinger's remark as I left the last meeting, a month before in Washington, where he said that: 'Well you'd better get back out because in the devil theory of history we have to have someone to blame'. And I remembered the joke that President Lincoln used to tell about the man who had been tarred and feathered and ridden out of town on a rail—and who had observed if it weren't for the honor of the thing he would just as soon walked. But my own feeling was one of enormous relief, that everything that I tried to do in those last three weeks of avoiding a panic in Saigon and of getting all of the Americans out and arranging to get a considerable number of Vietnamese out, that at least avoided a departure in total dishonor, and for that I was grateful. And I remember the feeling of enormous gratitude to the staff which on the whole performed superbly, superbly.

Index of contributors

Ball, George, 61–2, 77–8, 85–6, 91–2, 93–5, 108–10, 125–6, 131–2
Bowie, Robert, 32–3, 34, 35, 40–1
Bundy, William, 67–9, 87–8, 116–17, 120–3, 185–6

Colby, William, 53, 57, 76–7, 84–5, 193–7

Don, Tran Van, 14–15, 47–8, 97–9, 233–4
Duncanson, Dennis, 3–4, 19–20, 21–4

Eden, Anthony, 36
Ellsberg, Daniel, 173–81

Fairbank, John, 51–2
FitzGerald, Frances, 157–60
Frankel, Elliott, 156–7
Fulbright, William, 50, 111–12, 240–1

Galbraith, John, 79–80, 161–2
Gelb, Leslie, 169–72
Greenfield, James, 181–5

Hilsman, Roger, 63–4, 83–4, 87, 89–91

Ky, Nguyen Cao, 47, 212–25

Lansdale, Edward, 15–16, 42–7, 55–6
Letourneau, Jean, 31
Lodge, Henry Cabot, 95–7

McCarthy, Eugene, 162–7
Mansfield, Michael, 54–5, 81, 83, 243–4
Martin, Graham, 228–33, 234–8, 245–6
Minh, Ho Thong, 48–9, 54

Nolting, Frederick 'Fritz', 64–5, 69–71, 75–6, 82, 86
Nutter, Warren, 188–9, 192, 198–9, 201–2, 204–7, 209–10

Patti, Archimedes, 6–14
Pleven, René, 30, 33

Rostow, Walt, 105–6, 123–4
Rusk, Dean, 17–18, 26–7, 49–50, 52–3, 65–6, 80, 82, 86, 92–3, 113–16, 244–5

Sainteny, Jean, 4–6, 16, 28–30
Schumann, Maurice, 33–5
Small, William, 153–5
Szulc, Tad, 199–201, 203–4, 207–8

Taylor, Maxwell, 66–7, 71–5, 102, 107, 118–19, 150–1, 239–40
Thompson, Robert, 36–7, 56, 103–5, 124–5, 190, 197, 204, 241–2

Warnke, Paul, 128–31, 208–9
Westmoreland, William 'Westy', 134–149, 151–2

Yarmolinsky, Adam, 59–61

Selective index of persons referred to in text

Note: Asterisked page references are given to the American Presidents, the South Vietnamese Chief of Police and the Vietnamese Emperor, where they occur unnamed in the text.

Acheson, Dean, 26, 27, 131, 132
Attlee, Clement, 18

Ball, George, 61, 77, 85, 86, 89, 91, 108, 110, 125, 131, 132, 141, 142
Bidault, Georges, 33
Bowie, Robert, 32, 34, 40
Brezhnev, Leonid, 200
Bundy, McGeorge, 76, 77, 107, 115, 132, 139
Bundy, William, 67, 87, 116, 185
Byrnes, James, 26

Carter, James, 128, 177
Chiang Kai-shek, 11, 13, 19
Chou En-lai, 198
Christian, George, 154
Churchill, Winston, 2, 17, 231
Clifford, Clark, 128–31, 176
Colby, William, 53, 76, 77, 84, 85, 132, 193
Conein, Lucien, 99
Cronkite, Walter, 154

Dai, Bao, 4, 13, 15, 31, 46, 53, 55*
Diem, Ngo Dinh, 45, 46, 49, 53–8, 70, 71, 73–6, 80–99, 101, 102, 116, 133, 135, 136, 141, 150, 163, 164, 211, 212, 215, 216, 233
Dinh, Ton That, 98
Dillon, Douglas, 132
Don, Tran Van, 14, 47, 97, 233, 234
Dong, Pham Van, 42
Donovan, William, 6, 7, 16
Dulles, John Foster, 31–6, 39–42, 45, 46, 50, 51, 134
Duncanson, Dennis, 3, 21

Eden, Anthony, 36, 40

Eisenhower, Dwight, 31, 34, 62, 64, 65, 95, 134
Ellsberg, Daniel, 159, 168, 172, 173, 181
Ely, Paul, 34

Fairbank, John, 51
FitzGerald, Frances, 157
Ford, Gerald, 121, 233, 235, 237*
Forrestal, Michael, 87
Frankel, Elliott, 156
Fulbright, William, 50, 111, 113, 163, 167, 177, 180, 181, 240

Galbraith, John, 78, 161
Gard, Robert, 171
Gaulle, Charles de, 25
Gelb, Leslie, 169, 176
Giap, Vo Nguyen, 5, 11, 15, 33, 43, 242
Gilpatric, Roswell, 78, 91
Goldwater, Barry, 110, 117, 140, 170
Goodwin, Richard, 161
Greene, Graham, 15, 42
Greenfield, James, 181
Gruening, Ernest, 164, 167

Haig, Alexander, 203
Halperin, Mort, 176
Harkins, Paul, 133, 137
Harriman, Averell, 63, 64, 89, 91, 92, 136, 225
Heuvel, William vanden, 161
Hilsman, Roger, 62, 64, 66, 89, 91, 95
Hitler, Adolf, 153
Hope, Bob, 107
Hull, Cordell, 2, 7, 17, 25
Humphrey, Hubert, 166
Huong, Tran Van, 238

Johnson, Alex, 107

SELECTIVE INDEX OF PERSONS 249

Johnson, Lyndon, 72, 80, 100–2, 105–113, 117–32*, 134, 138*–42*, 149–151*, 160–4, 166, 170, 176, 178*, 180, 186, 187, 191, 193, 211, 219, 221, 241, 244

Kennedy, John, 36, 50, 54, 58–75, 77–82, 84, 85, 87, 90–4*, 96, 99–101, 105, 111, 116, 119, 134, 135, 137, 139, 141, 142, 244
Kennedy, Robert, 61, 127, 162, 170
Khanh, Nguyen, 163, 217
Khrushchev, Nikita, 41, 63, 66–8
King, Martin Luther, 162
Kissinger, Henry, 167, 171, 176, 177, 190, 198–201, 203–5, 207, 220, 241, 245
Krulak, Victor, 85
Ky, Nguyen Cao, 47, 191, 193, 211, 212

Laird, Melvin, 198
Lam, Tran Van, 236
Lansdale, Edward, 15, 42, 47, 219
Lenin, Vladimir, 3, 20–2, 38
Letourneau, Jean, 31
Lincoln, Abraham, 245
Lodge, Henry Cabot, 92, 95, 97–9, 219
Luan, Nguyen Ngoc, 155*, 238
Luce, Henry, 51

McCarthy, Eugene, 161, 162
McCarthy, Joseph, 50; McCarthy Period, 50–2, 175
McCloy, Jack, 131
McCone, John, 93
McGovern, George, 162, 167
McNamara, Robert, 78, 82, 88, 91, 92, 109, 121, 126, 128, 137, 138, 141–4, 164, 168–71, 173, 174, 185, 244
McNaughton, John, 171, 173–5
Mansfield, Michael, 54, 81–3, 113, 167, 243
Mao Tse-tung, 22–4, 27, 30, 103, 198
Marshall, George, 18, 26, 27; Marshall Plan, 26, 27
Martin, Graham, 228, 236, 245
Minh, Duong Van 'Big Minh', 99, 216, 217, 238
Minh, Ho Chi, 2–5, 7–30, 37, 39, 42, 43, 46, 49, 51, 53, 57, 124, 169, 212, 213, 215, 220, 227
Minh, Ho Thong, 48
Morse, Wayne, 114, 163, 164, 167
Mountbatten, Louis, 25

Nehru, Pandit, 23, 79
Nixon, Richard, 35, 36, 72, 126, 162, 164, 166, 173, 177, 180, 186, 187, 190, 191, 193, 196–200, 204–8, 210*, 220, 222, 232–5, 239
Nolting, Frederick 'Fritz', 64, 65, 69, 82, 86, 87, 95
Nhu, Madame, 83, 85, 94
Nhu, Ngo Dinh, 83, 85, 86, 89, 93, 94, 97–9
Nutter, Warren, 192, 199, 204, 209

Patti, Archimedes, 2, 5, 6, 12, 15, 16
Pleven, René, 30, 33

Quat, Phan Huy, 217

Radford, Arthur, 34
Reston, James, 68
Rockefeller, Nelson, 190
Roosevelt, Franklin, 2, 3, 6, 7, 11, 16–18, 24, 25, 121
Rostow, Walt, 71, 78, 79, 105, 112, 123, 176; Taylor/Rostow Mission, see under Taylor, Maxwell
Rowan, Harry, 178
Rusk, Dean, 17, 18, 49, 50, 61, 65, 78, 80, 86, 89–93, 95, 96, 108, 113, 124, 130, 154, 163, 166, 176, 244
Russo, Anthony, 178

Safer, Morley, 152, 153
Sainteny, Jean, 2, 4, 5, 11, 12, 16, 28, 29, 198
Schlesinger, Arthur, 161
Schumann, Maurice, 33, 34
Sheehan, Neil, 183
Small, William, 152
Smith, Bedell, 50
Smith, Hedrick, 183
Stalin, Joseph, 2, 25, 50, 51
Stevenson, Adlai, 162
Sukarno, Achmed, 69
Szulc, Tad, 199

Taylor, Maxwell, 66, 71, 75, 78–80, 102, 106, 108, 125, 133, 150, 151, 217, 218; Taylor/Rostow Mission, 69, 71, 72, 75–80
Thieu, Nguyen Van, 193, 202–5, 208, 211, 216, 217, 220, 224–9, 233, 234, 236, 238, 239
Thompson, Robert, 36, 37, 56, 103, 189, 191, 204, 241, 243

Thorez, Maurice, 28
Tito, Josip, 23, 169
Trueheart, William, 87
Truman, Harry, 3, 17, 23, 25, 26, 31; Truman Doctrine, 50, 61, 134

Vance, Cyrus, 107, 225

Walt, Louis, 152

Warnke, Paul, 128, 176, 208, 209
Westmoreland, William 'Westy', 118, 124, 126, 127, 129–31, 133, 134, 145, 147, 149, 151
Wheeler, Earle, 143
Wyatt, Ben, 235, 236

Yarmolinsky, Adam, 59, 61, 62